DANA CLAXTON

STEIDL | SCOTIABANK PHOTOGRAPHY AWARD

First edition published in 2021 on the occasion of the awarding of the
2020 Scotiabank Photography Award to Dana Claxton

Book design by Barr Gilmore
Project management by Ryan Burella
Edited by Laurel Saint-Pierre with additional essay editing by Candice Hopkins

All photography by Dana Claxton, unless otherwise noted
All digital colour work by Pauline Petit, Dana Claxton Studio at Studio 26 Artist Services
and Dan Ebert at Toronto Image Works
Additional colour work by Steidl image department
Production by Bernard Fischer, Gerhard Steidl
Production and printing by Steidl, Göttingen

Cover image: Dana Claxton, *Lasso*, 2018 (detail)

Steidl
Düstere Str. 4 / D-37073 Göttingen, Germany
Phone +49 551 49 60 60
steidl.de mail@steidl.de

ISBN 978-3-95829-882-8
Printed in Germany by Steidl

This publication was generously sponsored by Scotiabank.

Library and Archives Canada Cataloguing in Publication
Dana Claxton, 1959-
Dana Claxton: Scotiabank Photography Award
Contributing authors: Leila Timmins; Amy Kazymerchyk [et al.]

Scotiabank Photography Award: Dana Claxton
Exhibition curated by Gaëlle Morel
April 28 to August 7, 2021
Ryerson Image Centre
33 Gould Street, Toronto, Ontario M5B 2K3 Canada
www.ryersonimagecentre.ca

Ryerson Image Centre

SPONSOR'S FOREWORD

BRIAN J. PORTER, PRESIDENT AND CHIEF EXECUTIVE OFFICER, SCOTIABANK

Scotiabank is delighted to once again recognize outstanding contemporary photographers through our sponsorship of the Scotiabank Photography Award. This award, along with the Scotiabank CONTACT Photography Festival, celebrates the creativity and accomplishments of our most talented photographers.

We are very pleased to announce that Vancouver-based artist Dana Claxton is the recipient of the tenth annual Scotiabank Photography Award. For decades, Dana has made enormous contributions to contemporary Canadian art and photography and we are proud to share this collection of her work.

Scotiabank has a long history of supporting Canadian artists, culture and heritage in communities across our great country. We are committed to celebrating contemporary photography and helping to raise the profile of our artists here in Canada and around the world.

Congratulations to Dana for winning this year's Scotiabank Photography Award.

Scotiabank®

SCOTIABANK PHOTOGRAPHY AWARD

EDWARD BURTYNSKY, JURY CHAIR, SCOTIABANK PHOTOGRAPHY AWARD

On behalf of the Scotiabank Photography Award, we are pleased to present *Dana Claxton*, the tenth edition in a series of publications printed and distributed worldwide by Steidl Verlag, to celebrate our 2020 winner.

Founded in 2010, the Scotiabank Photography Award is an annual juried search for excellence among leading Canadian contemporary photographers. It recognizes a mature and accomplished body of work by an established Canadian photographic artist. In addition to this book, which celebrates the artists' vision, the award includes a Primary Exhibition in Toronto during the Scotiabank CONTACT Photography Festival.

The Scotiabank Photography Award is made possible by an exceptional team. We are indebted to publisher Gerhard Steidl and his staff; book designer Barr Gilmore and editor Laurel Saint-Pierre; Darcy Killeen at the Scotiabank CONTACT Photography Festival; Paul Roth, Gaëlle Morel and Valérie Matteau at the Ryerson Image Centre; Karen Machtinger and Marcus Schubert at Edward Burtynsky studio; and the team at Toronto Image Works.

Individuals throughout Scotiabank and in arts institutions and organizations across Canada have worked together to ensure that the Scotiabank Photography Award continues to have a sustainable, dynamic future. Thank you to every member of the Scotiabank team most sincerely, especially Brian Porter, Barbara Mason and John Doig. Thanks also to Gallant Law, Ryan Burella and Lauren Duffy for their work to advance the recognition and reach of the award, and to Joan Burgess for her ongoing commitment to the vision of the Scotiabank Photography Award and for maintaining the highest standards of excellence over the past ten years. Appreciation and thanks to our 2020 Scotiabank Photography Award Nominators: Wayne Baerwaldt, Independent Curator, 21C Curators Inc.; Jessica Bradley, Independent Curator & Consultant; Mary Bradshaw, Director of Visual Arts, Yukon Arts Centre; Noa Bronstein, Curator & Writer; Lorna Brown, Acting Director/Curator, Morris and Helen Belkin Art Gallery; Louise Déry, Director, Galerie de l'UQAM (Université du Québec à Montréal) and Associate Professor, Department of Art History, UQAM; David Diviney, Senior Curator, Art Gallery of Nova Scotia; Sky Goodden, Founding Publisher & Editor of Momus; Andrea Kunard, Associate Curator, Canadian Photography, National Gallery of Canada; Bernard Lamarche, Curator of Contemporary Art, MNBAQ (Musée national des beaux-arts du Québec); and Leila Timmons, Curator & Manager, Exhibitions and Collections, Robert McLaughlin Gallery.

We are grateful to each nominator for their thoughtful and extensive nomination. I would also like to thank our pre-eminent jury panel, Sophie Hackett, Candice Hopkins and Brian Sholis, for their expertise and collaboration. As Chair of the Scotiabank Photography Award jury, it is a privilege and an honour to contribute to the elevation of photography as a crucial art form in our time

Edward Burtynsky is regarded as one of the world's most accomplished contemporary photographers. His remarkable photographic depictions of global industrial landscapes are included in the collections of over sixty major museums around the world, including the National Gallery of Canada, the Museum of Modern Art and the Solomon R. Guggenheim Museum in New York, the Reina Sofia Museum in Madrid, the Tate Modern in London and the Los Angeles County Museum of Art.

CONTENTS

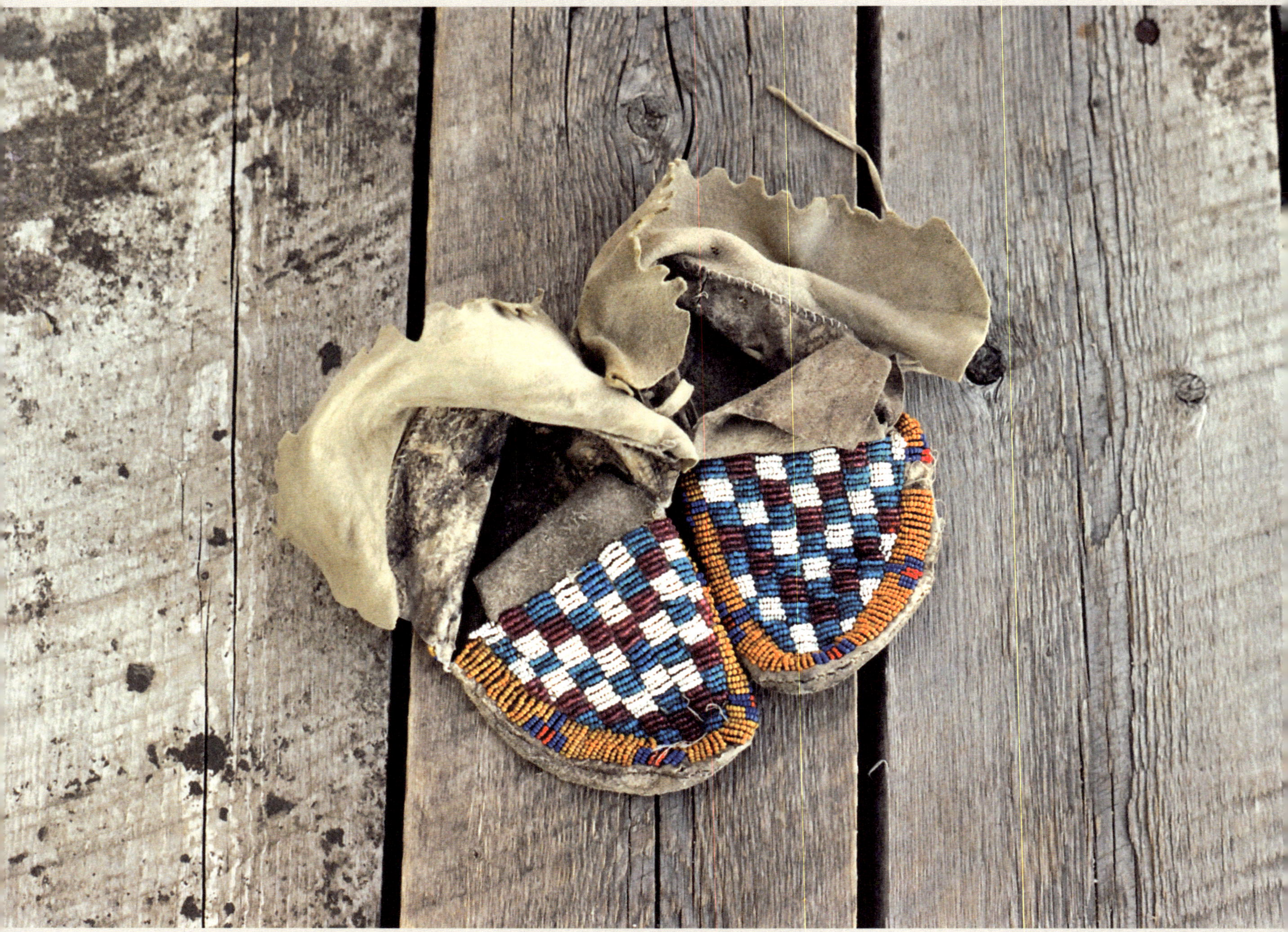

Ayuta Najin Ktewin—Killed the Enemy Who Stood Standing—Her Moccasins (My Great Grandmother), 1993–2021

INTRODUCTION

LEILA TIMMINS

"I'm known for speaking my mind," says Dana Claxton with a chuckle in a recent interview, "what's the point if you can't speak your mind?"[1] This sense of humour and clearheaded conviction have defined her multi-disciplinary practice for over thirty years. Working between performance, installation, film, video and photography, Claxton has built a body of work that explores art as a site of freedom and self-determination. Throughout her practice, she has been keenly aware of the power of representation. For her, "artworks have considerable potential to shift contemporary consciousness towards support of Aboriginal justice... as well as the potential for spiritual renewal, resolution and contemplation."[2]

Claxton, who is Hunkpapa Lakota Sioux, was born in Moosejaw, Saskatchewan in 1959 and traces her family roots in the area through her maternal lineage. Her great-great grandmother travelled into Canada with Sitting Bull after fleeing persecution from the US Army and settled in what is now the Wood Mountain reserve. Claxton draws on this family history in the early video works *I Want to Know Why* (1994) and *Sitting Bull and the Moose Jaw Sioux* (2004), both of which combine archival images, newspaper clippings and appropriated footage depicting the history of Lakota and Sioux re-settlement with intimate storytelling that narrates these histories of violence and dispossession. In a review of *Sitting Bull and the Moose Jaw Sioux* (2004), fellow artist and curator David Garneau remarked that:

> *Claxton's strategy is both good historical storytelling and creative art. The narrative is layered rather than linear, dialogic rather than authoritarian, and open-ended rather than contained. At least four accounts unspool at any one time. While they always complement each other and advance the story, the gentle polyphony encourages repeated viewings and the sense that we can gather only glimpses and should not imagine ourselves completely informed.*[3]

Mining historical images and pop culture to present more complex, authentic and nuanced narratives is a thread that continues through Claxton's practice. In the series *Indian Candy* (2013, pp. 127–133) important historical documents and pop-cultural representations of Indigenous people are remixed and edited with brightly saturated colour overlays. The signatures of Geronimo and Sitting Bull are enlarged and presented in brilliant blues and pinks, for example, and the words "Love Me" appear over an image of a toy doll adorned with beads and a headdress. Using the slick visual language of pop art and advertising to turn this found imagery into kitschy, highly aestheticized objects, Claxton comments on how value is assigned and questions which histories are taught and shared. The work is not an outright condemnation of the ways fictitious and harmful stereotypes of Indigenous people have circulated in the media, but rather builds on the media's power of seduction to reassert a more fulsome and historically accurate narrative. As Claxton describes it, she is "situate[ing] the works in vibrant juicy colours, as [if] to say this critical knowledge is delicious and sweet!"[4]

Claxton harnesses the seductive power of images and continues to use the language of popular media and advertising in order to comment on what is celebrated within contemporary culture and challenge notions of beauty and value. Many of her images are highly stylized studio portraits, shot in the style of fashion editorials, such as her iconic work *The Mustang Suite* (2008, pp. 105–111). Beauty, as reflected in the bold style of her imagery and the representation of strong Indigenous women, has been an ongoing aesthetic strategy to draw the viewer into the work where broader implications and challenges of the subject matter are revealed. As art historian Janice Hladaki notes, "with her alteration techniques, Claxton insists that an aggressive record of violence lurks behind the representation of a benevolent prosperity and benign social order."[4]

More than a critique of the enduring legacies of colonialism, Claxton's work explores the pleasure of beautiful objects and how aesthetic value can be held within communities in ways that eschew connoisseurship and consumption. Sioux leader and politician Jodi Archambault Gillette describes how the beauty of Indigenous cultural objects is central to the way knowledge is shared: "The transmission of Lakota cultural memory [is] not only a way of showing love, but of actually loving—a performative act of generosity and respect. A responsibility and a gift-giving that is also a way to survive... imparting a clear message: 'we have survived, we are here today, well-adorned, in joyous celebration of our heritage as Native Americans.'"[6] In Claxton's work and in Lakota cultural memory, gift giving, knowledge sharing and aesthetics are folded together to create a way of being that is celebratory and embodied.

The gifts of being well adorned and joyous are exemplified in Claxton's photograph *Cultural Belongings* (2016, pp. 152–153). The back-lit portrait presents a woman covered with multitudes of beaded objects and regalia. The woman has long black hair and is posed dancing towards the edge of the frame. She wears a sleeveless dress and high heels, with a densely beaded veil shielding her face. In front of her, she holds a horse-head dance stick and behind her, on a long buckskin robe, she carries a number of beaded, quilled and painted objects including barrettes, bark baskets, drums, belts and satchels. Positioned within a gallery, the work provokes questions about why cultural belongings are still held within museum collections and comments on the ways in which Indigenous women have typically been represented within these spaces. This photograph was first shown in the exhibition *Made to Be Ready* at SFU Galleries. The title, a clever inversion of Duchamp's *readymade,* implies that these everyday and ceremonial objects do not need to be elevated to the status of high art because they are already there. Claxton also calls her back-lit photographs fireboxes (rather than lightboxes) as a subtle but defiant way to sidestep the legacy of photo conceptualism, popularized in part by Jeff Wall's large-scale lightboxes. It is a legacy that arguably still looms large in Vancouver, where Claxton lives, but this is a weight she chooses not to carry.

Claxton has focused instead on creating new conditions for her work to be understood. In the related series *Headdress* (2019, pp. 157, 159, 161, 163, 165), she features portraits of Indigenous womxn[7], heavily adorned with what she calls "cultural abundance." The plumes of beaded and embroidered objects completely veil their faces, rendering them unrecognizable, their identities only alluded to in the titles of the works: *Jeneen, Dee, Shadae, Connie.* Each one is a friend and colleague of Claxton and the intimacy of these relationships comes through despite their covered faces. Collaboratively, they have selected objects and jewelry from their personal collections—often gifts from family and friends—to adorn themselves and the images are a powerful testament to the connections these womxn have to the makers of these objects and to each other. *Jeneen* (2019, p. 157) pictures the artist Jeneen Frei Njootli, a former student of Claxton's who is now fellow faculty in the visual art program at the University of British Columbia. Through her work and teaching, Claxton has helped shape a new generation of artists, but this image shows that the spheres of influence and support have been reciprocal.

This movement from the personal to the collective is a strategy Claxton uses to drive powerful political messages. In the series *NDN Ironworkers* (2018, pp. 181–185), a group of fit young men wearing work boots and safety harnesses pose casually for the camera. Critic Robin Laurence notes that the men, drawn from Vancouver's community of Indigenous ironworkers, are, "completely defying any of the cultural stereotypes that might be assigned to them... [as they] undertake demanding, dangerous and well-paid labour in the construction industry."[8] This series also points to the history of Mohawk "skywalkers" (steel workers) in New York and Ontario, and a wider solidarity between workers.

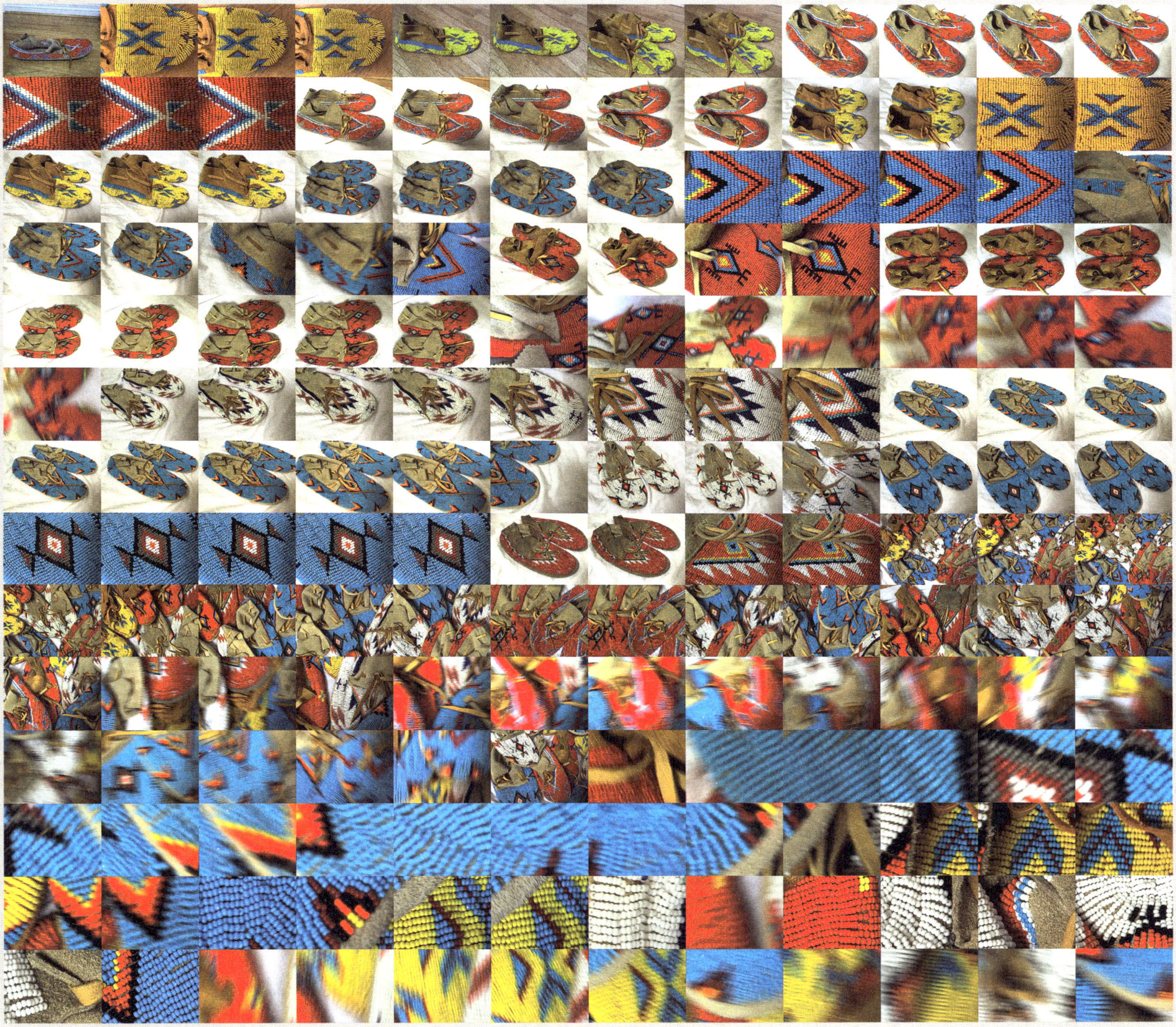

Wood Mountain Moccasins 1 (For Grace Peigan Moccasin Maker), 2017–2021

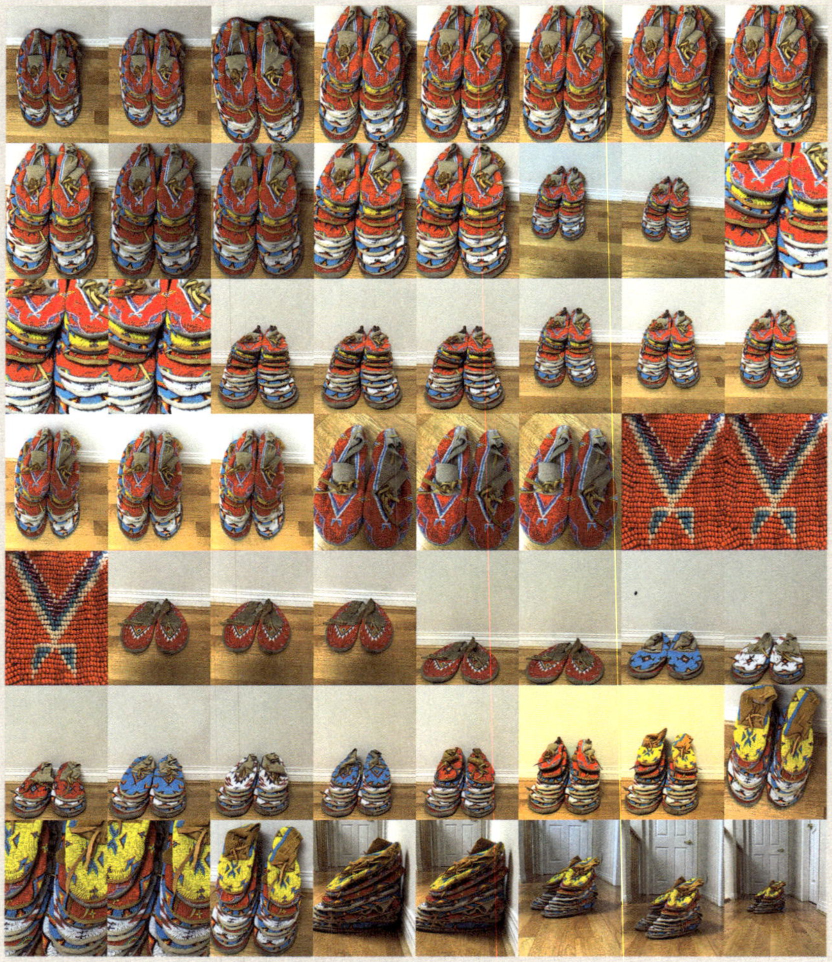

Wood Mountain Moccasins 2 (For Grace Peigan Moccasin Maker), 2017–2021

Claxton's text-based work *Red on Red: Ode to Gramsci* (2017), inspired by the Italian philosopher Antonio Gramsci, also makes use of collective strategies. The large red banners reference Gramsci's writing, alluding to both the working class and the collective power of language and art to shape culture. According to Claxton: "The red on red suggests I am following the red thread back, but in my case, as a Hunkpapa Lakota Sioux woman, I am following both the red thread and the red sinew. I am suggesting that indigenous knowledges, which are shaped by the collective commons, run parallel to Gramscian ideas."[9]

In some sense art is, by definition, communal. It wishes for community, according to the late poet Mary Oliver, and is for anybody and everybody that has hunger for it.[10] Claxton acknowledges how much we expect from art, and how much it gives us.[11] While her photographs challenge the viewer to look, think and act, they are also generous in what they provide.

NOTES

1. Dana Claxton, Governor General's Award in Visual and Media Arts video, 2020, https://en.ggarts.ca/dana-claxton.
2. Dana Claxton, "Medicine Making," *The Medicine Project* online exhibition. https://themedicineproject.com/curatorial-essay.html
3. David Garneau, "Dana Claxton: Sitting Bull and the Moose Jaw Sioux," *Vie des Arts* 197, 2004, 93.
4. Dana Claxton, artist statement, danaclaxton.com.
5. Janice Hladaki, "Remembering Otherwise: Counter-Commemoration and the Re-Territorialization in Indigenous Film and Video Art," *Revista de Estudios Globales y Arte Contemporáneo* 2, no. 1 (2014): 108.
6. Jodi Archambault Gillette, in *Dana Claxton: Fringing the Cube*, exh. cat. (Vancouver: Vancouver Art Gallery, 2018), 64.
7. Claxton adopts this spelling in relation to this body of work.
8. Robin Laurence, "Dana Claxton," *Border Crossings*, 150, May 2019.
9. Dana Claxton, artist statement, danaclaxton.com.
10. Mary Oliver in conversation with Krista Tippet, *On Being* podcast, "Mary Oliver: Listening to the World," February 5, 2015.
11. Dana Claxton, Governor General's Award in Visual and Media Arts video, 2020, https://en.ggarts.ca/dana-claxton.

Leila Timmins is a writer and curator with a Bachelor in Art History from the University of British Columbia, and a Master in Art History from the University of Toronto with a focus on contemporary Canadian photography. She is currently the Curator and Manager of Exhibitions and Collections at the Robert McLaughlin Gallery in Oshawa. Leila also sits on the Board of Directors of DACHI, the Education & Community Engagement Commitee at the AGO, and is a founding member of EMILIA-AMILIA.

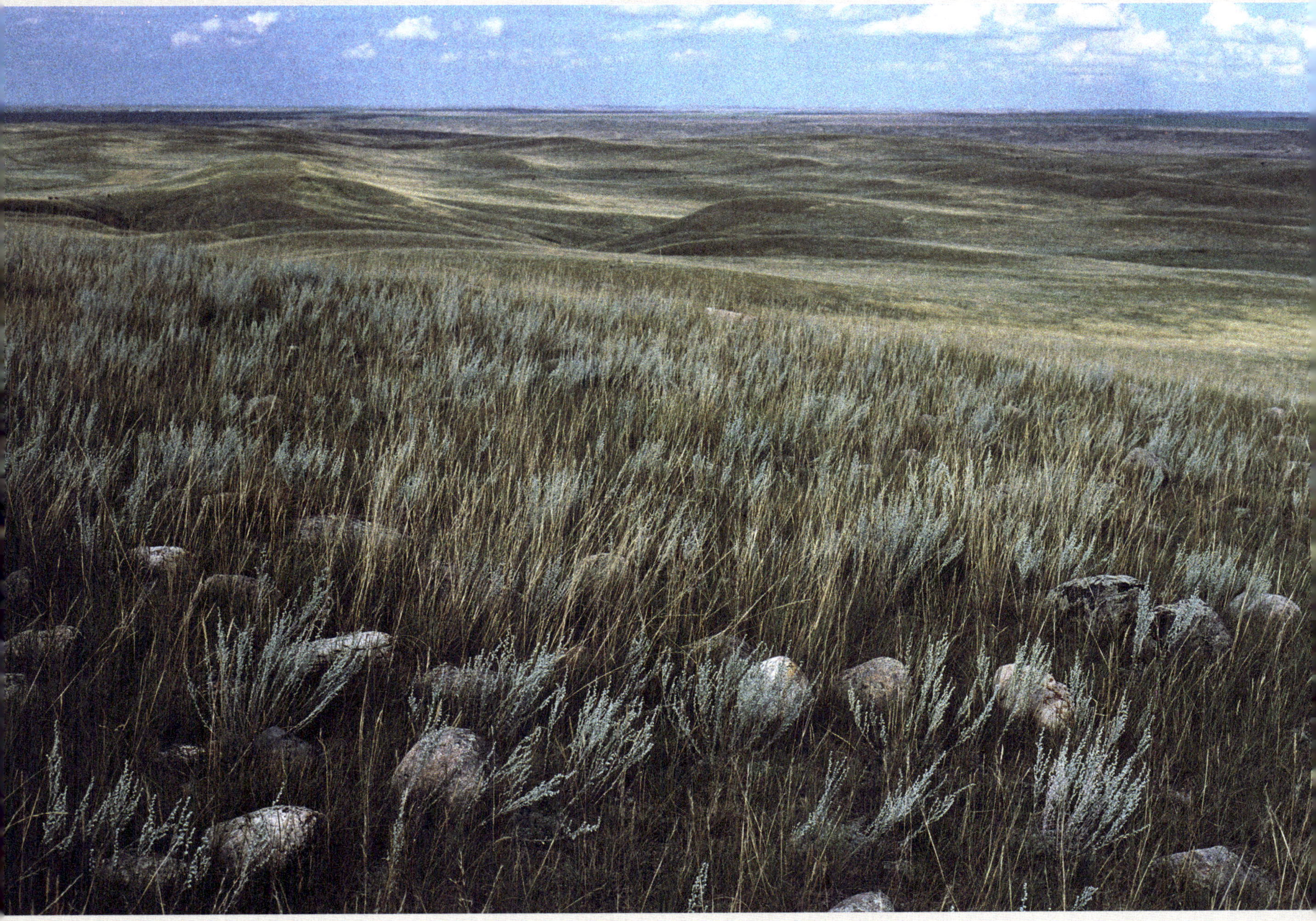

Cabri Lake 1, 1995–2021

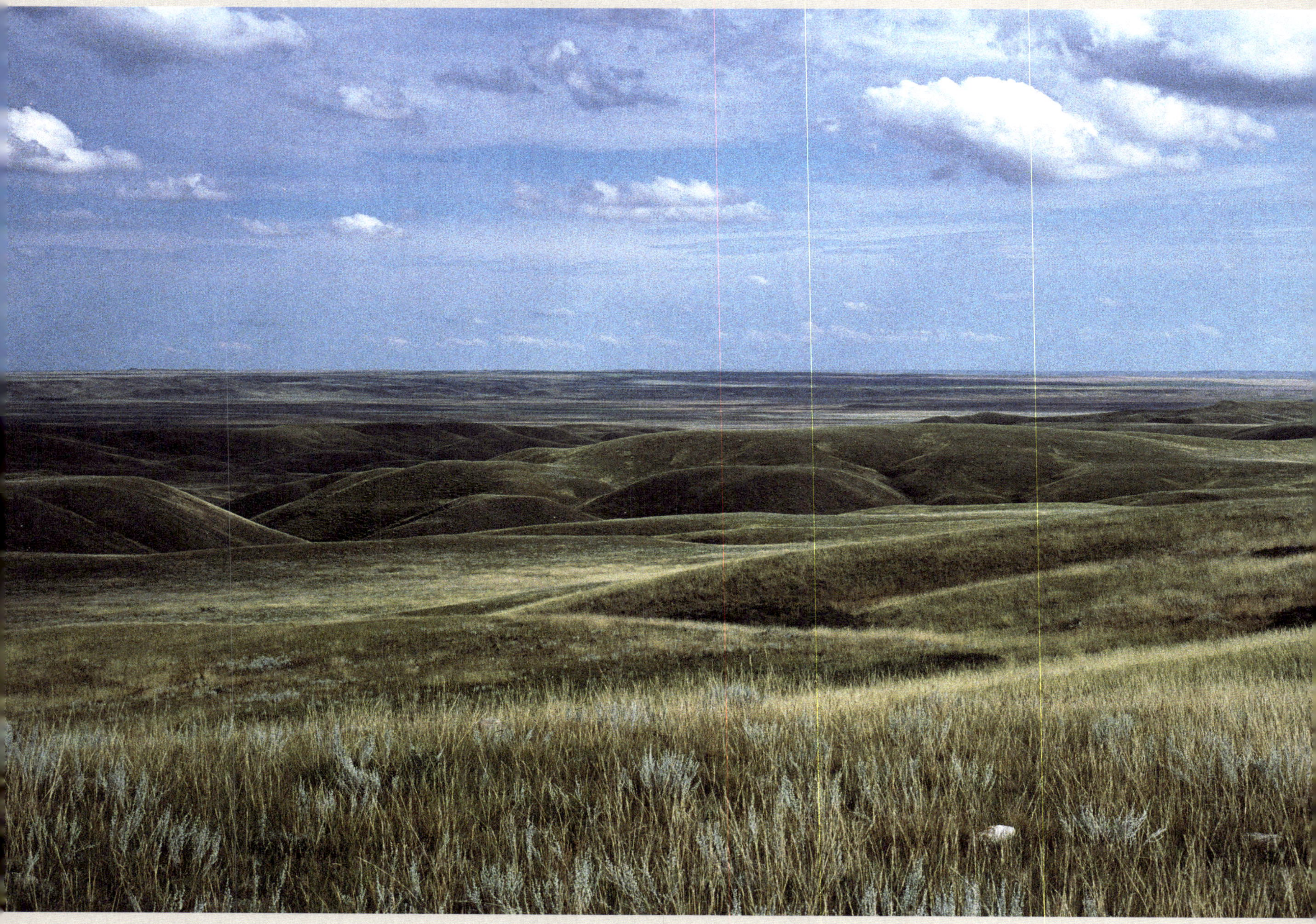

Cabri Lake 2, 1995–2021

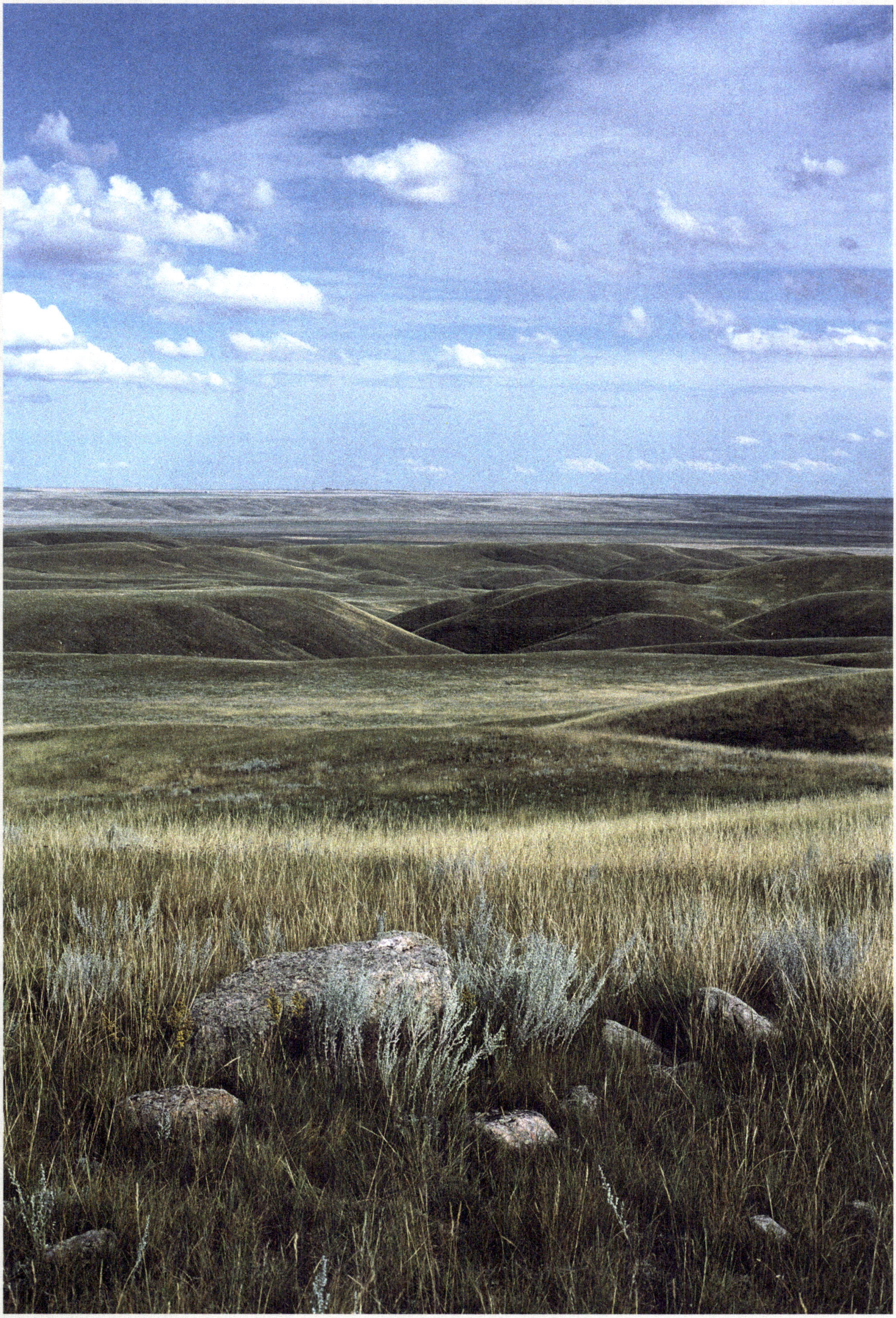

Cabri Lake 3, 1995–2021

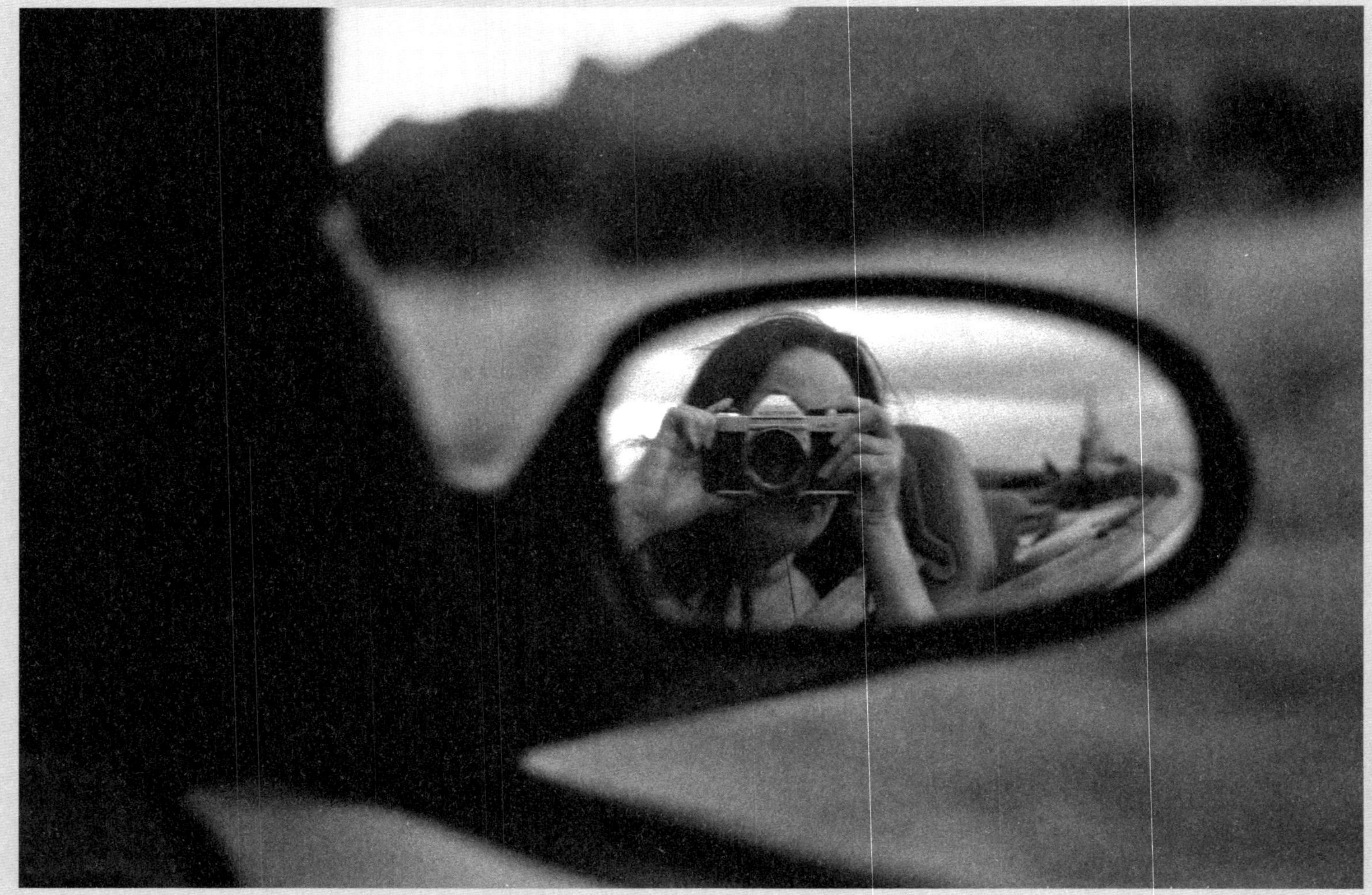

Self Portrait in Kaui, 2009–2021

EVERYTHING YOU NEED TO KNOW IS IN THE SKY

AMY KAZYMERCHYK

In the late 2000's, Dana Claxton took a photo of herself in the side mirror of a moving convertible. The landscape around the mirror is out of focus. We see a wash of three tones that suggest tall grasses in the foreground, a grove of trees in the mid-ground and hills rising above the horizon. The mirror is in focus, and we glean the stain of an overcast sky in the distance. Claxton's reflection is the focal point of the image. Her hands elegantly clasp the metal body of the 35mm camera. It covers most of her face and the eye of its lens is aligned with her own. The photograph spatially and temporally situates her in the territory, showing what's ahead, behind and above her. What she is traveling towards and where she has been.

I encountered this image amongst contact sheets and test prints in Claxton's archive. She does not consider it an artwork, but it embodies the consciousness of her practice. The photographs around it had been taken on various trips, sometimes alongside the production and presentation of artworks that had sharpened into focus more quickly. They captured lightning storms, cloud formations and scattered stones in Saskatchewan, fashion and architecture in New York, and museums in Rome and London. Together they pictured a life lived with and through art. They could be considered un-realized artworks, but they may have simply been in retreat, awaiting the right conditions to emerge.

Encountering these images led me to reflect on how *movement* catalyzes and shapes Claxton's practice. It is expressed in how she moves across territories, under the sky and with the elements; and between temporalities, genealogies and paradigms. Claxton's engagement with a range of conceptual and formal influences is a dynamic form of mobility, as is the circulation of formal motifs and conceptual patterns across varied media. These expressions of movement are synthesized by the propulsive energy of the intuitive, responsive and relational methods that guide her practice.

Movement in Claxton's work often takes the form of walking, a modality that allows her to shoot in scale with her body, unencumbered. The agility that walking offers is expressed in the technical qualities and formal composition of many of the images. A photograph may be taken from a raked angle that draws attention above or below the eye line, and the horizon may be off balance, or the subject out-of-focus. The way one walks in the world conditions how the eye drifts, frames and focuses. Walking as a means of cultivating insight and wisdom is practiced in numerous lineages including that of Plains nations such as the Lakota, which Claxton has inherited.[1]

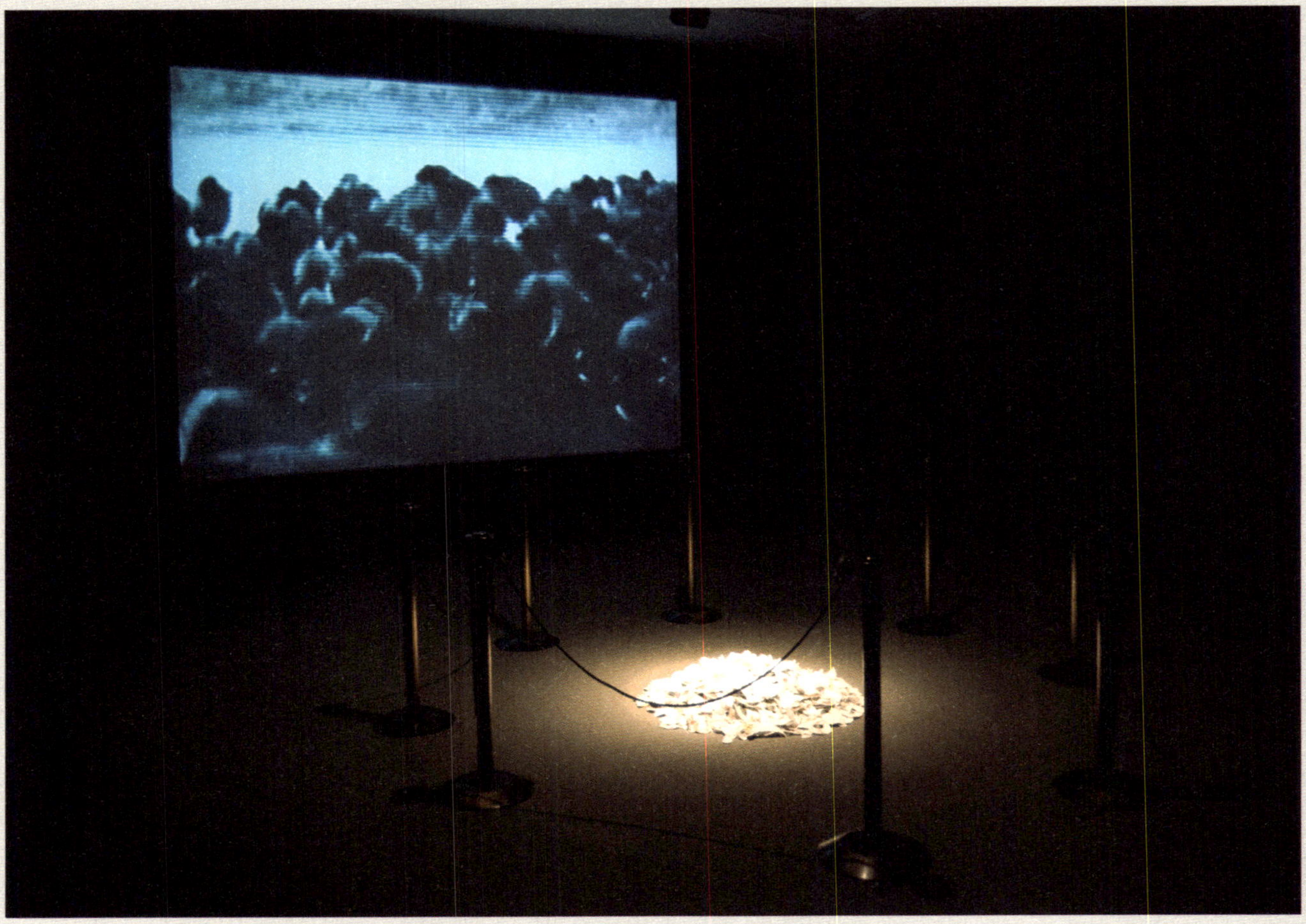

Installation view of **Buffalo Bone China** (1997) at MacKenzie Art Gallery, 2000. Photo by Don Hall / Courtesy of the MacKenzie Art Gallery.

•

Claxton's genealogy is braided with that of the Hunkpapa Lakota Sioux who walked north from the Black Hills to the Cypress Hills with Sitting Bull in 1877 to escape colonial terror and were forced to settle between Moose Jaw and Wood Mountain in southern Saskatchewan.[2] The Sioux are identified as the Tatanka Oyate or Buffalo People and their way of life—including their shelter, food, clothing, music, dance and ritual—is inherited from the buffalo.[3] They align with the wisdom, courage and fortitude that guide the animal's movement across an expansive territory and with the generosity of its provision. Colonial policy stopped Indigenous people and the buffalo from moving freely across the plains, instigating borders, reservations, warfare, murder and starvation. Highly strategized policies recognized that the lifeforce of the Sioux and the buffalo were intrinsically linked, and that the decimation of one would take the breath out of the other.[4] Both the Sioux and the buffalo showed physical and spiritual agility in the face of capture. Walking is a means of survival for Indigenous people across the Americas, as the legacy of Sitting Bull attests,[5] and mobility as resilience is a fundamental value within Sioux philosophy that shapes Claxton's vision.

The buffalo's propulsive lifeforce resonates in the video element of *Buffalo Bone China* (1997) through the visual and aural rhythms of a migrating herd. In this work, the renewal of the buffalo's energy is also transfigured through its spiritual release from the constraint of the china made from its bones. This early work inaugurated what would develop into Claxton's 'Plains Projects,' which highlight the resilience and beauty of Plains people, their culture and their lifeforce.

The breadth and visibility of the plains' horizon suggest an expansive range of movement. From the perspective of the plains, it's much easier to visualize the earth's circumference in all directions. The distinctions between subjective positions such as front–behind, left–right or above-below are muted. This can cause vertigo at first, but disorientation soon settles into a unique sense of emplacement, cultivated by the territory's spatial relativity. The reflectivity between the earth and sky both focuses and diffuses one's relation to them, establishing a strong sense of connectivity. The horizon's expanded sense of time, space and relationality permeates Claxton's moving image works and influences the form of their presentation.[6]

In the installation *Landscape #1* (2004), one video is presented as a large projection and a second one appears on a small monitor. The projected video opens with an establishing shot of a prairie around Cabri Lake, Saskatchewan.[7] The sky is bright blue and patterned with clouds that cast shadows on the rolling coulees.[8] Over the horizon, a sequence of black and white archival footage of settler homesteads, agricultural infrastructure and religious buildings appears in a binocular shaped, picture-in-picture frame. The camera then drops from the horizon to the ground and tracks over low-lying stones that are covered in lichen and nestled amongst wild grasses. The texture, colour and motion in this tracking shot emphasise the perspectival rift between Claxton's breathing image and the atrophied archival footage. The video on the monitor doubles the prairie landscape, creating a second instance of binocular vision. Two lines of text alternate in the lower third of the screen, "Walk each step as a prayer / I give you these offerings." The repetition of these lines sets the intention of the peripatetic tracking shot in the large projection and implies a continuum between those who walk, have walked and will walk this territory, regardless of restrictions.

In 2015, Claxton returned to Cabri Lake, where part of *Landscape #1* was filmed, to shoot the two-channel installation *Landscape Revisited* (2015). In it, the landscape is presented across adjacent screens that are approximately life size. Claxton's figure is pictured walking away from, then towards the camera, enacting a cycle of retreat and return.

Claxton has also taken colour and black and white photographs at this location. Images in the *Cabri Lake* series (1995–2021, pp. 13–15) show stones amidst grasses and the prairie under calm or turbulent skies. The high contrast black and white images illuminate the distinct textures of the grasses and lichens and the undulation of the coulees. Like both the establishing shot and the tracking movement in *Landscape #1*, they are clearly taken from the perspective of a standing person in moments in which walking has been halted. A viewer's relative familiarity with and relation to the territory in the photographs, may effect their interpretation of the works. Some aspects of the images may be immediately recognizable while other elements may be less legible.

One work in the series, *Cabri Lake (BW Panorama)* (2000–2021, pp. 26–28), is sutured together from multiple exposures and depicts a richly textured territory of undulating coulees covered in prairie grass. The shape and texture of the blades of grass express a relation to the fringe that adorns Lakota clothing, tack, instruments and other belongings. Grass's flexibility and tenacity in the face of the elements inspires the form and spirit of fringe, which, Claxton says, keeps the wearer "keenly aware of the connection between his or her body and the elements."[9] Wind also shapes grass into tufted patterns that resemble buffalo fur, which is equally resilient to the elements. This effect is visible in the photograph *Tatanka Wanbli Chekpa Wicincala (Robe)* (2006, p. 91). Hides and fringe are are evidence of the reciprocity between humans, animals, elements and plants in this territory.

In the landscape near Cabri Lake, the intricate formation of lichen on stones and the flora that surround them evoke the vivid composition and colouring of beadwork in Plains design. Speckled, blooming and orbiting patterns in rose, mint, olive, pumpkin, graphite and umber form on the stones. Beadwork flourishes throughout Claxton's works and the specificity of Lakota design is featured in a series of photos documenting beaded moccasins titled *Wood Mountain Moccasins 1 & 2 (For Grace Peigan Moccasin Maker)* (2017–2021, pp. 9–10). Each print is composed of a grid of small adjoining frames. The movement expressed in some of the frames and across their sequencing propels the moccasins into motion—as if they are being danced—and gives the composition a cinematic feeling. This sensation is emphasized in a single-channel video that Claxton made by montaging the still images.

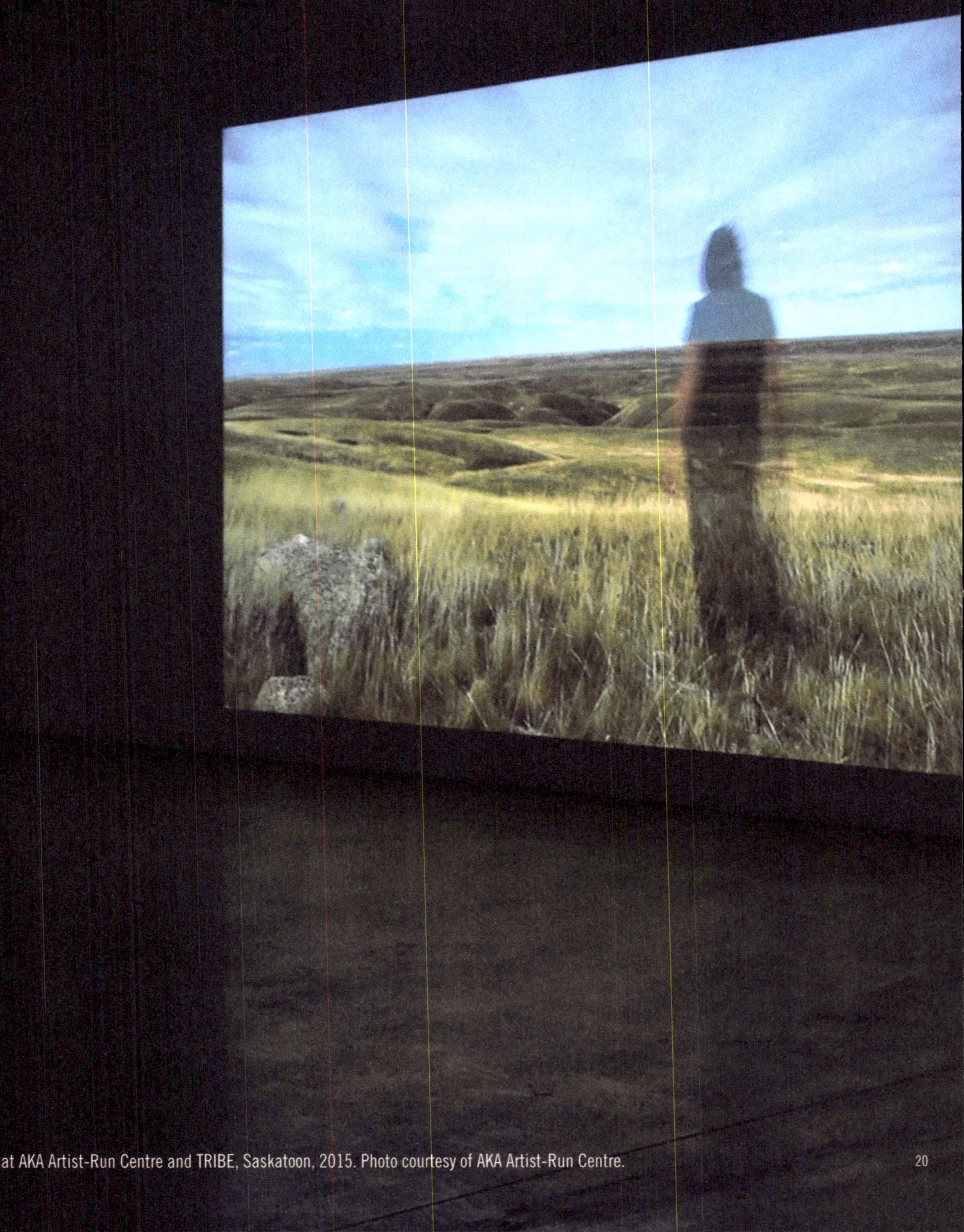

at AKA Artist-Run Centre and TRIBE, Saskatoon, 2015. Photo courtesy of AKA Artist-Run Centre.

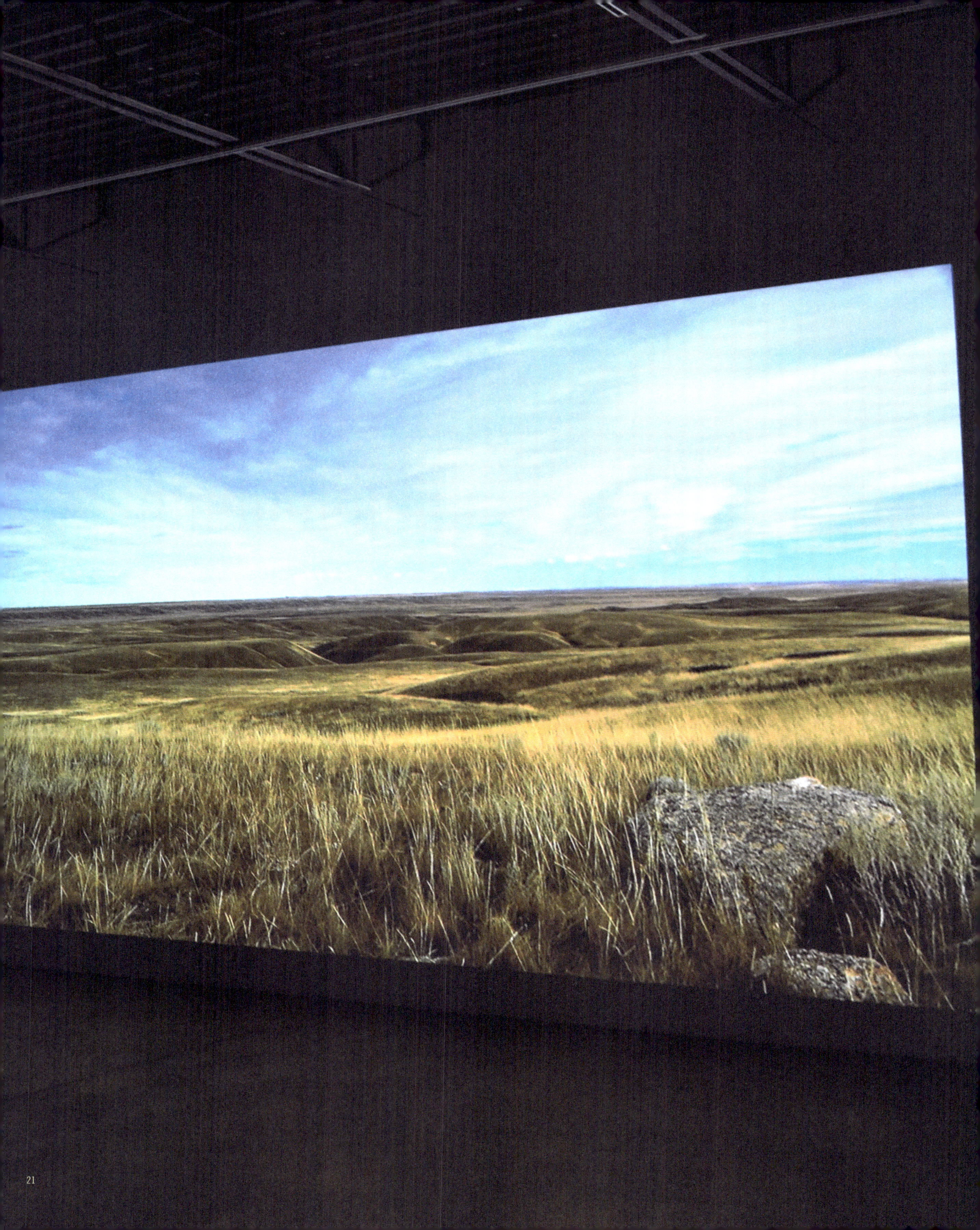

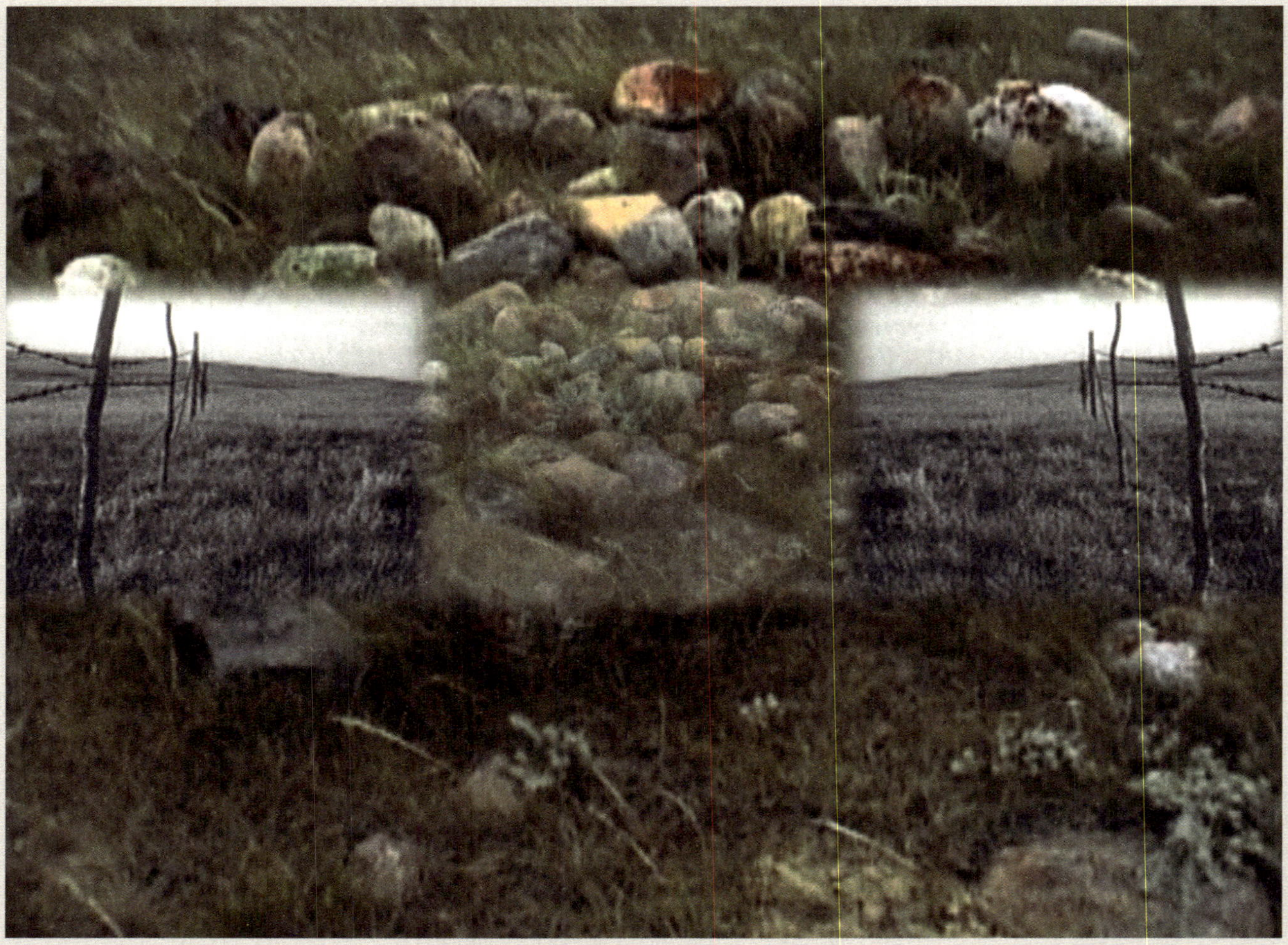

Video still from **Landscape #1**, 2004

The territory in *Cabri Lake (BW Panorama)* is marked with deep furrows caused by the migration of buffalo over centuries.[10] The furrows were instrumental in shaping the coulees and buttes, and in scattering and fertilizing prairie grass seed. Earth and rock markings from 500 tipi rings can also be found on the site. These circular ruts and stones trace the presence of Plains people across the territory. Neither of these features is visible from a distance, but the texture and dimension of animal and human movement can be seen in the photograph's tonality. The condition of 'not visible,' particularly in images of landscapes in North America, in relation to Indigenous life, is hegemonically rendered as absence, loss, yearning or past. Cree Filmmaker Tasha Hubbard synthesizes an alternative paradigm that resonates with Claxton's methodology. She reframes 'not visible' as "patterns of emergence and retreat, re-emergence and renewal," which emphasize visibility as a process of circulation rather than a state of permanence.[11]

In her writing, Hubbard draws from Plains origin stories that convey how buffalo emerged from under the earth to support the livelihood of Plains people. In turn, they may also retreat underground to hide during various times of crisis—such as colonialism—and re-emerge when it is safe.[12] Hubbard observes that this cyclical sense of renewal is inscribed in the repetition of the running buffalo in Claxton's *Buffalo Bone China.*[13] The quietude of the *Cabri Lake* images does not preclude them from portraying this dynamic process. Like Claxton's own image in the car mirror, the buffalo that grazed this territory may simply be caught in a reflection that is poised between hindsight, insight and foresight.

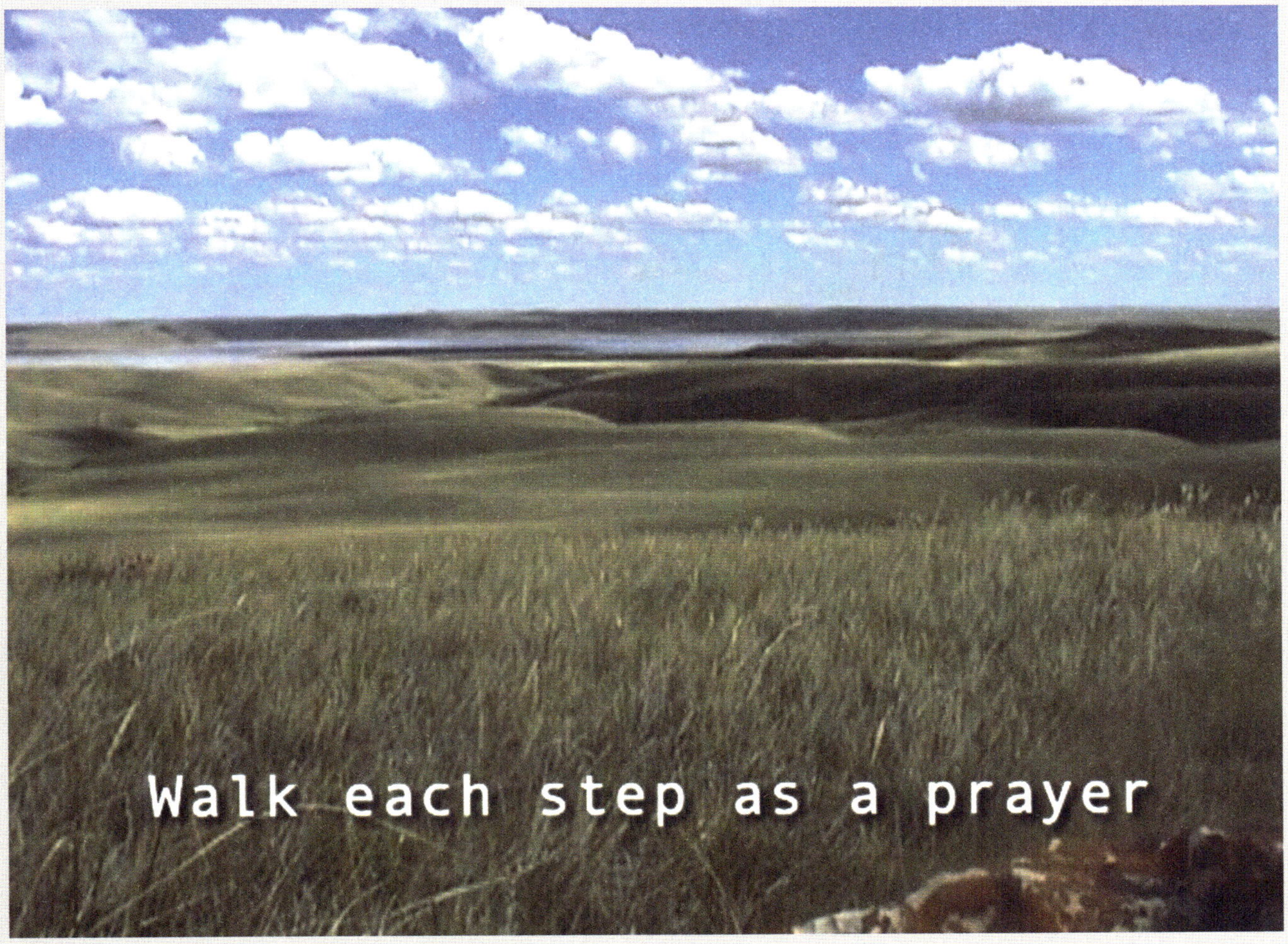

Video still from **Landscape #1**, 2004

Since the mid 1990s, Claxton has traveled internationally to support the presentation of her work. On two of these occasions, she reprised walking as modality and method to explore her emplacement in global cultural centres. The *Paris* series (2006, pp. 39–72) was shot when she accompanied the presentation of *Rattle* (2003) at the Le Havre Biennale and the *Manhattan* series (2015-2021, pp. 74–83) was created in New York when she performed *Fringed* (2015) at the Metropolitan Museum of Art. For each series, Claxton articulated an intention then set out with a 35mm camera to respond to what she encountered.

Claxton was inspired to highlight her presence as a contemporary Native artist in Paris and New York and to draw attention to the influence of Indigenous aesthetics in cosmopolitan culture.

She had first explored this ethic on a trip to London, Rome and Paris in the 1990s with the painter Lawrence Paul Yuxweluptun. The *Sauvage au Musée* series (1994-2021, pp. 196–197) portrays Yuxweluptun looking at paintings by masters in Europe's most prestigious museums. Claxton was drawn to document Native artists as actants in, rather than subjects of, aesthetic culture. An essential aspect of such autonomy is the right to create art that preserves and evolves lineages of Indigenous visual culture in dialogue with Euro-American aesthetics. "Indigenous artists were never supposed to visit the world's most prestigious cities and museums," she explains, "nor learn from their artworks, let alone present their own work there themselves."[14] To walk the streets of the centres of empire and re-frame the expressions of their design and habitudes is to perform resilience in the face of forced retreat.

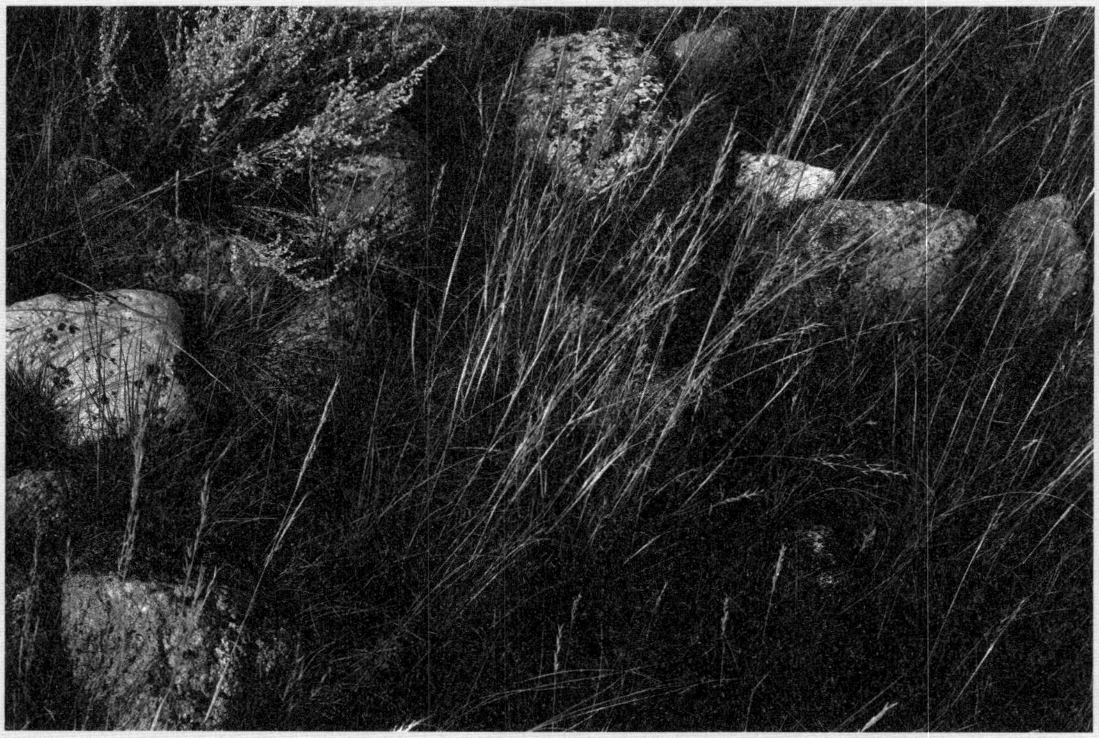

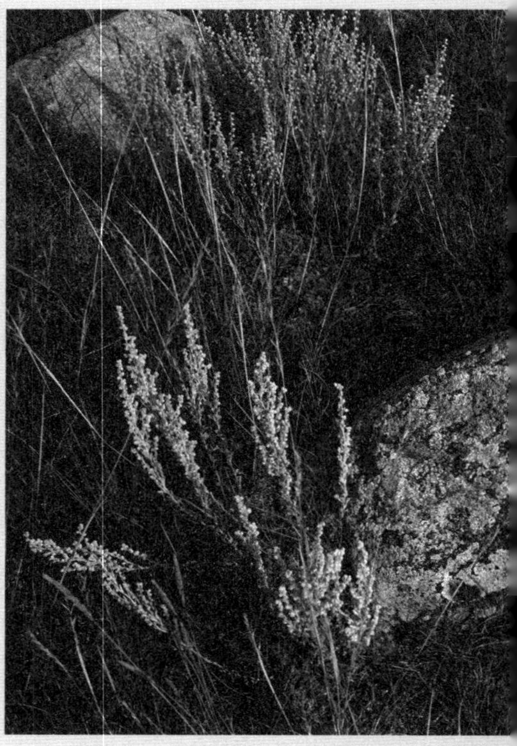

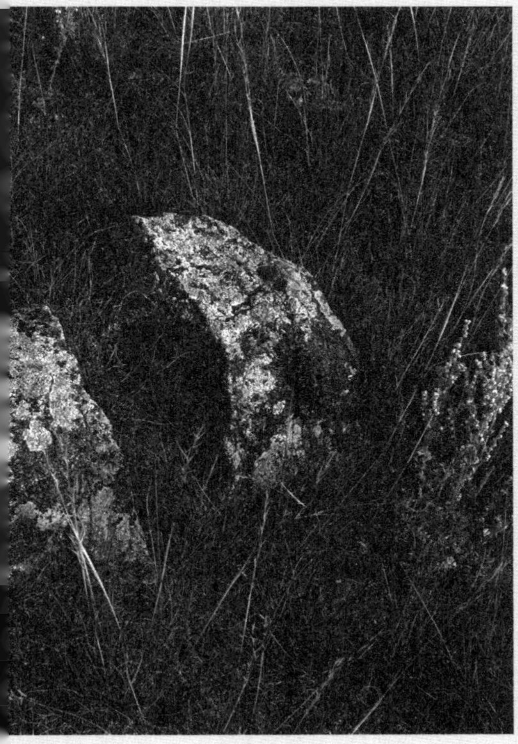

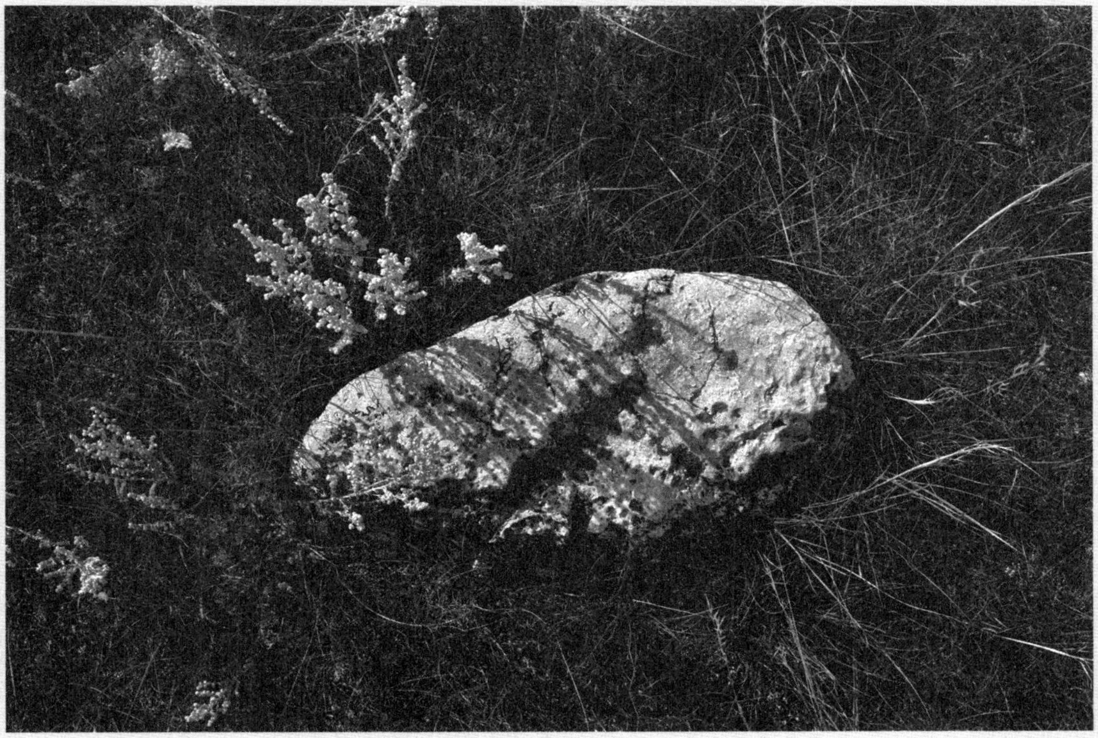

Stones 1–3, 2000–2021

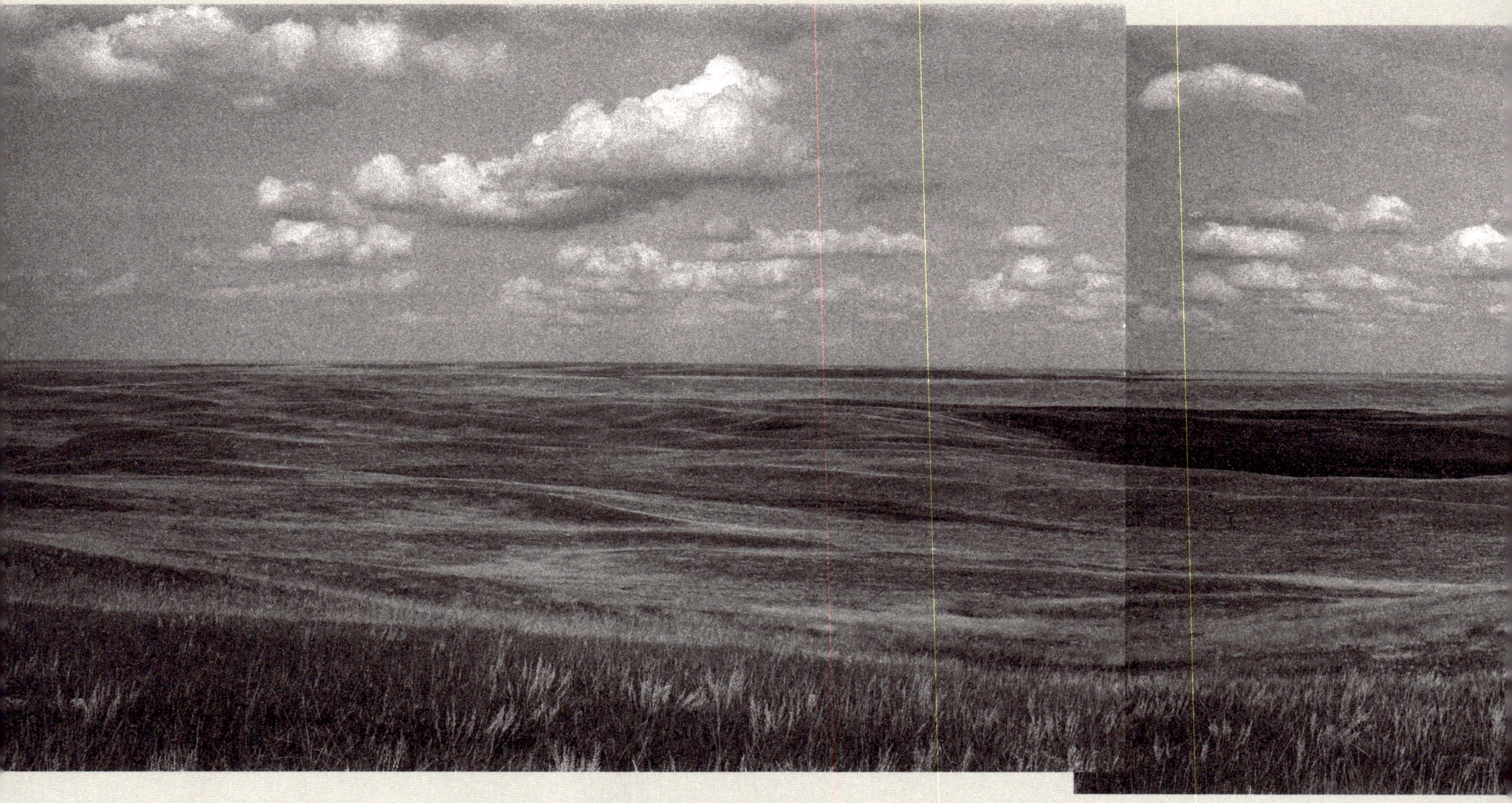

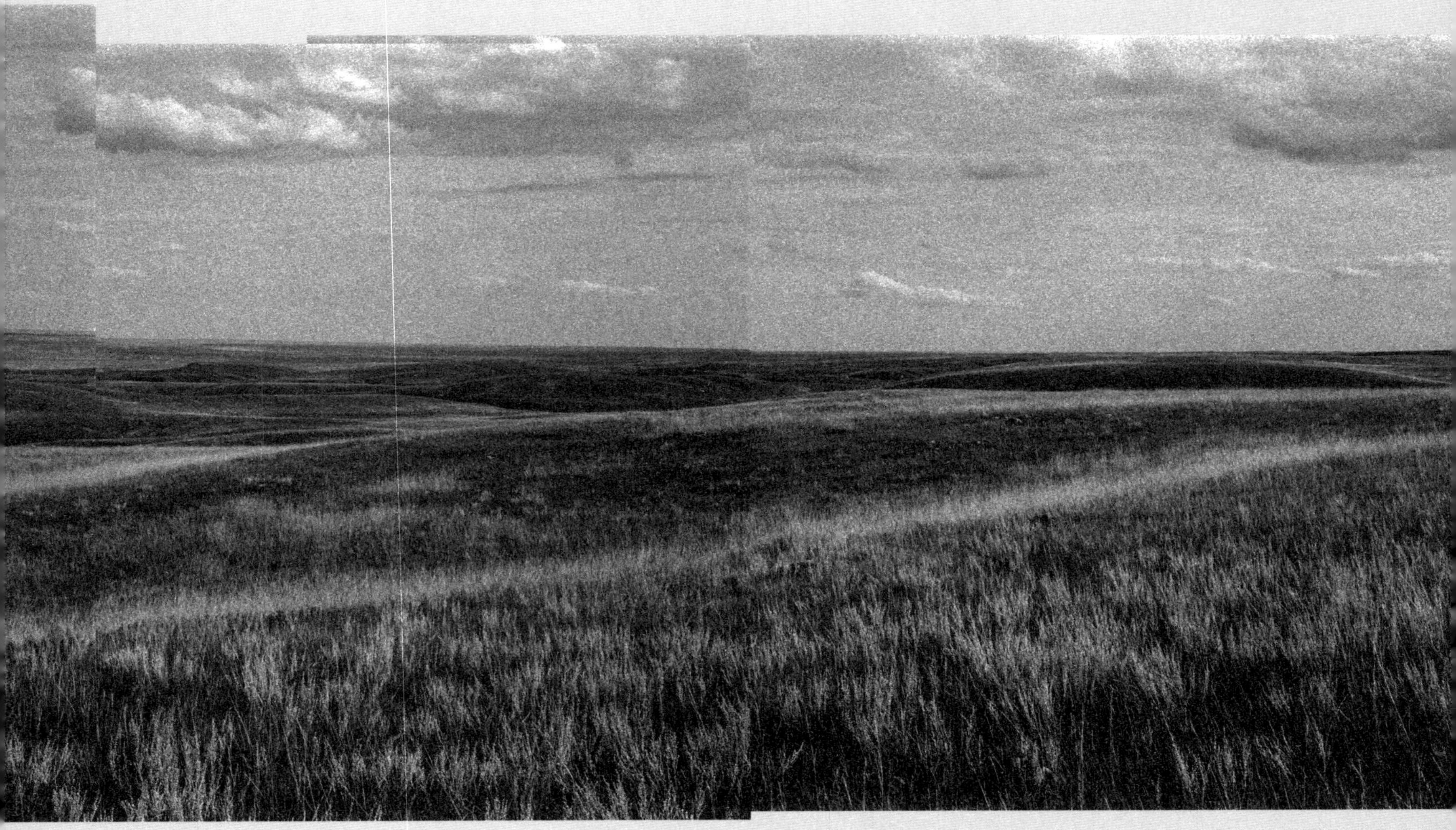

Cabri Lake (BW Panorama), 2000–2021

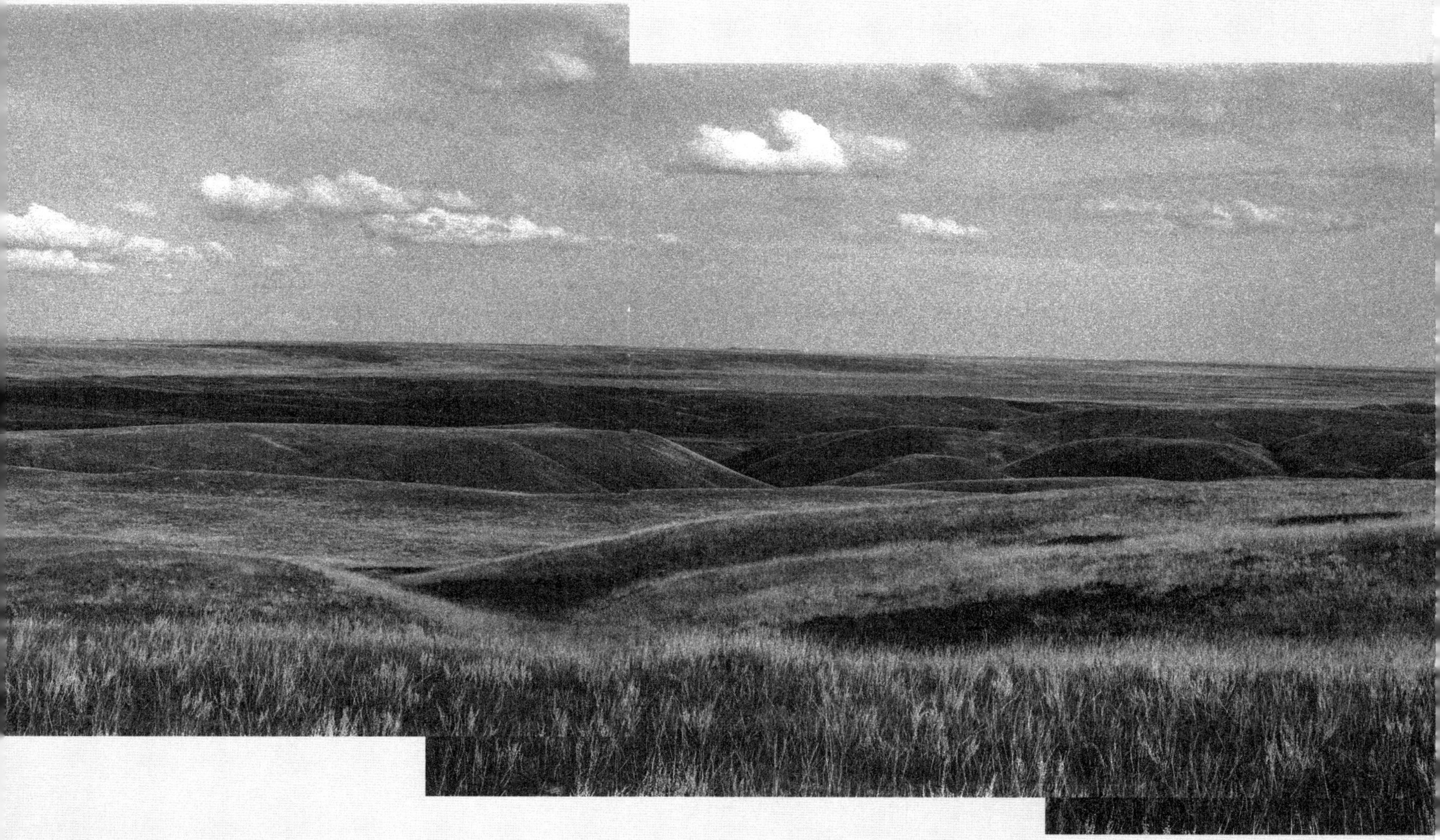

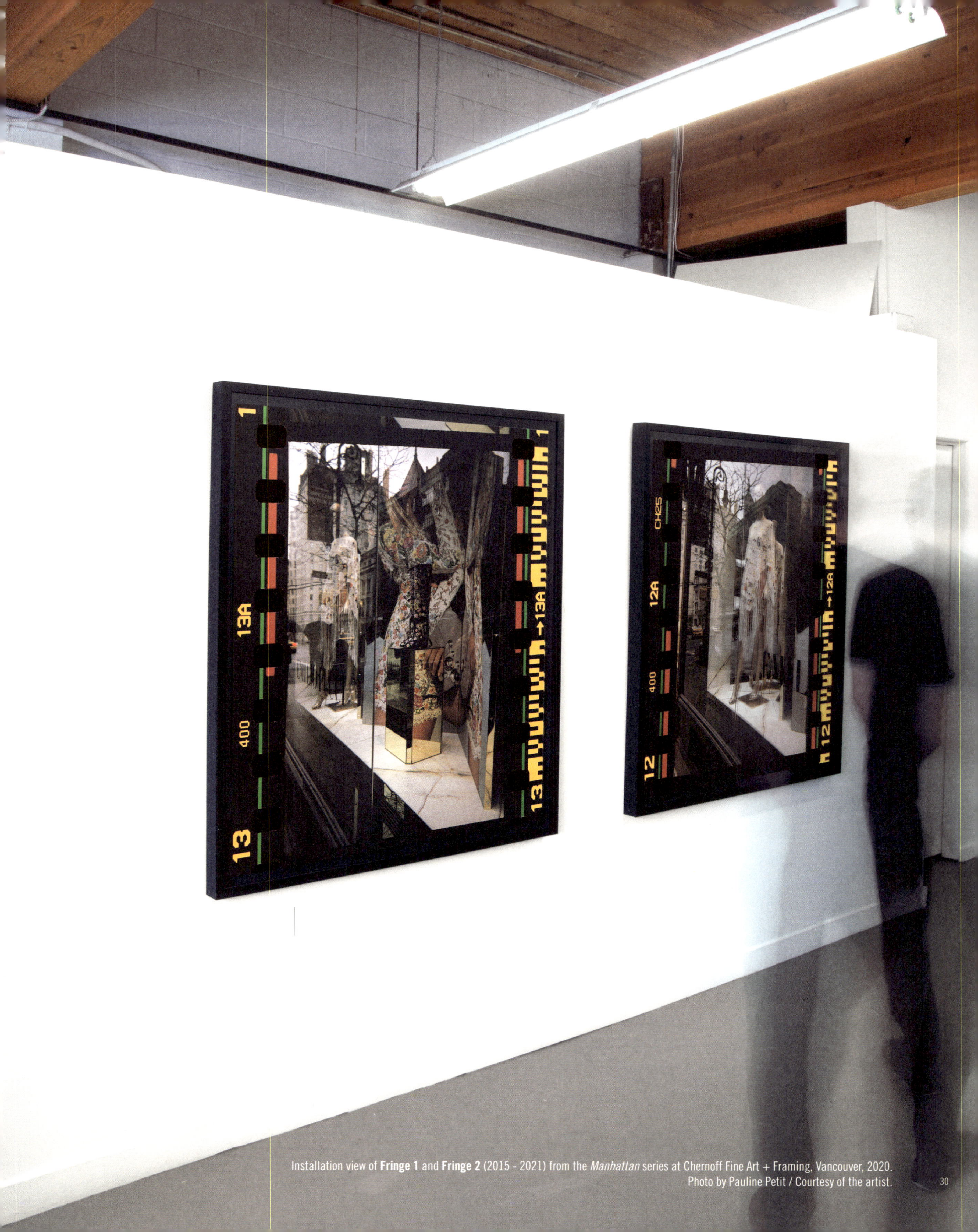

Installation view of **Fringe 1** and **Fringe 2** (2015 - 2021) from the *Manhattan* series at Chernoff Fine Art + Framing, Vancouver, 2020.
Photo by Pauline Petit / Courtesy of the artist.

The *Paris* and *Manhattan* series portray the freedom that is accessed through mobility. This freedom is expressed in the photographs' spherical perspective and formal agility. The images exude a verité quality that evokes both senses of *free*: inexpensive means of production and the autonomy of working with lo-fi, portable equipment.

The impetus for the *Paris* series was to look at 'Indians' in the streets. In these photographs, Claxton highlights subtle aspects of architecture, monuments, advertising and fashion that are imbued with concepts prominent in the imperial imagination such as solitude, wildness, freedom and captivity. Her attention to the sky in Paris is distinct from the myopia of the modernist Flaneur or the focus on street culture in dérive literature. The value of the sky's reflection is also expressed in her moving image installation *Rattle,* which was presented in France at the Le Havre Biennale. In the work, a close up of two rattles being shaken and a detail of beadwork are doubled and mirrored across four screens, creating a visual palindrome. Claxton has discussed how the doubling of images emphasizes the notion that creation on earth and in the sky reflect each other to create an existence of timelessness—continuum with no ending.[15]

In a number of the Paris photographs, she isolates historical and political statues from their socio-cultural context, such as a public square or building, by framing them against the sky. *Man and His Horse* (2006, p. 63), shows a monument of a man in a loincloth grasping at the reigns of his horse whose front legs are reared and mane wild, as if it is striving to free itself from the confines of the pedestal. In other photos, she highlights the energetic force of the sky. In *Cathedral Window 1* (2006, p. 42), the sun illuminates the intricate design of stained glass windows whose radial patterns echo Plains beadwork. *Paris Garden* (2006, p. 72) captures potted roses that have grown wild, reaching up to towards the sun beyond the wrought iron balustrade of a balcony.

Figurations of stoic women also feature prominently in the *Paris* series. Joan of Arc is portrayed twice. In *Peasant Warrior* (2006, p. 41), she is captured from a low angle, with hands clasped in prayer and eyes cast skyward. In *A Horse and His Man or Woman* (2006, p. 60), she is glimpsed from a distance, armoured on her horse and positioned to charge into battle. In *Nurse* (2006, p. 40), a young woman with a long braid resting over her breast is also shot from a low angle. Her solemn eyes are cast downward towards the camera and her hand rests on a sword.

The impetus for the later *Manhattan* photographs was to look for evidence of fringe in the city. The series was inspired by Claxton's performance at the Metropolitan Museum of *Fringed,* in which she dances a garment of floor-length fringe. In the late 1980s, Claxton lived in New York where she was involved in fashion and design and she was drawn to the prominence of haute-couture there. *Fringe 1 and 2* (2015-2021, pp. 82–83) capture a window display of white lace Emilio Pucci dresses with vivid embroidery and beading, black high heel boots adorned with floral embroidery and a shawl edged in draping white fringe. The display also features a number of mirrored cubic forms that split and refract reflections of the mannequins, the lacework-embroidery and the surrounding architecture.

In *American Elm 1 and 2* (2015-2021, pp. 76–77), Claxton's eyes are drawn upward to the sinewy limbs of American elm trees in Central Park. She frames the branches so that their elongated fingers touch the sky, like Joan of Arc's praying hands. If these trees were exposed to plains' winds, one can imagine how their sinewy branches would sway like long fringe. A rhizomatic growth pattern also appears in *Upper East Side 1 and 2* (2015-2021, pp. 74–75) in the residue of wild vines on the side of a building. The sun dancing on the decrepit façade creates a shimmering aura of nature's resilience.

•

Claxton's attention to the lace and embroidery on the Pucci dresses in New York, the coloured stained glass in Paris and the beadwork on moccasins from Wood Mountain evolved into a series of prints, windboxes (printed silk banners) and fireboxes (Claxton's term for illuminated photographs, or lightboxes) that she produced from 2016 to 2019, including *Headdress* (2016–2019, pp. 151, 157–165), *The Protector* (2017, p. 135), *Buffalo Woman 1 & 2* (2016, pp. 144 and 147) and *Cultural Belongings* (2016, pp. 152–153). While most of the figures in the portraits are seen from the front, the woman in *Cultural Belongings* is shot in profile. Her body is directed forward, her leg is poised mid-step and her arm is outstretched, bearing a man's warrior horse dance stick. This composition embodies Claxton's commitment to 'walking in beauty,' which synthesizes the Lakota ethic of 'walking the good way' and the Diné Navajo philosophy of 'the beauty way'.[16] In this paradigm, beauty is rooted in spiritual, physical, relational and ethical balance, and in the equilibrium between goodness and adversity. Walking in beauty means facing life's complexity with courage, integrity and grace.[17]

Cultural belongings, like the ones featured in the trail of the eponymous photograph, play an active role in walking in beauty. As art historian Lynne Bell explains, "they are a central part of their owner's social lives: they are beautiful, they are 'carriers' of the culture's most important teachings, and they need to be taken out regularly so that they can breathe and dance."[18] Claxton observes this value by allowing her belongings to breathe in photographs, films, videos and performances. Some of her belongings have circulated through numerous works, such as her painted parfleche bustle holder, which was part of the performances *The Elsewhere* (2011) and *Fringed* and is featured in *Cultural Belongings* in the trail behind the figure. The beaded barrettes in *Rattle* are part of the headdress pictured in *Headdress*. Elemental energy is imbued in illuminated fireboxes, such as *Headdress* and in the loose hanging flexible silk of the windboxes *Buffalo Woman 1 & 2*.

Perhaps the first time the headdress breathed in Claxton's practice was in the performance of *Buffalo Bone China* in 1997. The performance begins with Claxton, adorned in a white work-suit, smock and face shield, approaching a table. She selects bone china from a second table set off to the side, buries it under a pile of sawdust in front of her, then smashes it with a mallet. After a few cycles of this sequence, she brushes the sawdust aside, collects the shards and tenderly wraps them in purple cloth. Thinking along with Hubbard, Claxton's burial of the buffalo bones in sawdust serves to guide them into retreat before her mallet releases them from colonial capture, for proper burial and mourning.

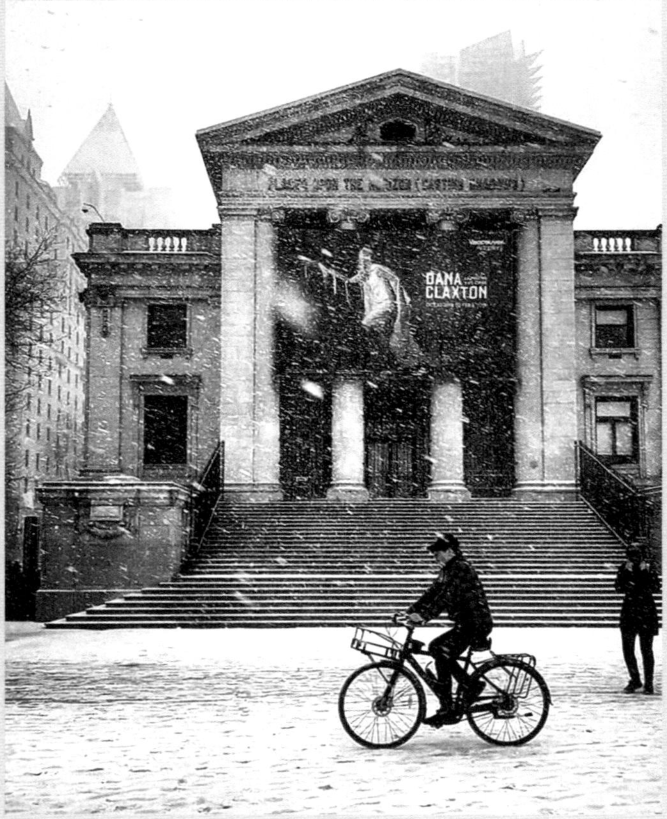

Promotional banner for *Dana Claxton: Fringing the Cube*
at the Vancouver Art Gallery, Vancouver, 2018.
Photo by Angela Code.

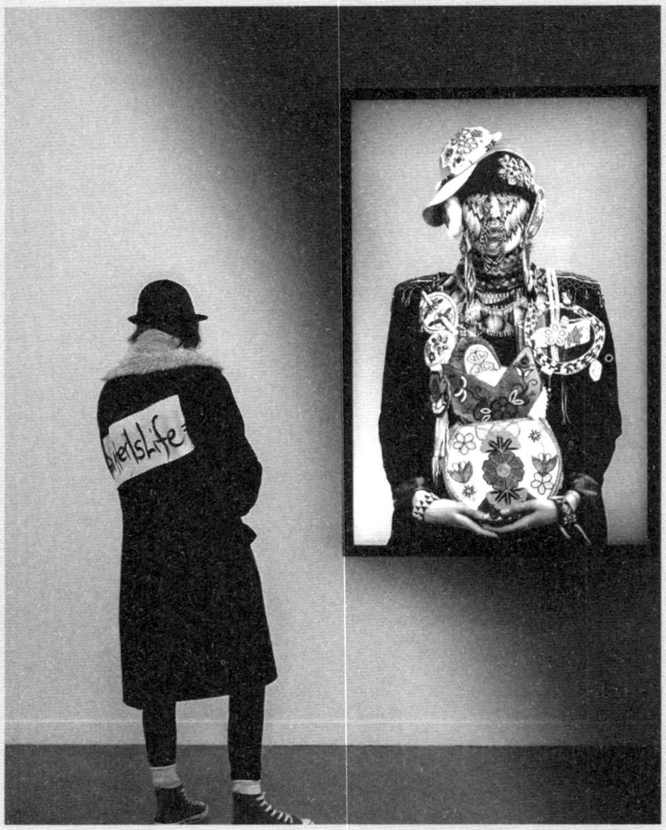

Installation view of **Headdress – Jeneen** (2018)
at the Vancouver Art Gallery, Vancouver, 2018.
Photo by Alex Ballingall.

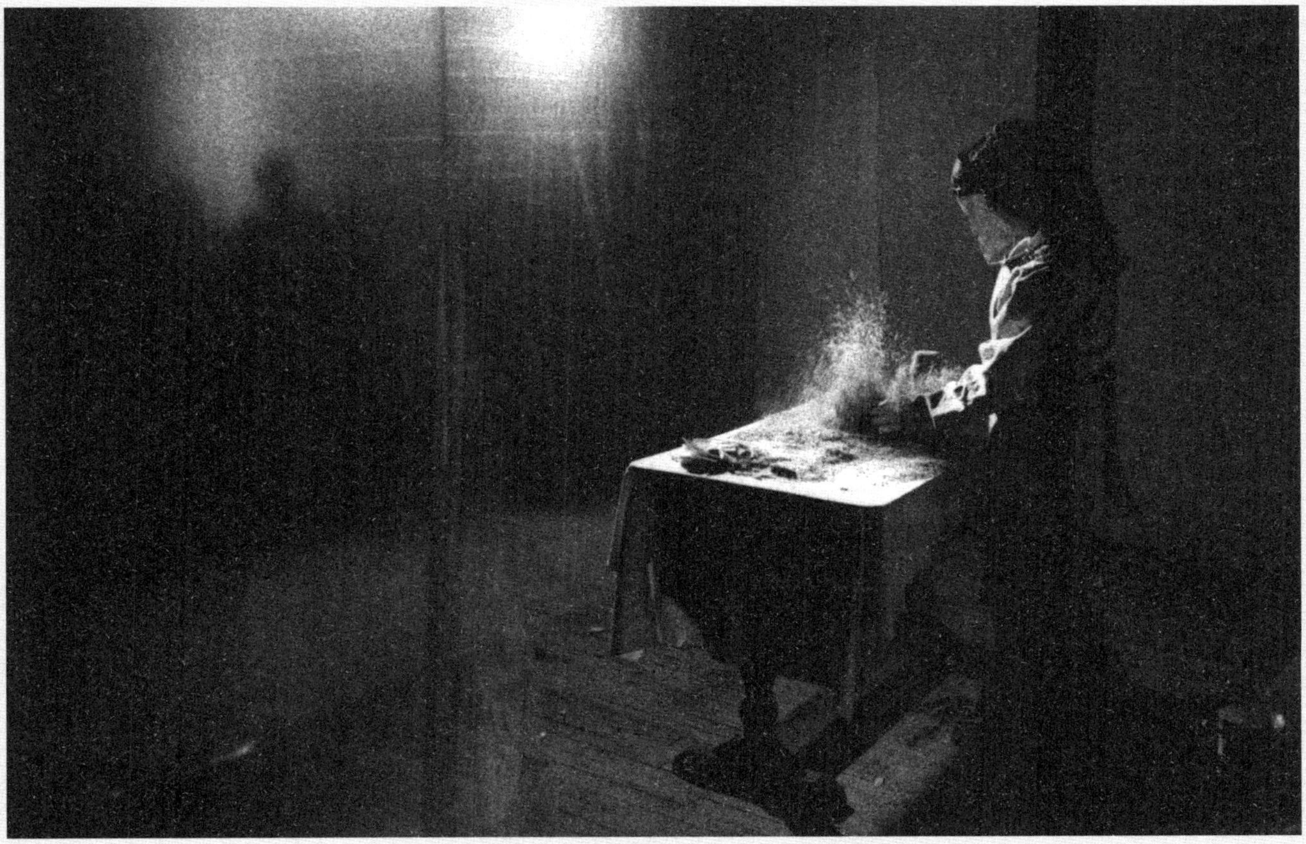

Performance of **Buffalo Bone China** (1997) at TRIBE/AKA Artist-Run Centre, 1997. Photo by Bradley LaRocque.

In the second part of the performance, Claxton wears a headdress edged in fringe that resembles the face shield. She enters a second tableau and places the bundles on a blanket, in front of a video of running buffalo. Claxton's use of similar garments for labouring and for ritual acknowledges the relation between the enduring labour of restitution, and the sacred value of self-determination and self-sufficiency.

Twenty years after the performance of *Buffalo Bone China*, the headdress form re-emerges in a series of studio photographs. In *Headdress*, the sitter wears a composition of Claxton's belongings that the artist composed. In subsequent photographs, modeled after the original but named for the person portrayed, the sitters are adorned in their own personal collections. They are poised and confident and face the camera head-on. They see the camera, but its access to them is obscured. The viewer is confronted with the sitters' embellishment. Beauty in these images is visibly expressed in the aesthetic wonder of the beadwork, the sitters' composure and the formal composition. The aesthetic expression of the belongings in the photographs is an active gesture of resistance and resilience.

In conversation with writer Aruna D'Souza about the tension between Indigenous women and mainstream second wave feminism in the 1960s and 70s Claxton said, "Indian women didn't want to burn our bras—we wanted to bead them! Meaning we want to maintain culture as our cultures were criminalized and we were placed into 'zones of indistinction' by the state, church, all institutions including the academy and art history."[19] Indigenous women articulated colonialism as the primary oppressive force in their lives, that displaced them from their land, disrupted their relations with extended family, partnerships and their own children and dispossessed them of their rights to self-sufficiency and cultural continuity. Reconnecting with these relations, rites and title is a priority for establishing Indigenous women's sovereignty. The bracelets, cuffs, necklaces, hats, brooches, bags and earmuffs in the *Headdress* series (pp. 157–165) were made by the sitters' friends, family and teachers. Portraiture's frequent emphasis on the singular figure is socially expanded through their presence. None of these women walk alone. Their beauty is upheld by the collective cultural resilience that made and circulated their belongings.

•

Photographs such as the *Headdress* series were taken in large studio spaces that offer Claxton plenty of room to improvise with actors and models, and to choreograph lighting and camera positions. She likens the scope of these spaces to the breadth of the plains. Describing how she moves between production conditions, artistic mediums and technical disciplines, she explains that she doesn't distinguish them as separate architectures, mediums or disciplines. She considers them equally, as *realms* that overlap, collide, echo and influence one another. For her, the sky, a film set, a composition of stones and dance choreography can be envisioned as a constellation of harmonized forces.

The studio as realm is evident in the film *The People Dance* (2001) and the accompanying photographs (pp. 84-89). The black and white 16mm film draws on the lineages of the Sioux Sundance and Powwow dance, and the prophecy of the White Buffalo Calf Woman. It features two protagonists named 'Man' and 'Woman.' Woman is a spectre of the sacred relation who appeared to the Lakota in the mid-eighteenth century when the people were suffering from famine, after being pushed west from the woodlands into the open plains by Ojibwe, who were armed by the French. She gave the people the sacred pipe and seven sacred rites to cultivate resilience in the face of changing living conditions.[20] In the film, Woman gives Man a similar leather-bound bundle, guides him to listen to teachings of the sky, wind and water, then leads him to dance. After dancing with two dancers, Man carries a white stone and a framed photo of a white buffalo calf out of the darkness. The closing shot of the film is a long slow zoom out from a close up on the photo.[21]

Stones akin to the ones in the Cabri Lake photos make numerous appearances in *The People Dance*. Sweat lodge stones, flying stones, talking stones and grandfather stones are relations of *Iyan*, the first rock that existed in the void and birthed the world in Lakota cosmology. The film temporally shifts between the beginning of creation, the emergence of White Buffalo Calf Woman, the resilience of contemporary Indigenous men and women and the birth of the white buffalo calf. It expresses how the buffalo continues to re-emerge in support of Sioux's renewal, and demonstrates how movement shapes Claxton's vision.

A suite of six photographs was taken on the set during production. Each photograph portrays a distinct visual perspective. *Jingle Dress 1* (1998–2011, p. 84) is an omniscient view of the set from above that observes the lights, technical gear and crew behind the scenes. *Jingle Dress 2* (1998–2011, p. 85) captures the cameraman filming the dancer. *The People Dance (The Camera)* (1998–2011, p. 86) documents the apparatus of vision—the camera on a dolly-crane rig backstage.

These photographs draw attention to the apparatus of production, the perspective of the artist, the gaze of the camera and the power of the lens. Like Claxton's self-portrait in the car, they may also be viewed as traces of artistic consciousness. They highlight the apparatuses that have scrutinized and consumed Indigenous life. They reveal Claxton's reflexive observations on the conditions of image production and presentation. And they portray the studio as a dynamic realm where these conditions can be transfigured.

In *The People Dance*, Woman lays a path of stones for Man to follow as he learns to walk the good way. This is a path that Claxton's ancestors have walked for thousands of years. Her contemporary adaptation of the story of White Buffalo Calf Woman emphasizes walking as a modality that continues to cultivate reflection. In the film, Man repeats "everything I need to know is in the sky," as he practices listening to the teachings of sun, wind and water. These teachings inform how Claxton walks through the world and how she sees. They guide her to draw relations between the resilience of the material world, Lakota culture and artistic production, to lay a path into the future.

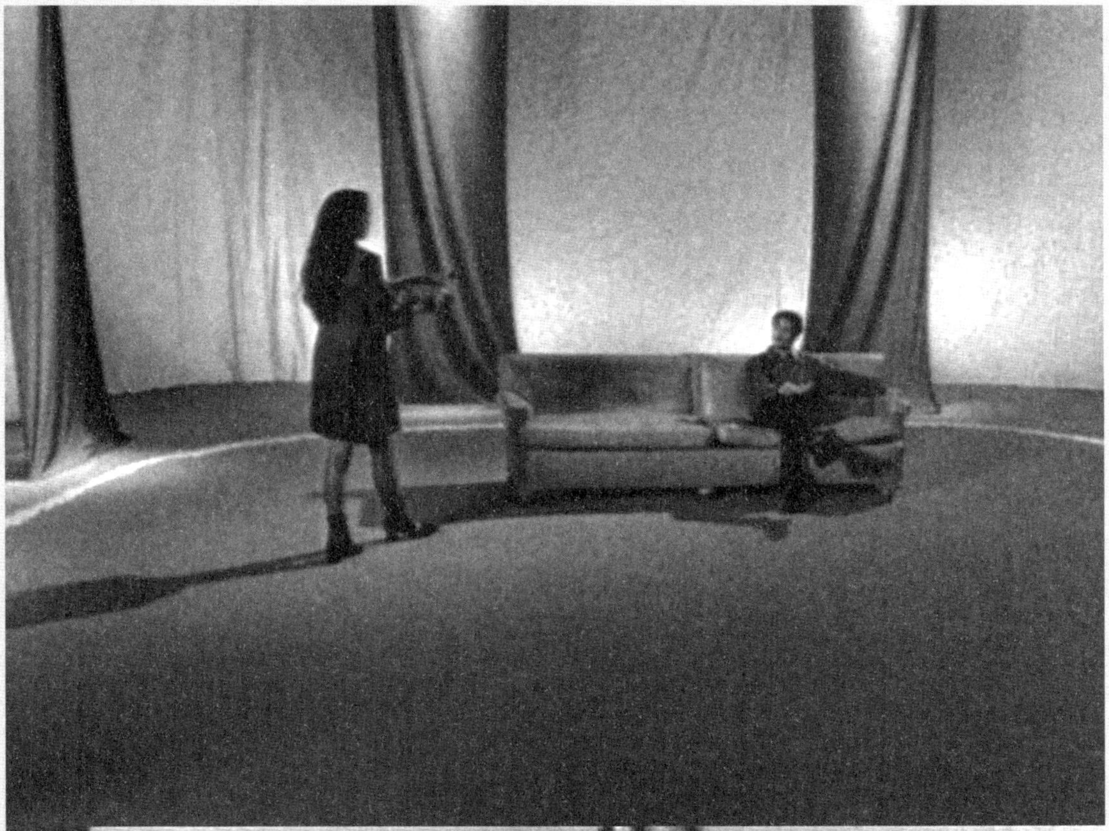

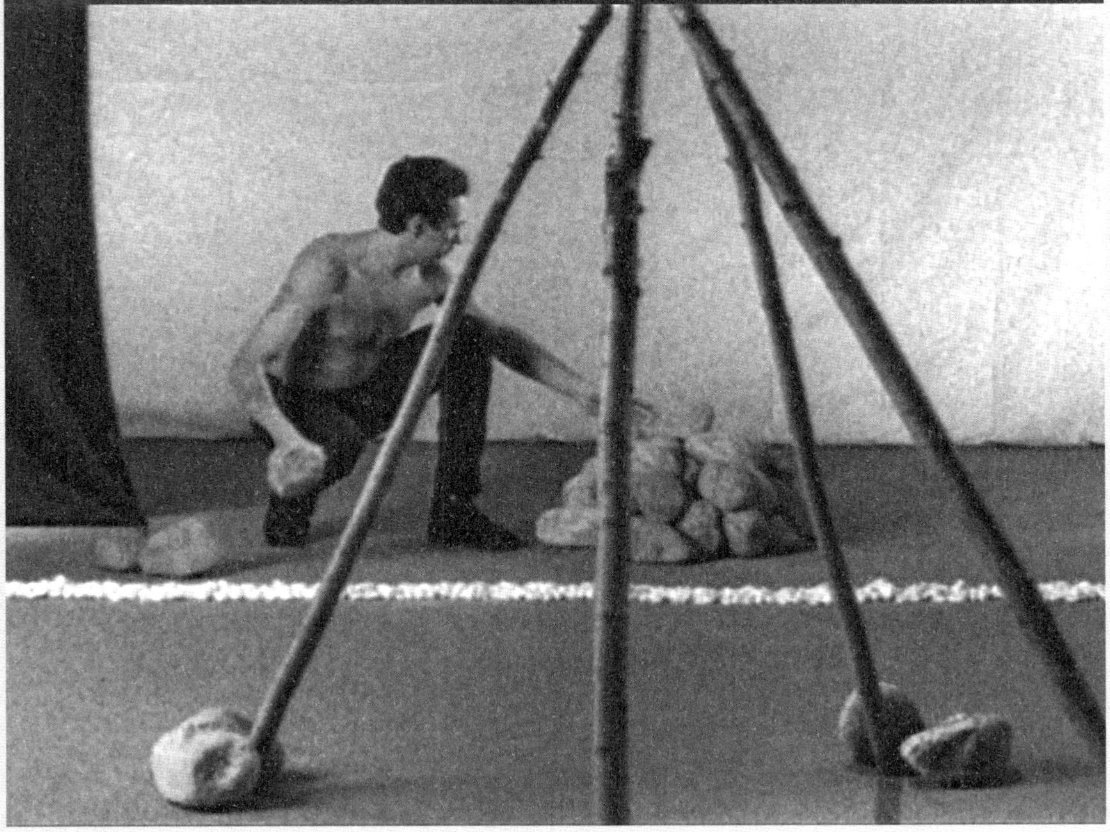

Stills from **The People Dance**, 2001. Courtesy Vivo Media Arts Centre.

NOTES

1. Oceti Sakowin (People of the Seven Council Fires) or the Sioux, are a confederation of plains Indigenous people that speak the related Siouan languages Lakota, Nakota and Dakota. A number of bands speak each language and they reside in different regions. The Western Sioux or Teton spoke Lakota, and Hunkpapa is one of the Teton's bands. Prior to colonization, the Sioux were nomadic across the 49th parallel. In Canada, there are multiple Nakota and Dakota reserves between Alberta and Ontario, but Wood Mountain in Saskatchewan is the only Lakota reserve—although Lakota people reside across the continent. Sioux is an abbreviation of Nadouessioux, a pejorative name thought to be introduced by Ojibwe and translated by French then English colonists. Although it is contentious amongst members of the nation, Claxton celebrates the term.

2. Sitting Bull led a group of Lakota north across the border following the Battles of the Rosebud and Little Big Horn—also known as Custer's Last Stand—both in 1876. Although the Sioux were victorious, the threat of government retaliation, the diminishing buffalo herds and settler expansion made life increasingly difficult. Sitting Bull refused to sign the Laramie Treaty of 1868 which ceded land to the government and restricted Sioux to reserves. In Canada, the Lakota also encountered the diminished buffalo herds and starvation. Some Lakota, including Claxton's relatives, stayed in Canada, though many returned with Sitting Bull to the USA in 1881.

3. The Sioux share the plains with other Indigenous cultural groups, including but not exclusively the Blackfoot, Cree, Ojibwe, Assiniboine, Crow and Cheyenne, who also have intrinsic relationships to the buffalo.

4. Tasha Hubbard quotes Mineconju-Lakota Spiritual leader Lame Deer to emphasize this context: "The buffalo was part of us, his flesh and blood being absorbed by us until it became our own flesh and blood. Our clothing, our tipis, everything we needed for life came from the buffalo's body. It was hard to say where the animal ended and the man began." in "'The Buffaloes are Gone' or 'Return: Buffalo'? The Relationship of the Buffalo to Creative Indigenous Expression." *The Canadian Journal of Native Studies* XXIX, 1&2 (2009): 68.

5. Following Sitting Bull's murder in 1890, Spotted Elk (Chief Bigfoot) walked another group of Hunkpapa Lakota from Standing Rock to Pine Ridge. Instead of safety, however, they encountered more violence at Wounded Knee. Since 1990 the *O'maka Tokatakiya (Future Generations Ride)* has gathered horse-back riders, walkers and runners to track over 300 miles between Sitting Bull Camp and Wounded Knee to commemorate the 1890 massacre. In 1972 eight organizations including the American Indian Movement (AIM) and the National Indian Brotherhood organized the *Trail of Broken Treaties* caravan from the west coast to Washington DC. It was followed by *The Longest Walk* from Alcatraz, CA to Washington in 1978 to protest the further erosion of treaty rights, and was repeated four times over the following forty years to address standards of living. In 2016, people walked from across the continent to Standing Rock, North Dakota to resist the Dakota Access Pipeline. In 2019, Women of All Red Nations (WARN), a women's faction of AIM, reunited to join the *Future Generations Ride* and honour Murdered and Missing Indigenous Women (MMIW). In Canada, *Walk4Justice* gathered people to walk from Prince Rupert, British Columbia to Ottawa, Ontario in 2011 to raise awareness of MMIW. In 2013, the Nishiyuu Walkers walked from Whapmagoostui, Quebec to Ottawa in support of *Idle No More*, which was echoed by Kwakwaka'wakw Chief Beau Dick's caravan from Alert Bay, BC to Ottawa in 2014.

6. In an August 2020 interview with the writer, Dana Claxton spoke about how the wide aperture of the sky and the movement of weather and celestial patterns have a cinematic quality. Quoting Métis Cree Filmmaker Loretta Todd, she said "the plains sky is the largest screen in the world."

7. Plains and prairies are related topographies. A plain is a vast stretch of land with little elevation or depression. Located at various altitudes, it can express a range of ecologies, whereas a prairie is primarily a perennial grassland. In North America, the Great Plains are demarcated by the Rio Grande in the south, the Mackenzie River delta at the Arctic Ocean in the north, the Canadian Shield in the east and the Rocky Mountains in the west. Both terms have also come to express complex social, economic and cultural regions. Colloquially, prairie tends to refer to Canadian geography and plains refers to American, though the latter also names a physiographic region that predates colonial borders. In this text I primarily use plains to recognize Indigenous ecological and social relations, and prairie when I'm specifically referring to grasslands.

8. In southwestern Canada coulees were formed by receding glaciers, which caused flooding and formed new water features that eroded and shaped the land.

9. Amanda Malcolm, "Dana Claxton to Perform Original Piece, *Fringed*, at the Met," The Metropolitan Museum of Art, March 12, 2015, http://www.metmuseum.org/blogs/now-at-the-met/2015/dana-claxton-performs-fringed/. In the performance, Claxton wears an embellished fringe garment with a projection of the plains grassland behind her, echoing her grandfather's participation in the men's grass dance, a northern Plains tradition in which the dancers wear brightly coloured fringe and dance together like wind in the grass.

10. To emphasize the temporal and spatial presence of the buffalo on the plains, Hubbard cites Métis writer Peter Erasmus's observations of their endurance. "Deep ruts scored the prairie grass where the buffalo had traveled for centuries in their migrations back and forth across the plains." 69.

11. Hubbard, 75.

12. Hubbard draws on writing by Marie Battiste, Vine Deloria Jr., Eleanor Verbicky-Todd, Neal Mcleod and Peter Vandall to express a complex temporality that resists equating the not-visible with past, absence and permanence. She writes, "It is precisely from this concept of shifting location, from loss to gain, death to renewal, from history to contemporary (and back again), that I wish to examine the context of the Buffalo's place in Indigenous Creative Expression… By engaging in a cycle of retreat and re-emergence, the Buffalo's agency in the acts of leaving and returning can clear space for a spirit of renewal for plains Indigenous People." 75–76.
13. Hubbard, 78–79.
14. Dana Claxton in an interview with the writer, August 2020.
15. Dana Claxton as quoted in Steven Loft, "Language of Intercession: Native Media and New Media Artists (Canada)" Dazibao, February 19 – March 19, 2005), accessed November 8, 2020. http://dazibao-photo.org/en/past/language-of-intercession-native-media-and-new-media-artists-en
16. 'Walking the good way' encompasses the Lakota cardinal virtues of generosity, wisdom, bravery and fortitude. Dana Claxton discussed these virtues in an interview with the writer in August 2020. The connection between these values, art and aesthetics in Lakota culture is expanded upon by Lakota anthropologist Bea Medicine in her essay "Lakota Views of 'Art' and Artistic Expression" in Claxton's publication *The Sioux Project—Tatanka Oyate* (Regina: Mackenzie Art Gallery; Vancouver: Information Office, 2020), 54–55.
17. Claxton embodies her great grandfathers name Oyewaste (Oye washday), which was later changed to Goodtrack, meaning 'walks a good way.'
18. "The Sioux Project—Tatanka Oyate—The Buffalo People," in *The Sioux Project—Tatanka Oyate*, 32.
19. Claxton continues "… We didn't want equal pay for work of equal value—we wanted to be able to have business on reserves, which was also against the law. We didn't want shared cooking in the kitchen, especially Lakota/Dakota/Nakota as in our feasting systems women cook as honoured positions and men serve the food, also as an honoured position. We didn't want to wear pants we wanted to wear our traditional dresses. (I still know many mostly white feminists who won't wear dresses for political reasons.) The dress is also spiritual—Also, hence now the ribbon skirt "movement." The struggles of western feminisms were so different. NDN women wanted to raise their children in the home–cuz of child removal, break up of families, etc. I think this is why on many levels I can't identify with western feminism. Class, race and location weren't really part of white liberal feminism—poverty on reservations was not part of the beginnings of feminism." Aruna D'Souza, "The Fourth World and the Second Wave: On (Non) Encounters between Native Women and Feminism," in *Art for a New Understanding: Native Voices 1950s to Now.* eds. Manuela Well-Off-Man, Mindy N. Besaw, Candice Hopkins (Fayeteville: University of Arkansas Press; Bentonville: Crystal Bridges Museum of American Art, 2018), 67.
20. Mark St. Pierre and Tilda Long Soldier. *Walking in the Sacred Manner: Healers, Dreamers, and Pipe carriers—Medicine Women of the Plains Indians* (New York: Touchstone, 2015), 38–39.
21. This sequence references White Buffalo Calf Woman's prophecy that the birth of a white buffalo calf would be a significant message for the Sioux. White calves were born in the United States in 1994 and 1996, just prior to the film's production.

Amy Kazymerchyk is a curator who pays particular attention to moving image practices and their encounters with cinema, performance and visual art. She has been the Curator of SFU Galleries' Audain Gallery, Events and Exhibitions Coordinator at VIVO Media Arts Centre and Programmer of DIM Cinema at The Cinematheque.

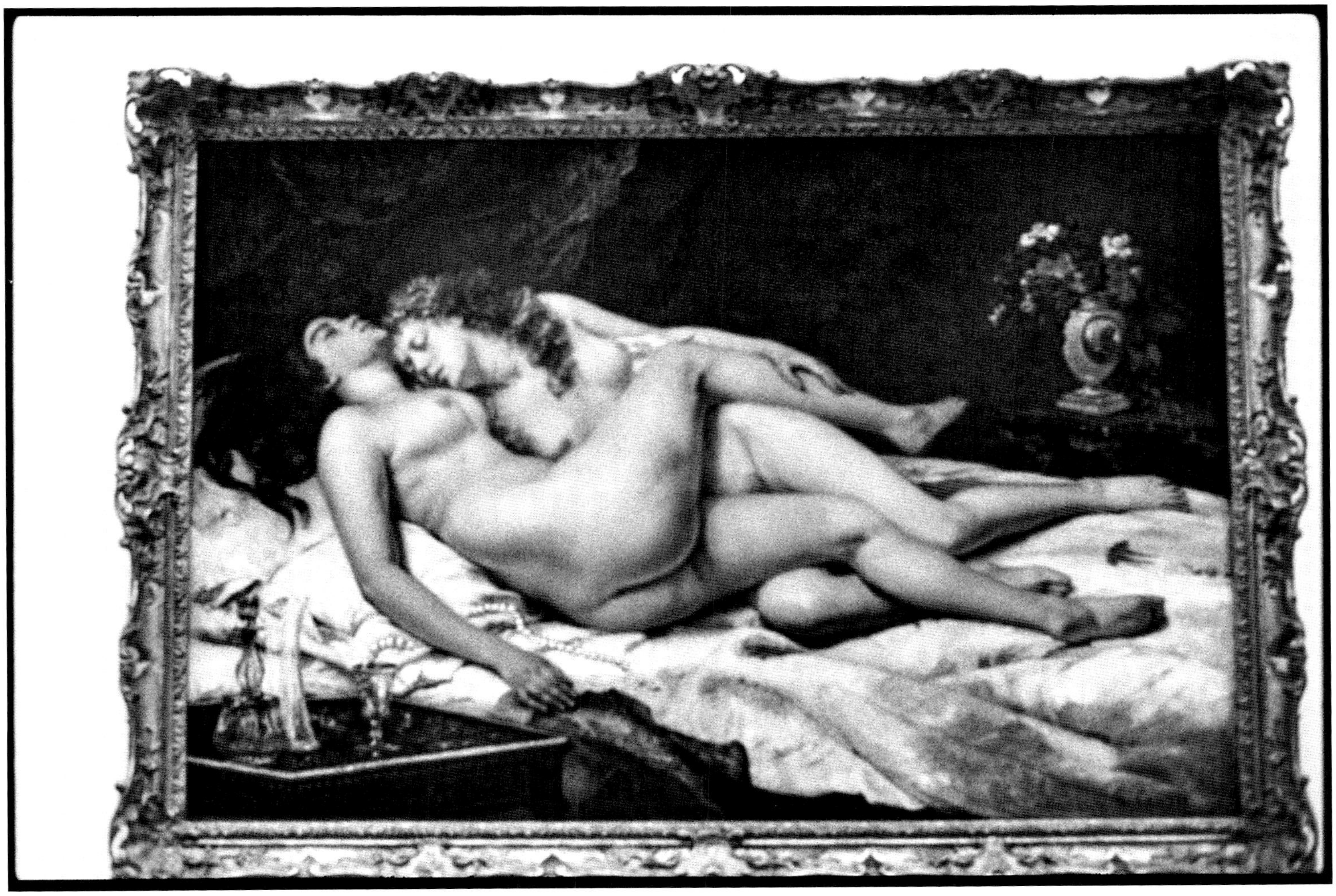

She Loves Her, *Paris* series, 2006

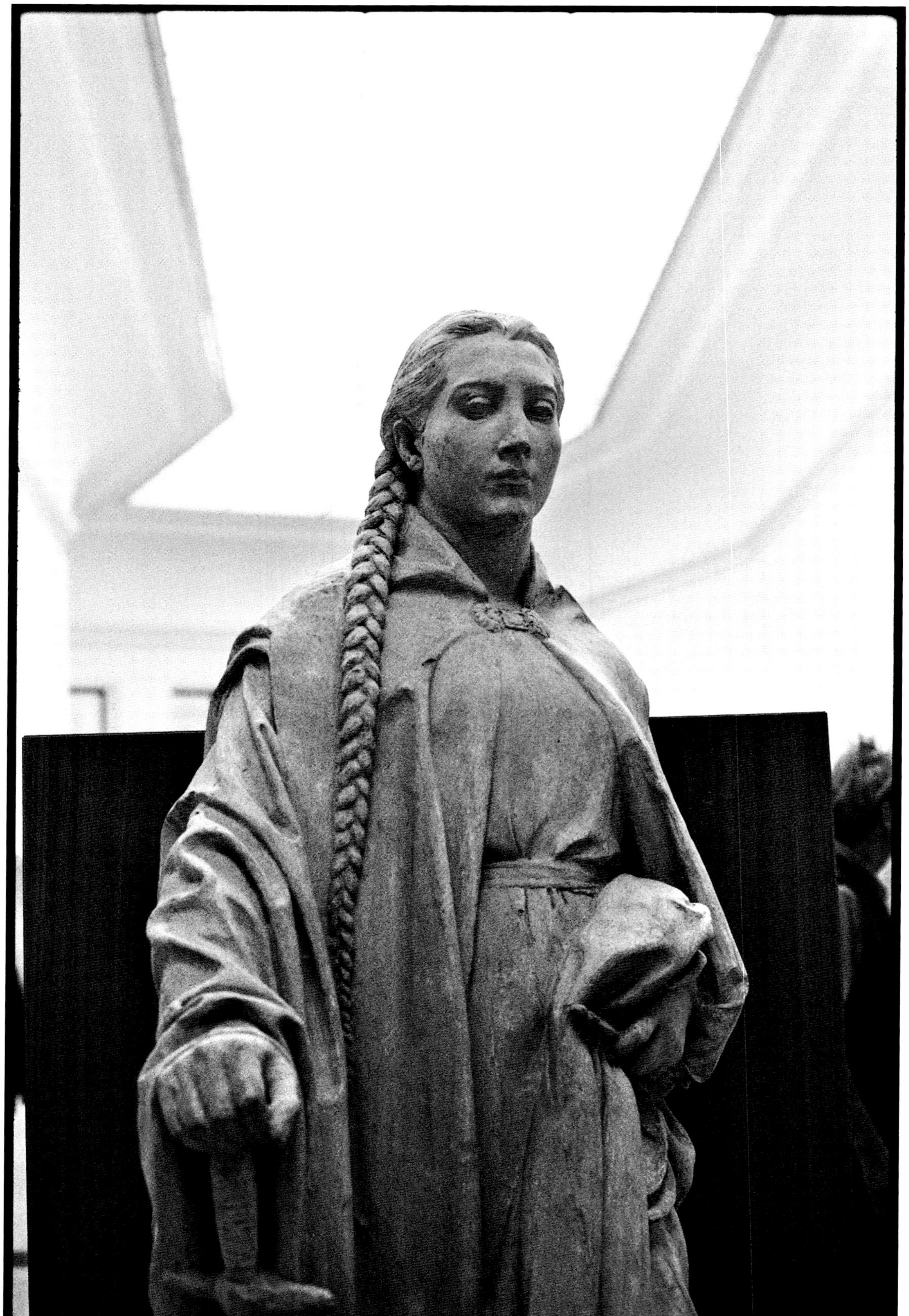

Nurse, *Paris* series, 2006

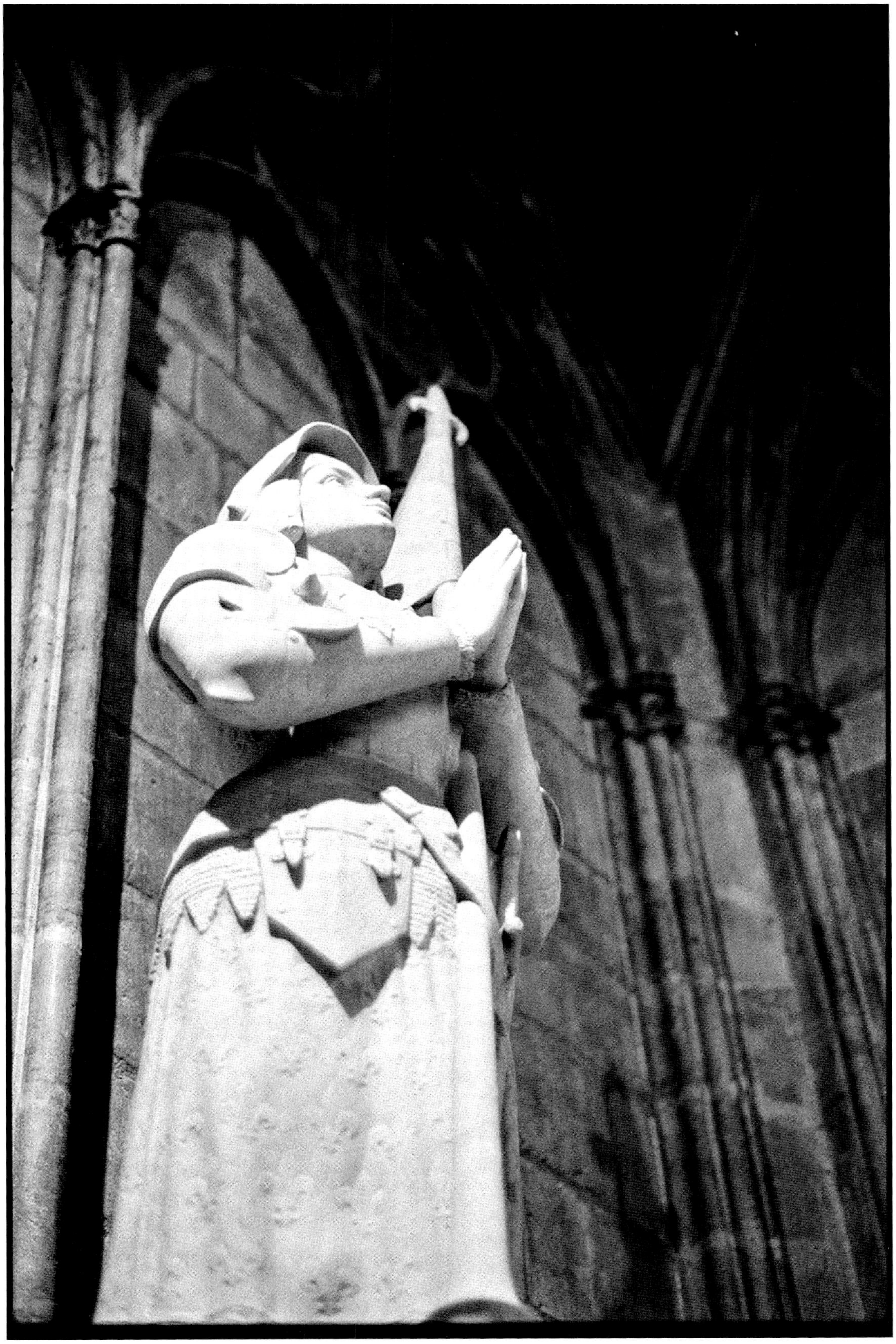

Peasant Warrior, *Paris* series, 2006

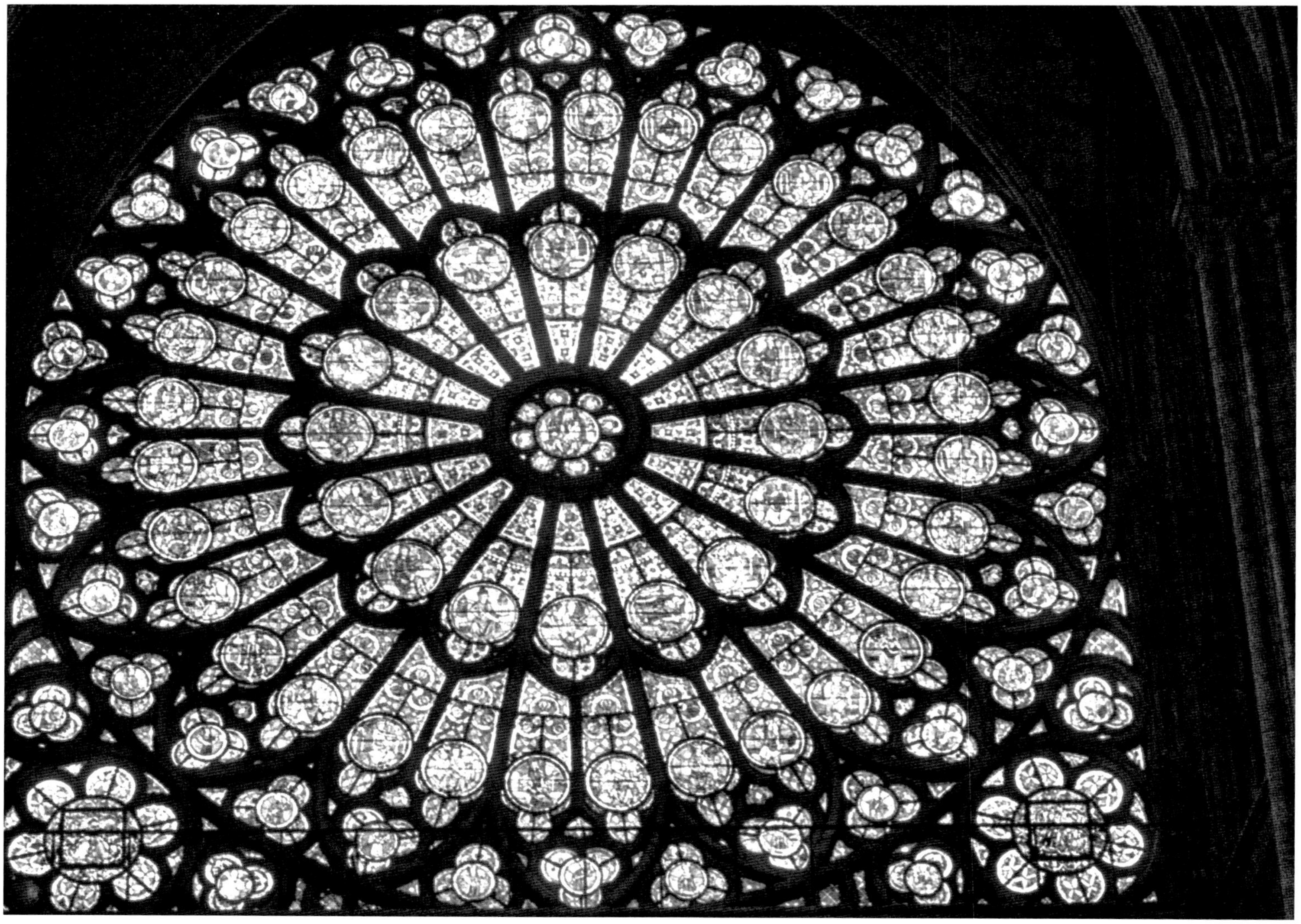

Cathedral Window 1, *Paris* series, 2006

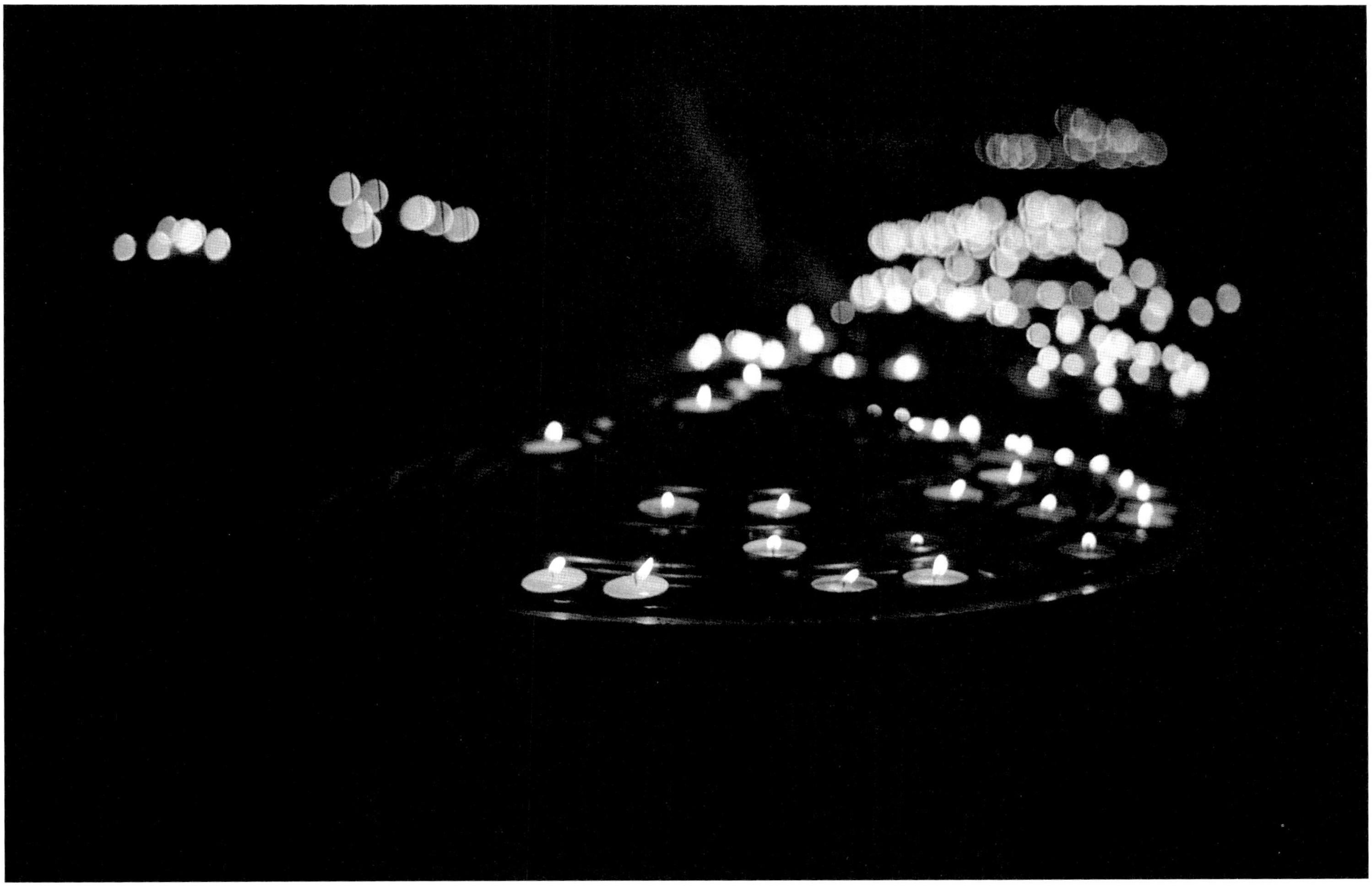

Candles at Notre Dame, *Paris* series, 2006

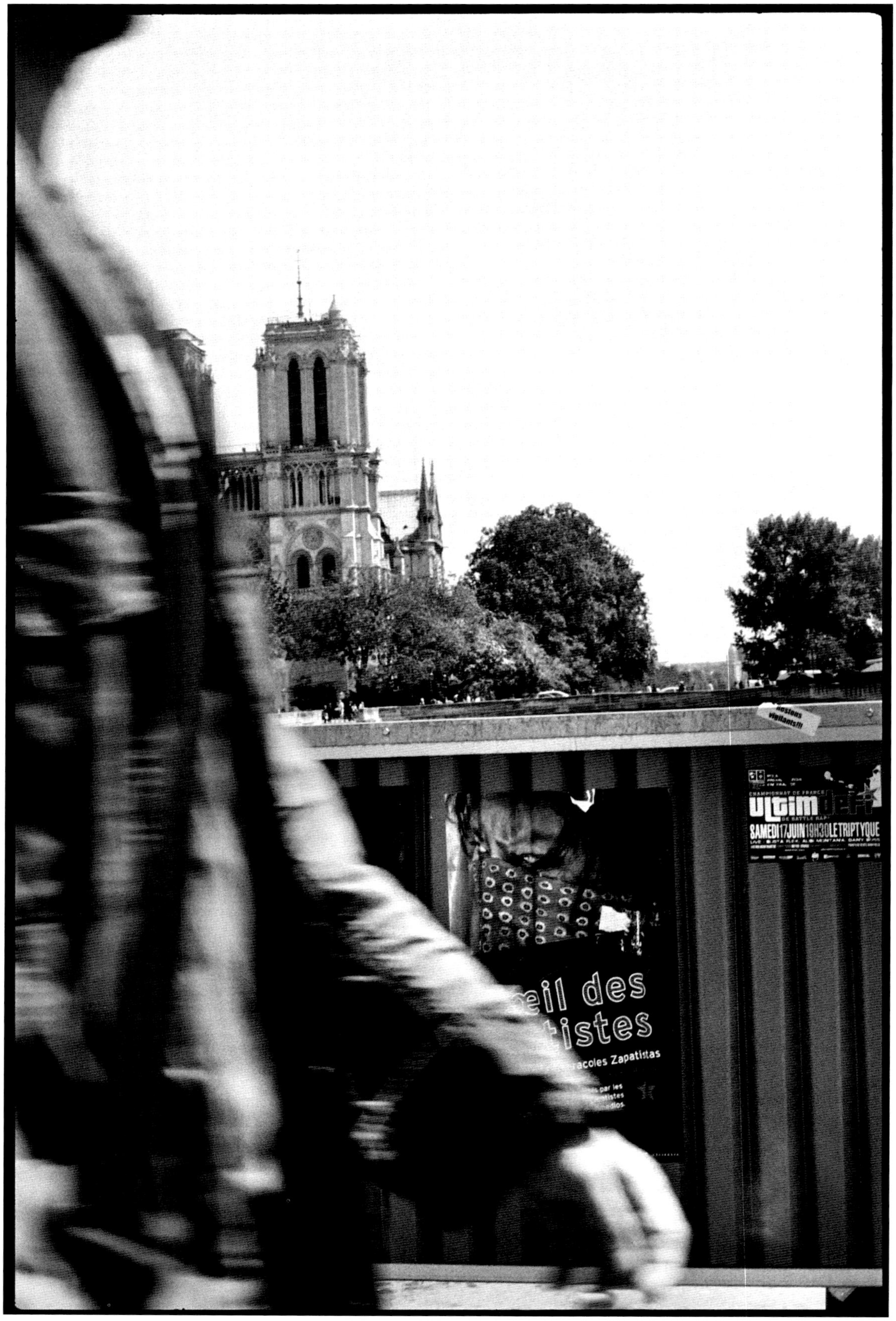

This Image Took My Breath Away (Zapatista on the Seine River), *Paris* series, 2006

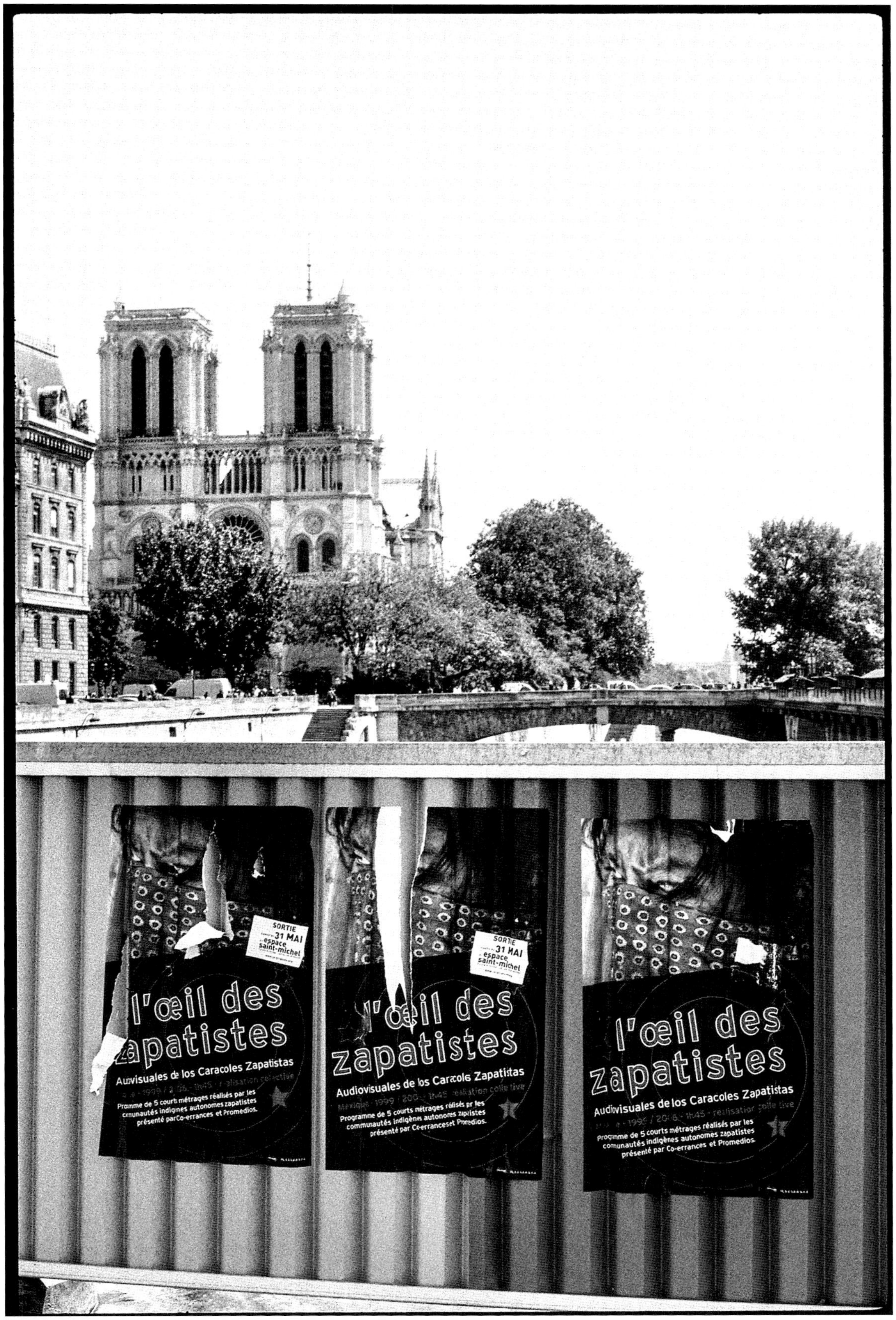

Zapatista on the Bridge, *Paris* series, 2006

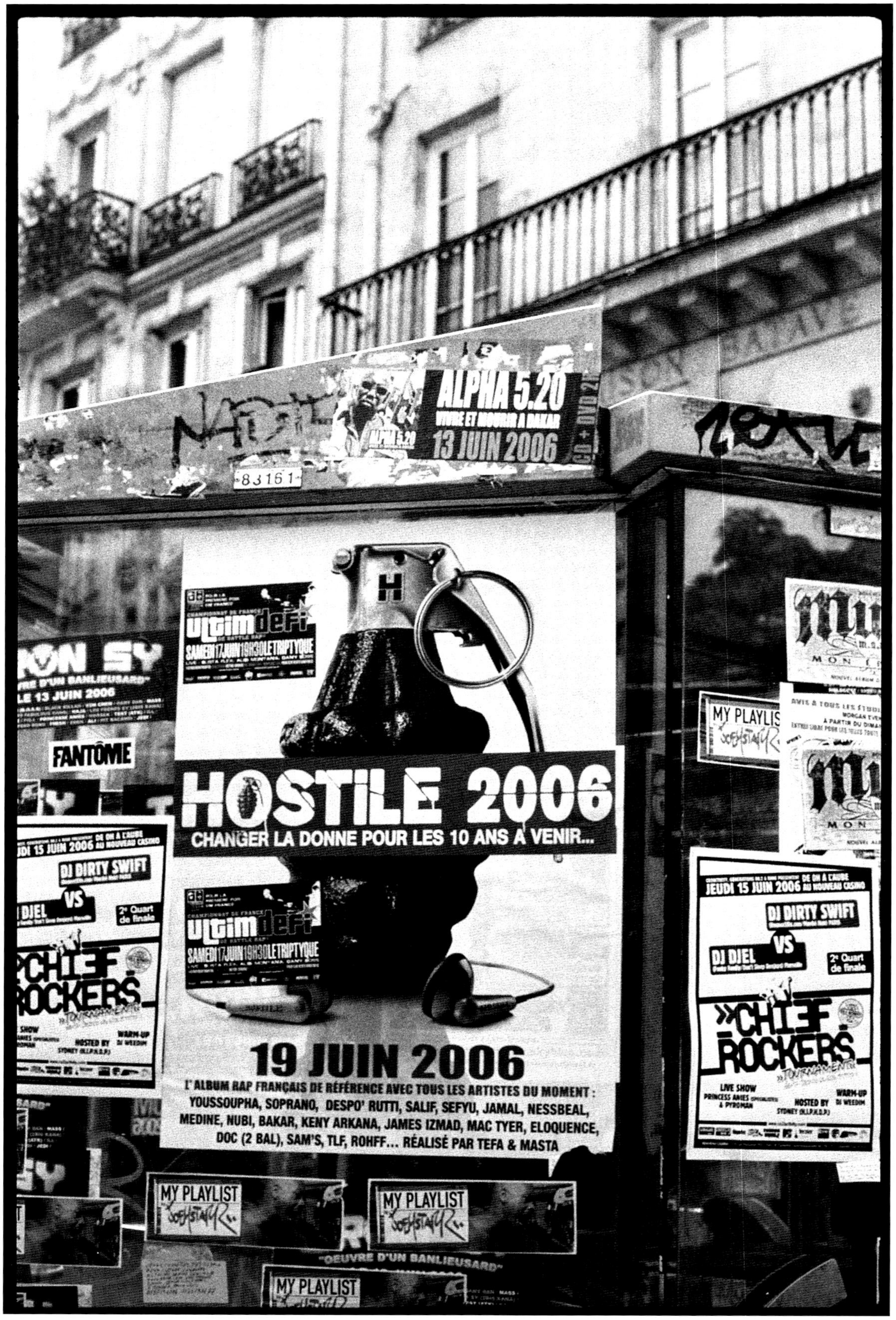

Hostile, *Paris* series, 2006

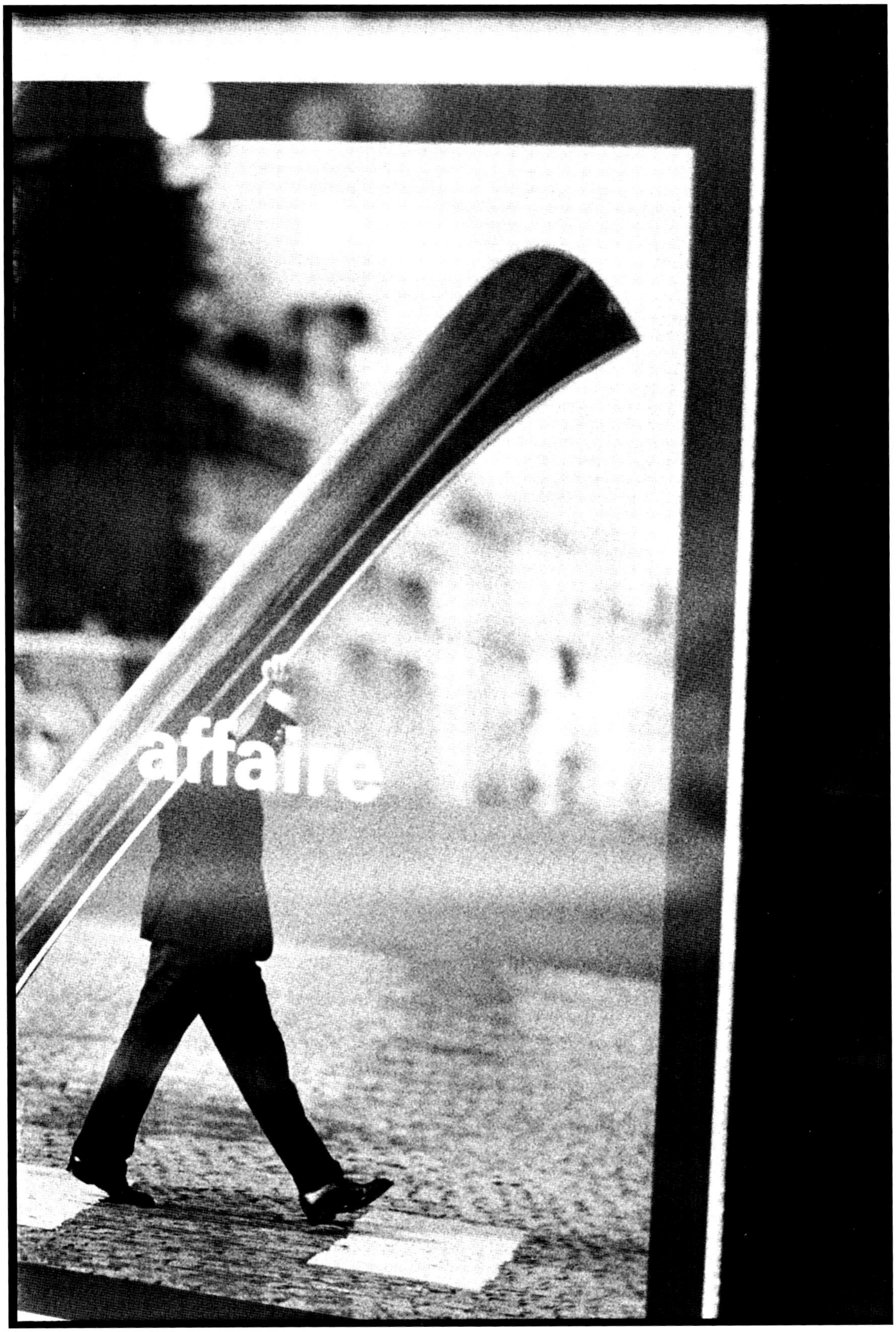

Canoe, *Paris* series, 2006

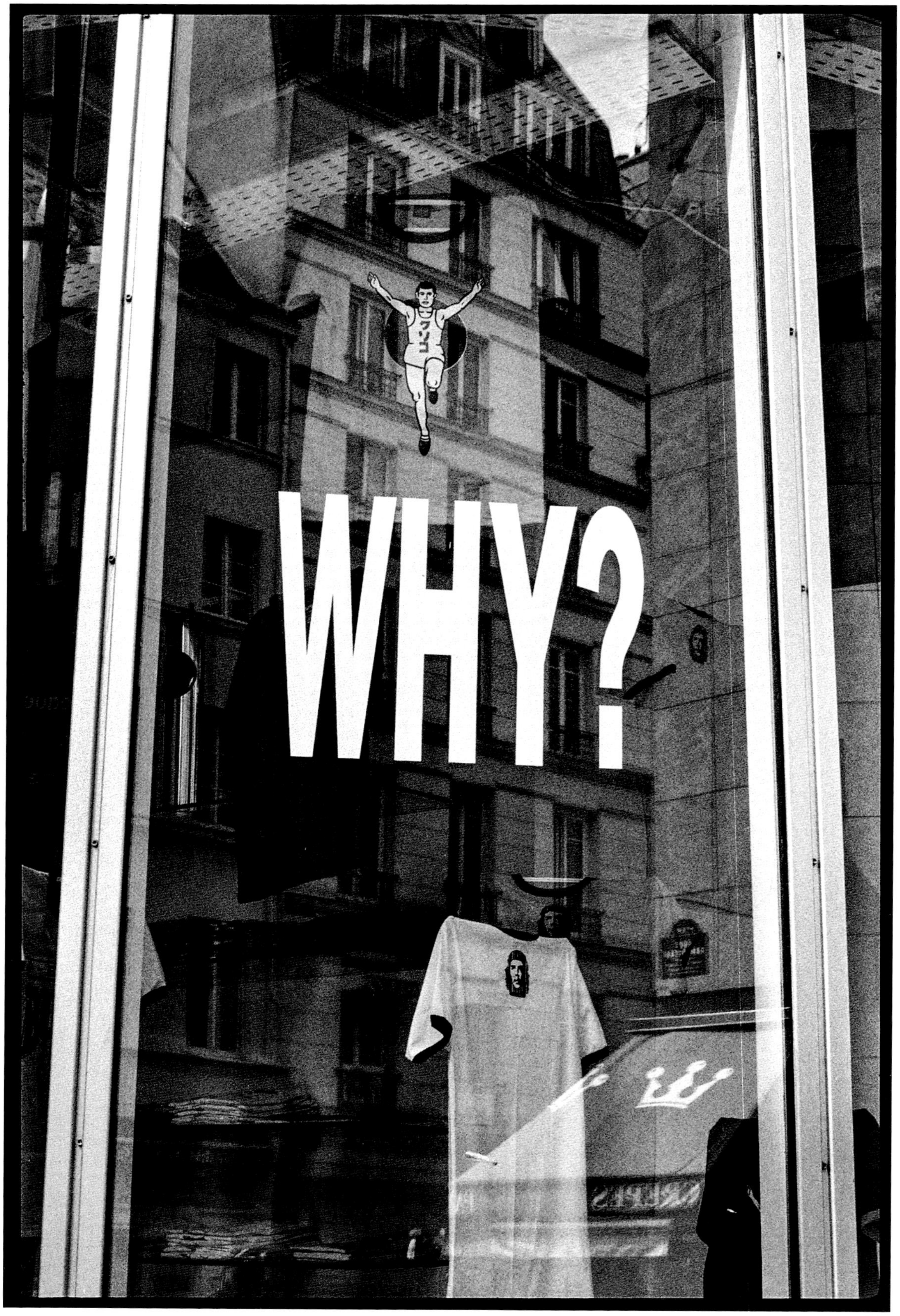

Why?, *Paris* series, 2006

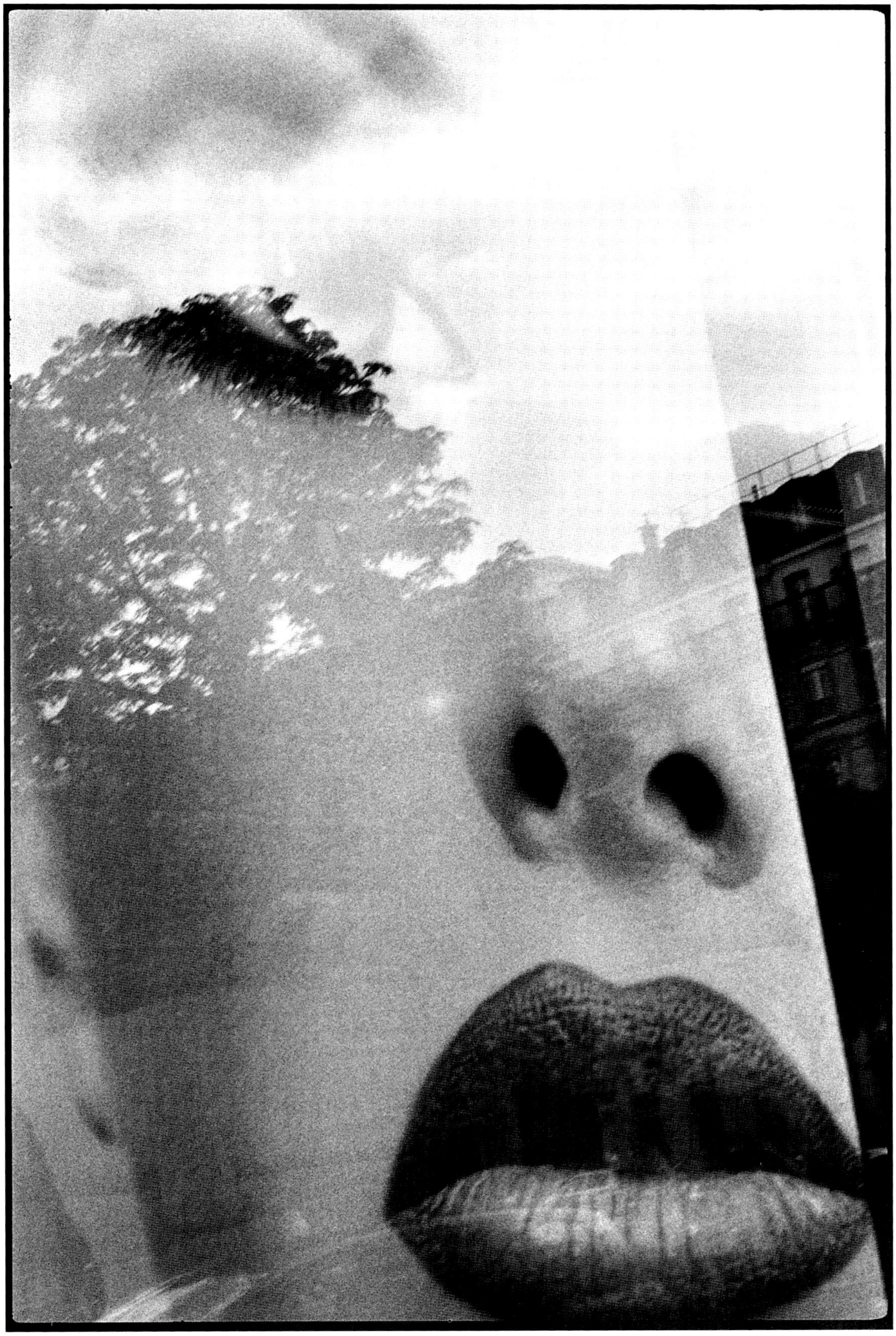

Kiss Me, *Paris* series, 2006

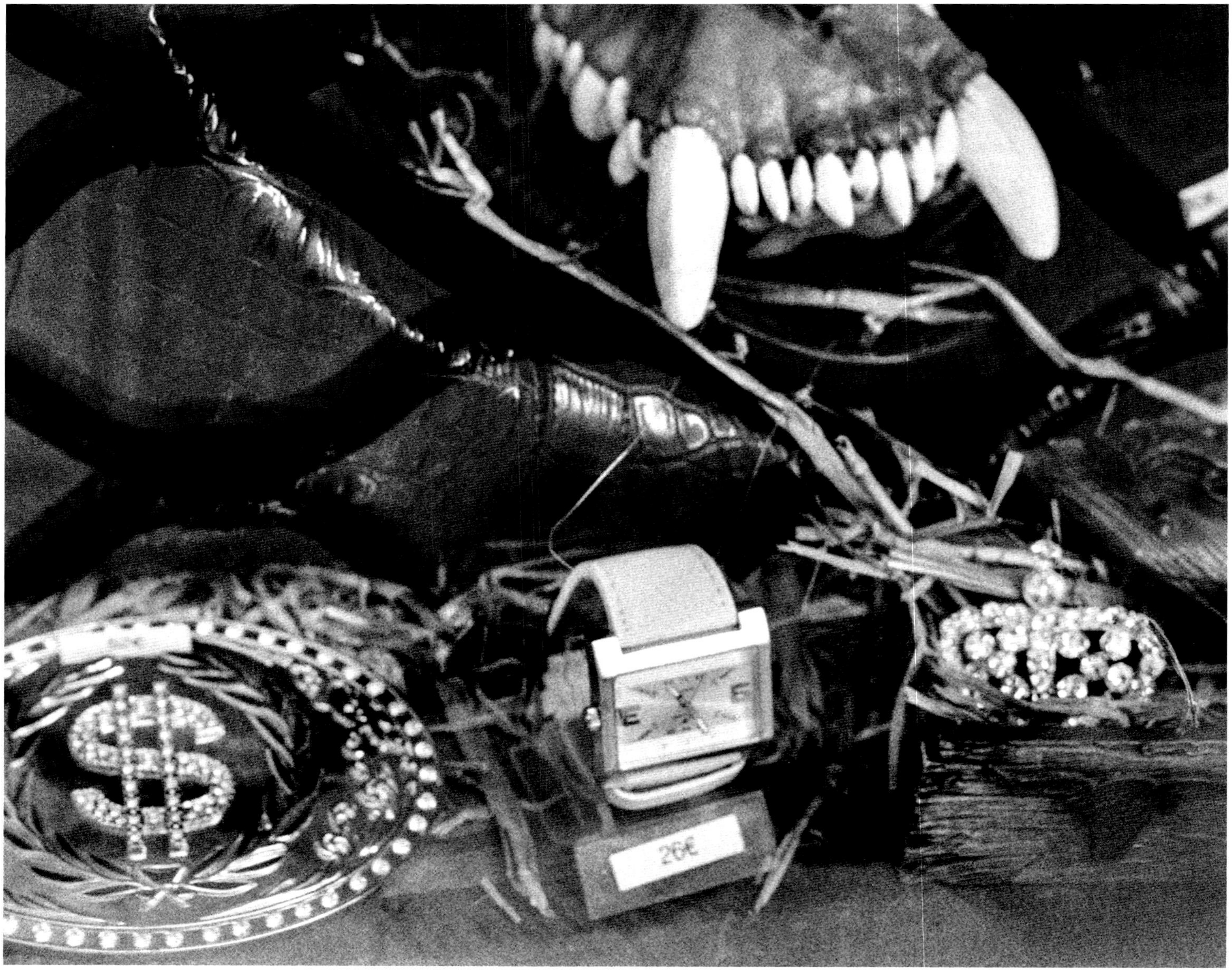

Excess, *Paris* series, 2006

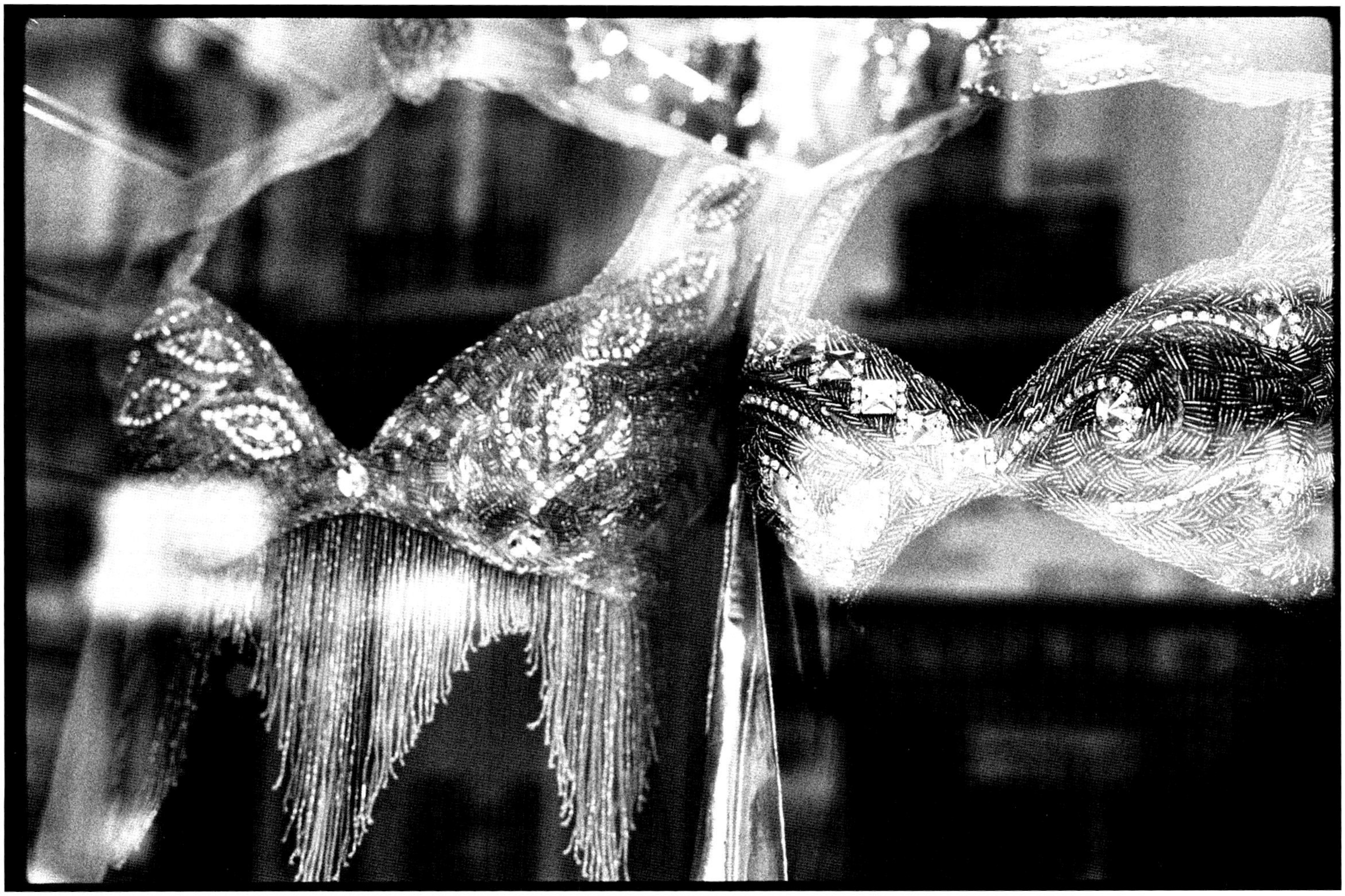

Beaded Bras, *Paris* series, 2006

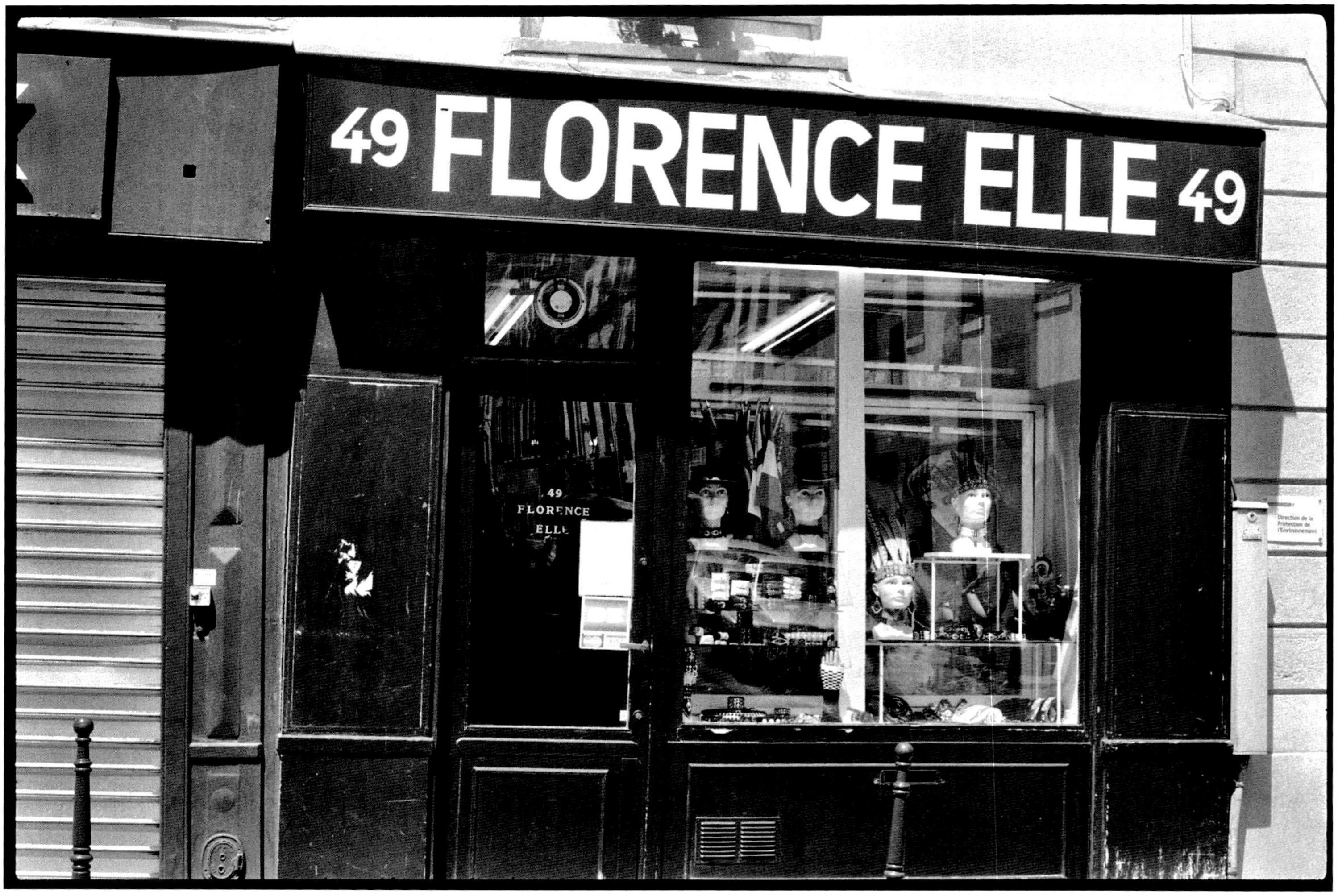

More Cowboys and Indians, *Paris* series, 2006

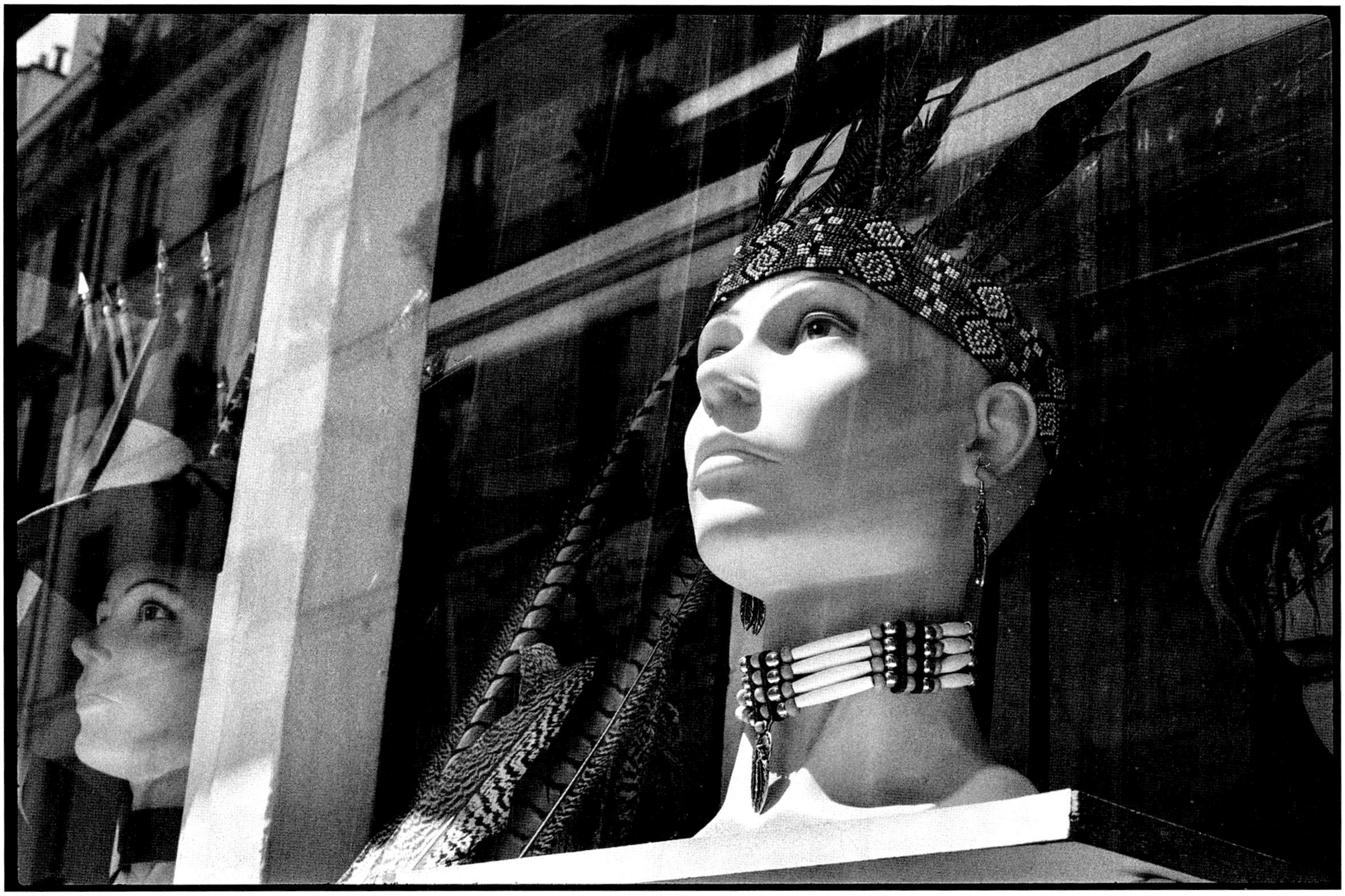

Beads and Feathers (Head), *Paris* series, 2006

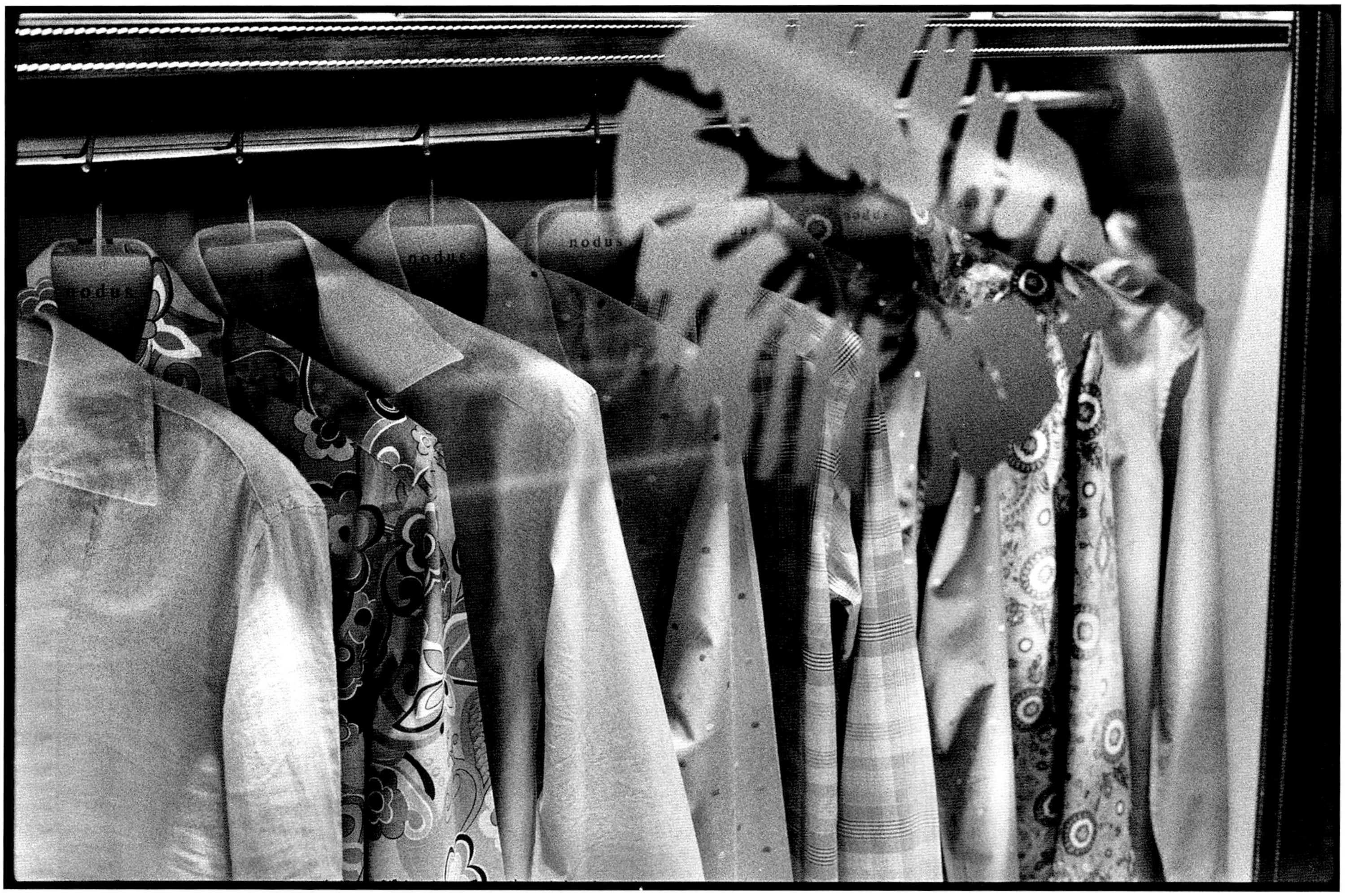

Coloured White Collar, *Paris* series, 2006

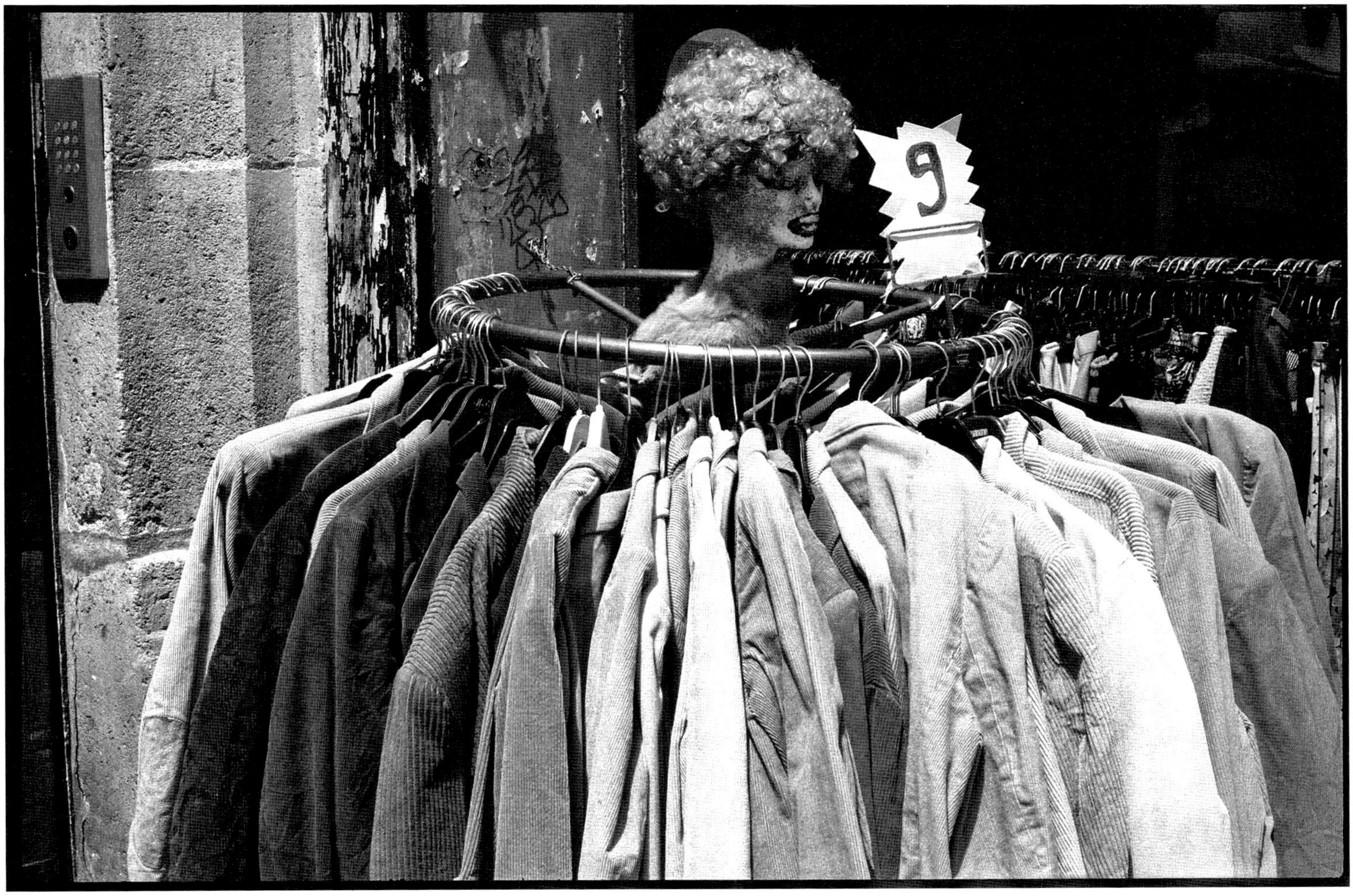

Nine Dollar Jacket, *Paris* series, 2006

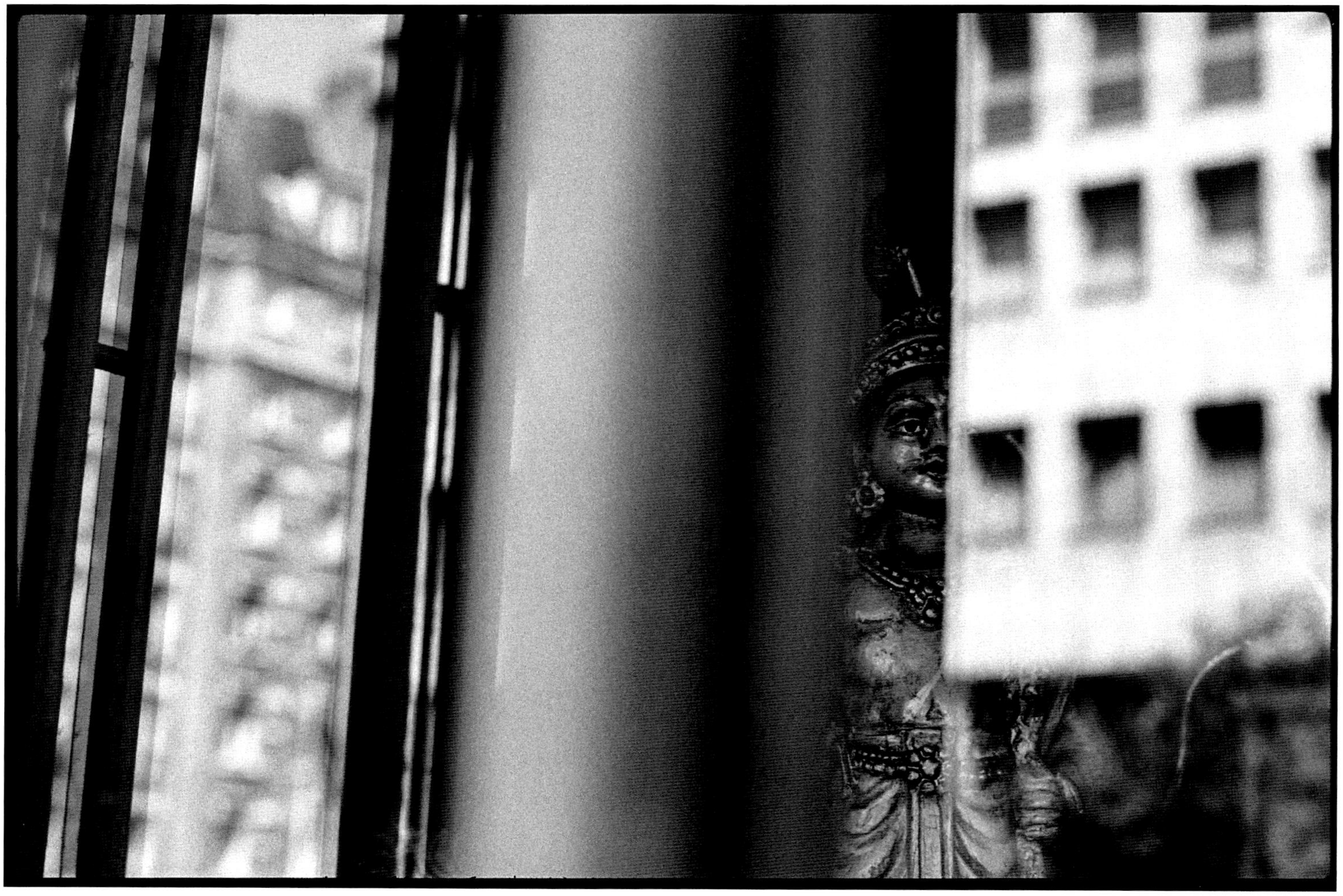

A Deity, *Paris* series, 2006

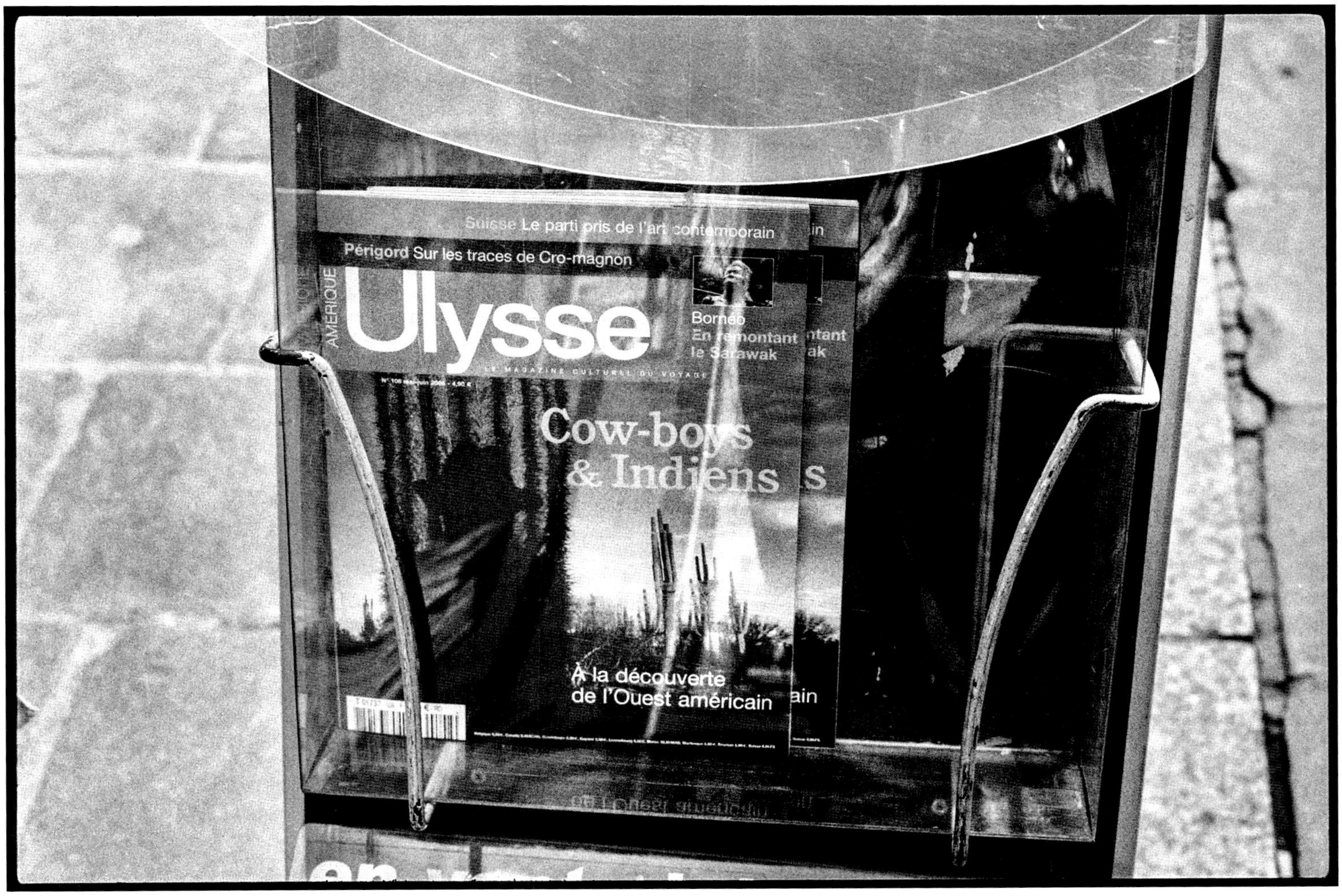

Cowboys and Indians (Magazine Cover), *Paris* series, 2006

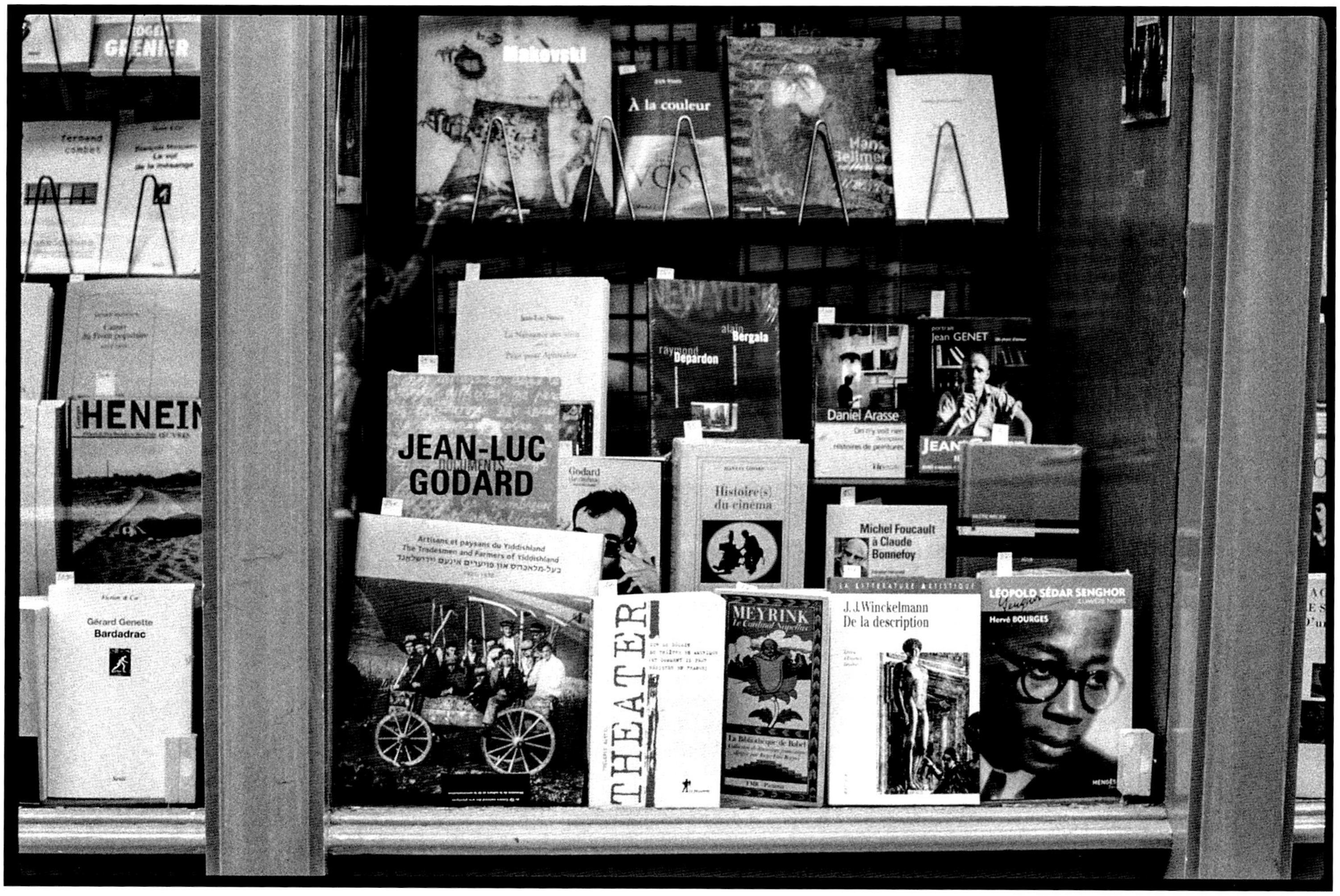

Books, *Paris* series, 2006

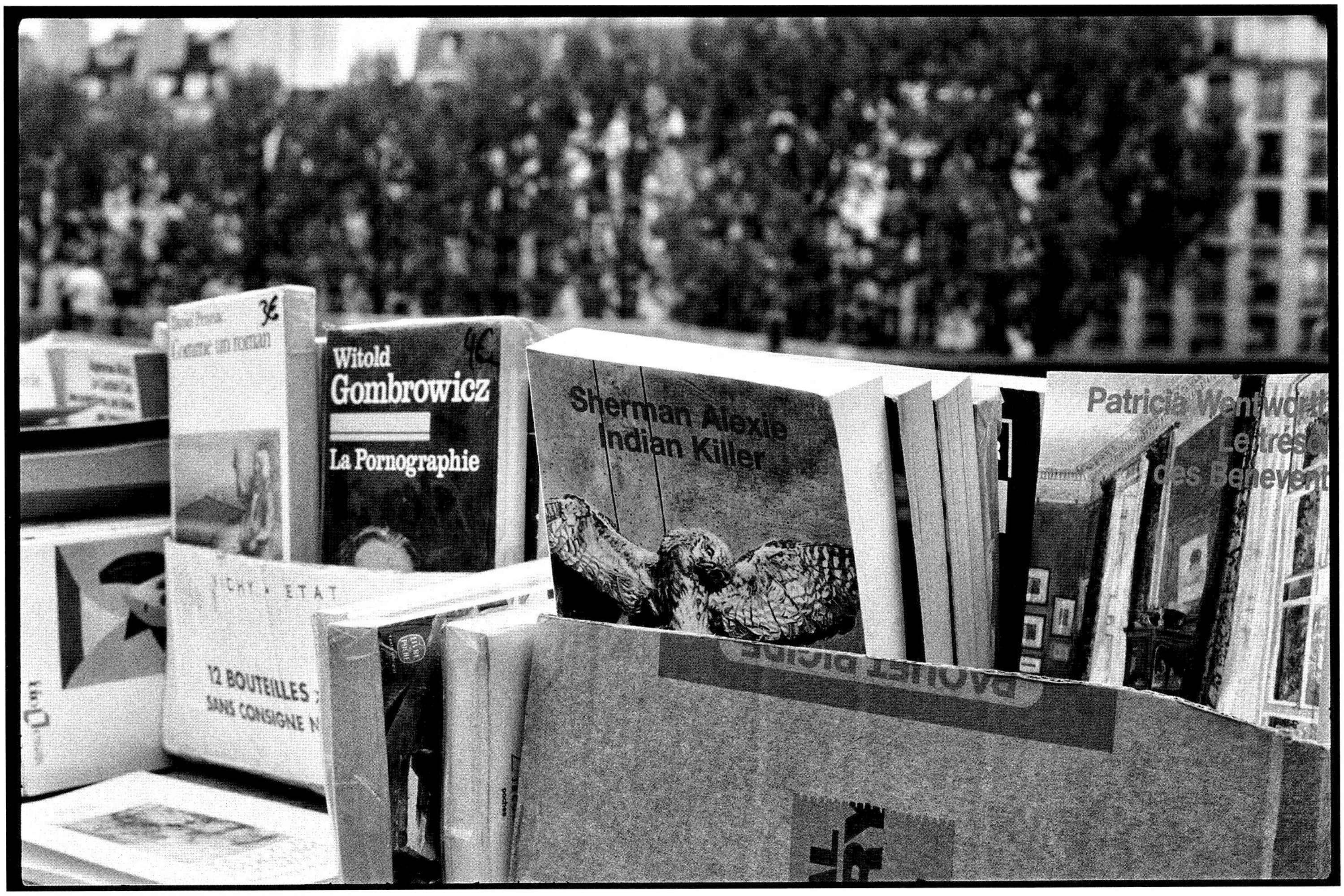

Book Seller Kills an NDN, *Paris* series, 2006

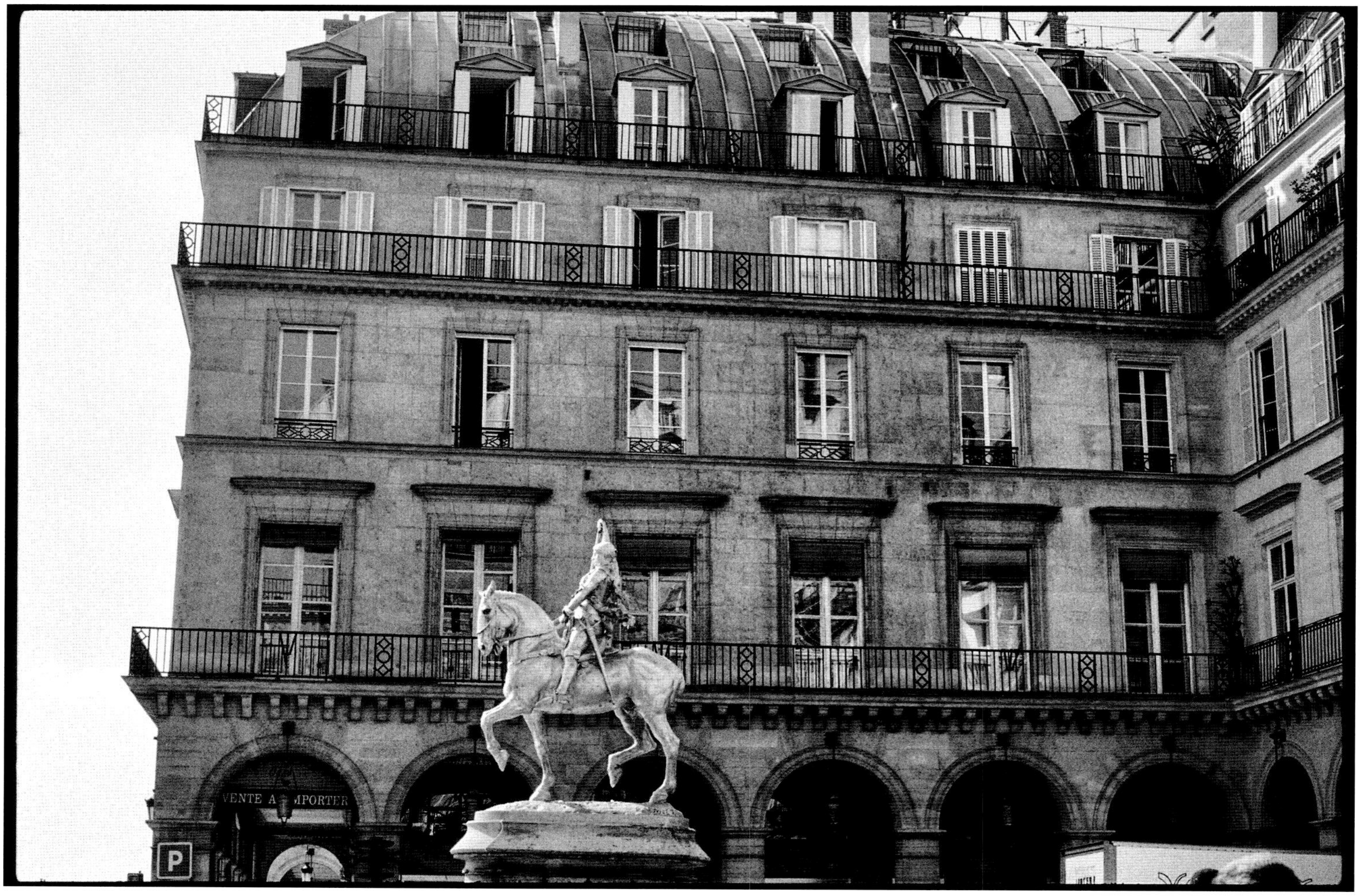

A Horse and His Man or Woman, *Paris* series, 2006

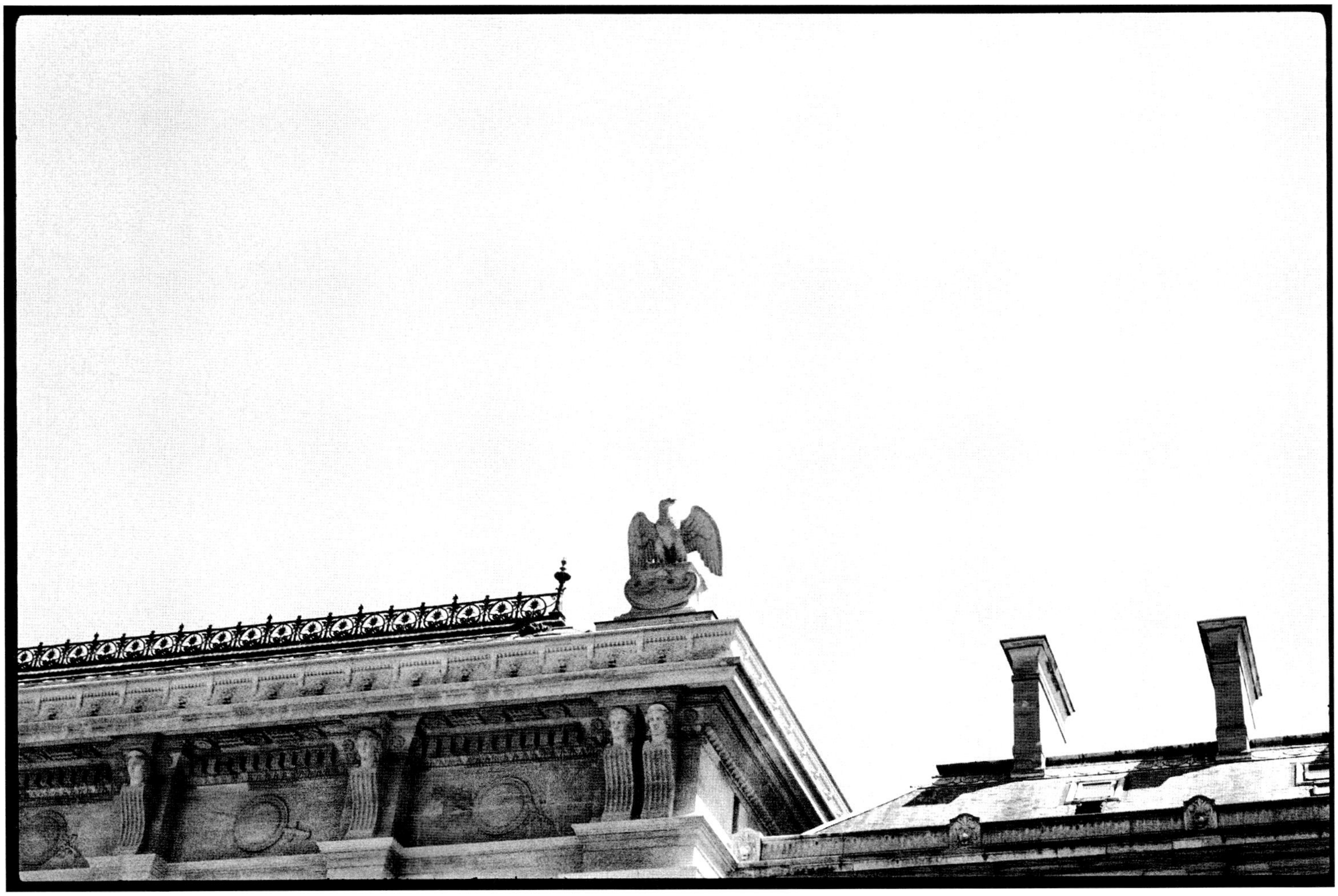

Paris Rooftop, *Paris* series, 2006

Backwards Man, *Paris* series, 2006

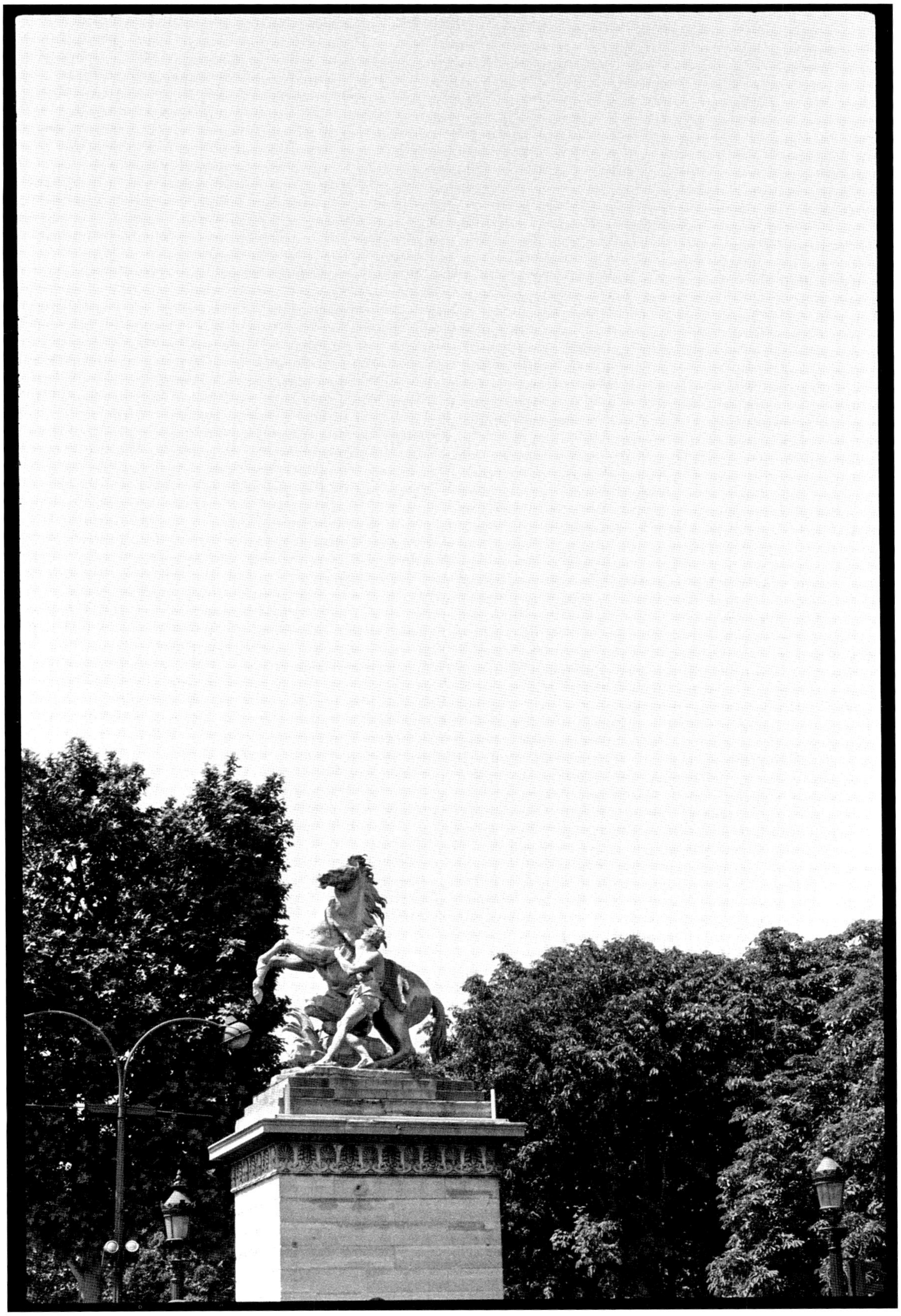

A Man and His Horse, *Paris* series, 2006

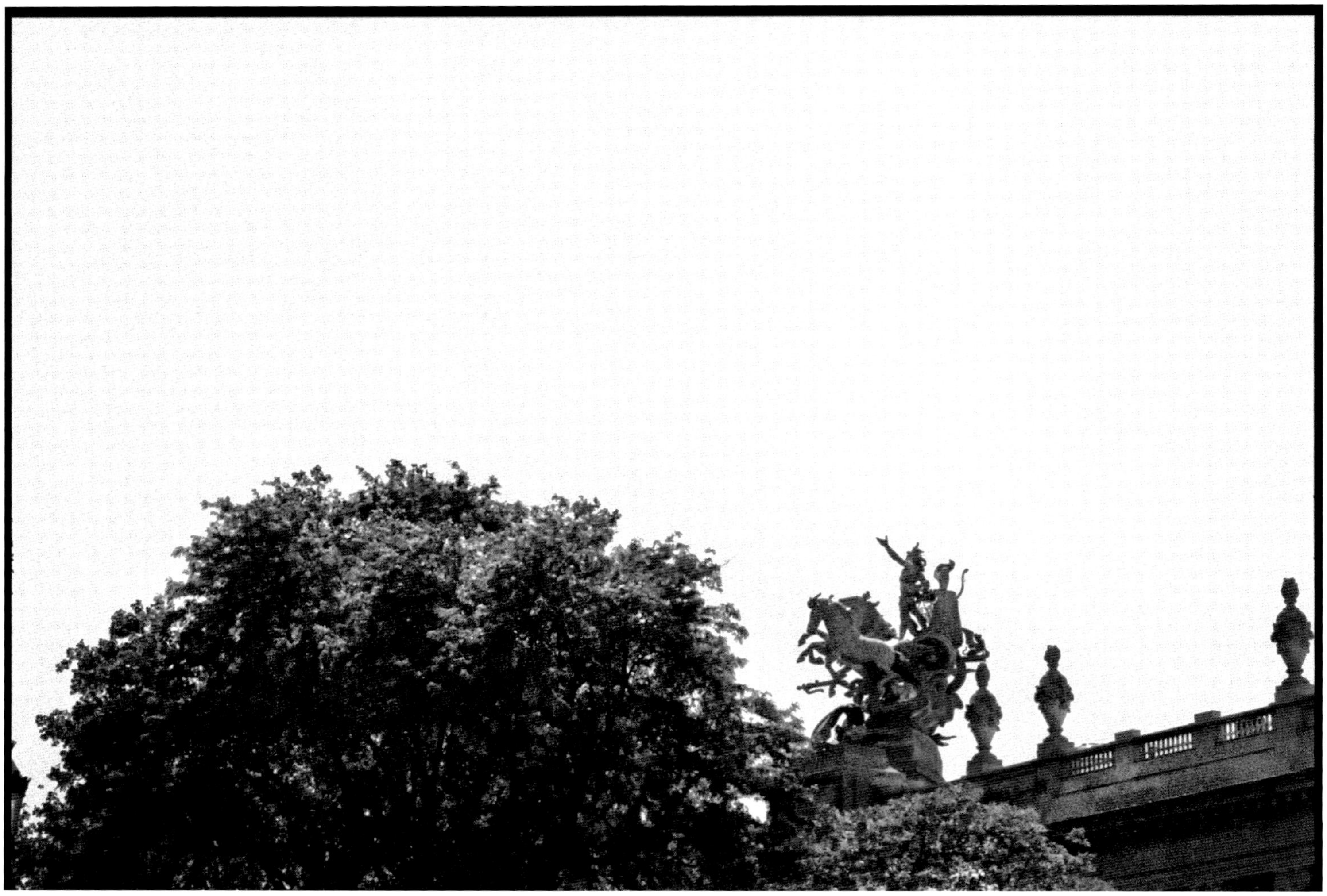

A Man and His Horses, *Paris* series, 2006

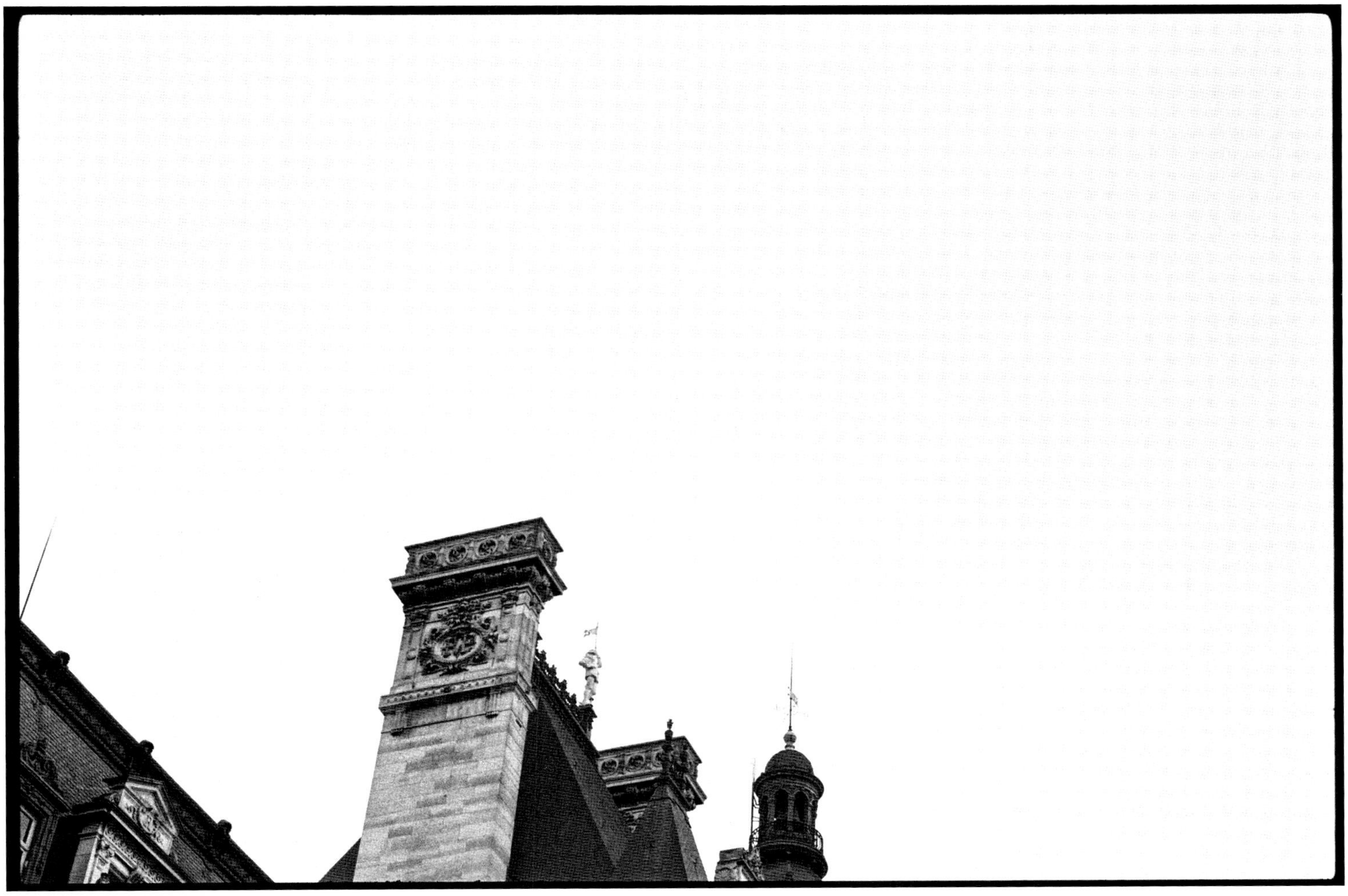

Jet in Sky 1, *Paris* series, 2006

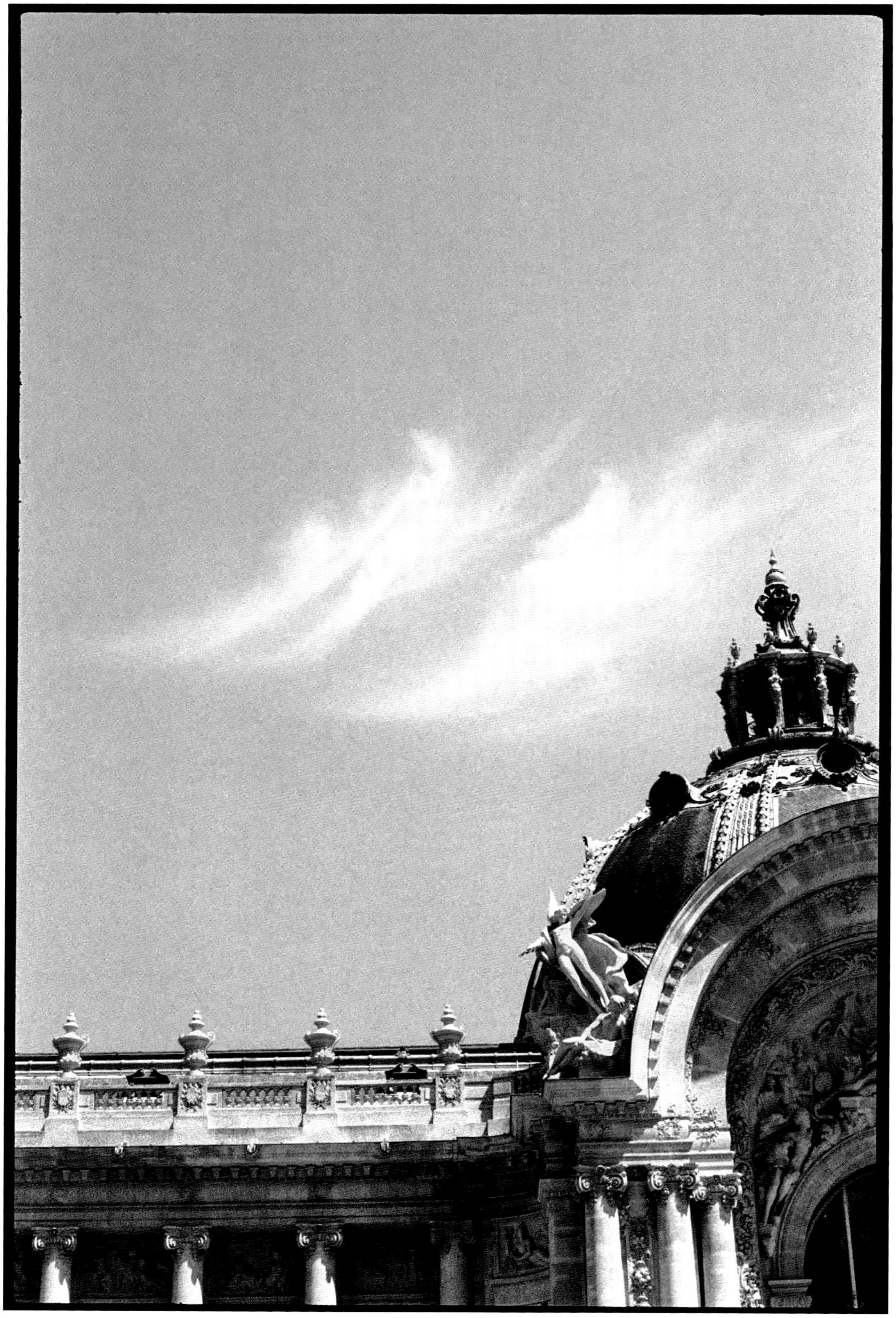

Two Dancing Clouds, *Paris* series, 2006

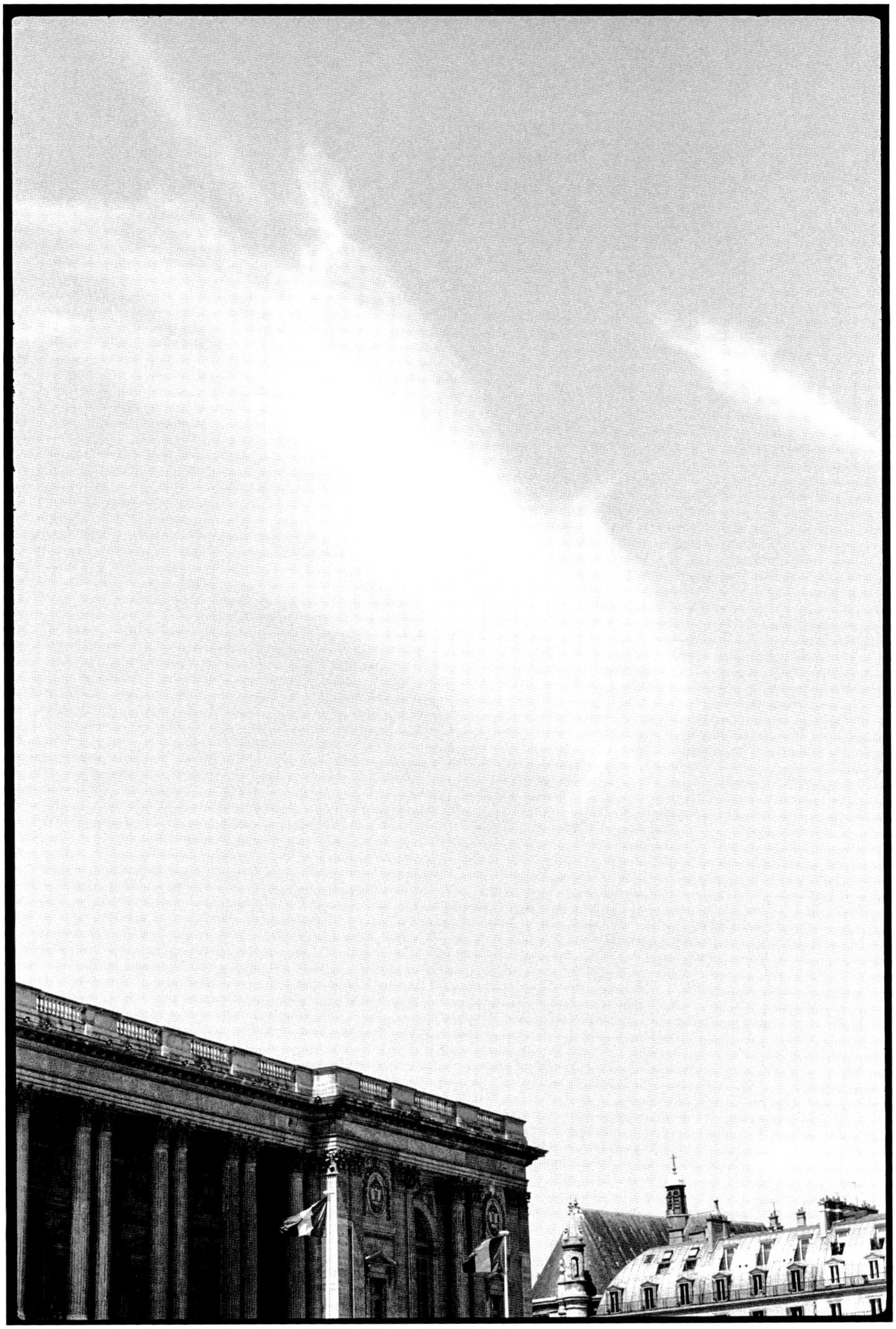

Bird Cloud, *Paris* series, 2006

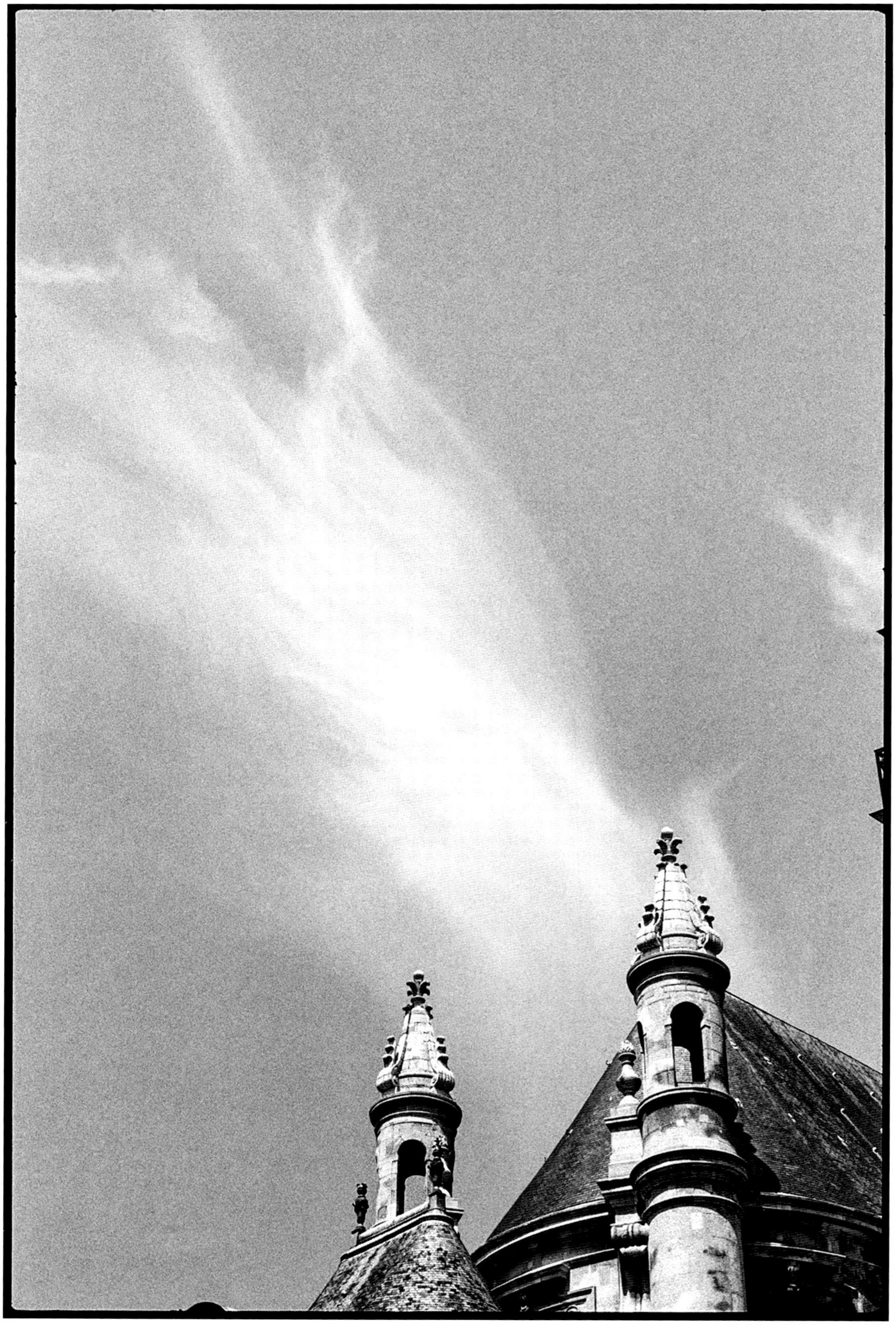

The Sky, The Sky, *Paris* series, 2006

Jet in Sky 2, *Paris* series, 2006

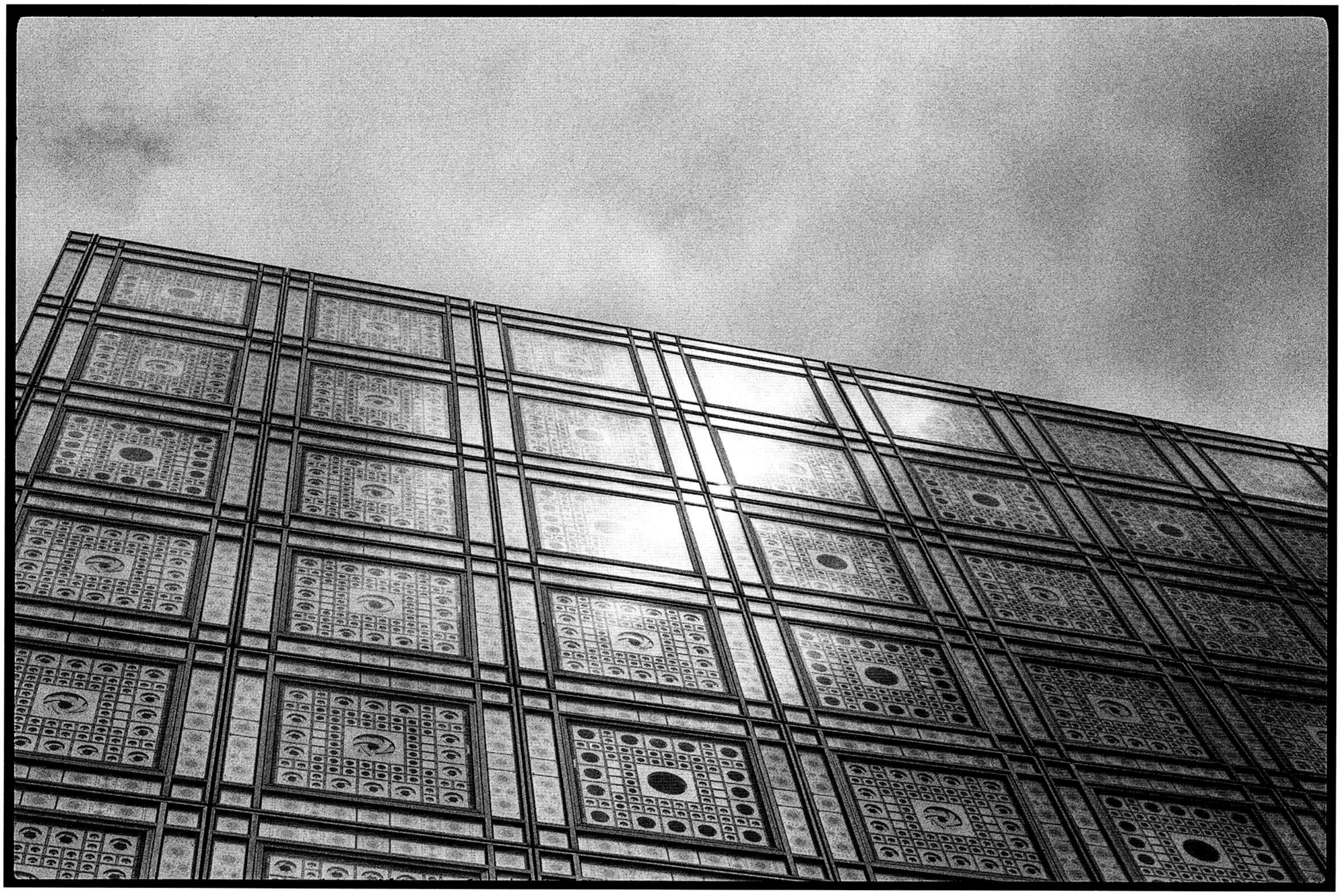

Eastern Math, *Paris* series, 2006

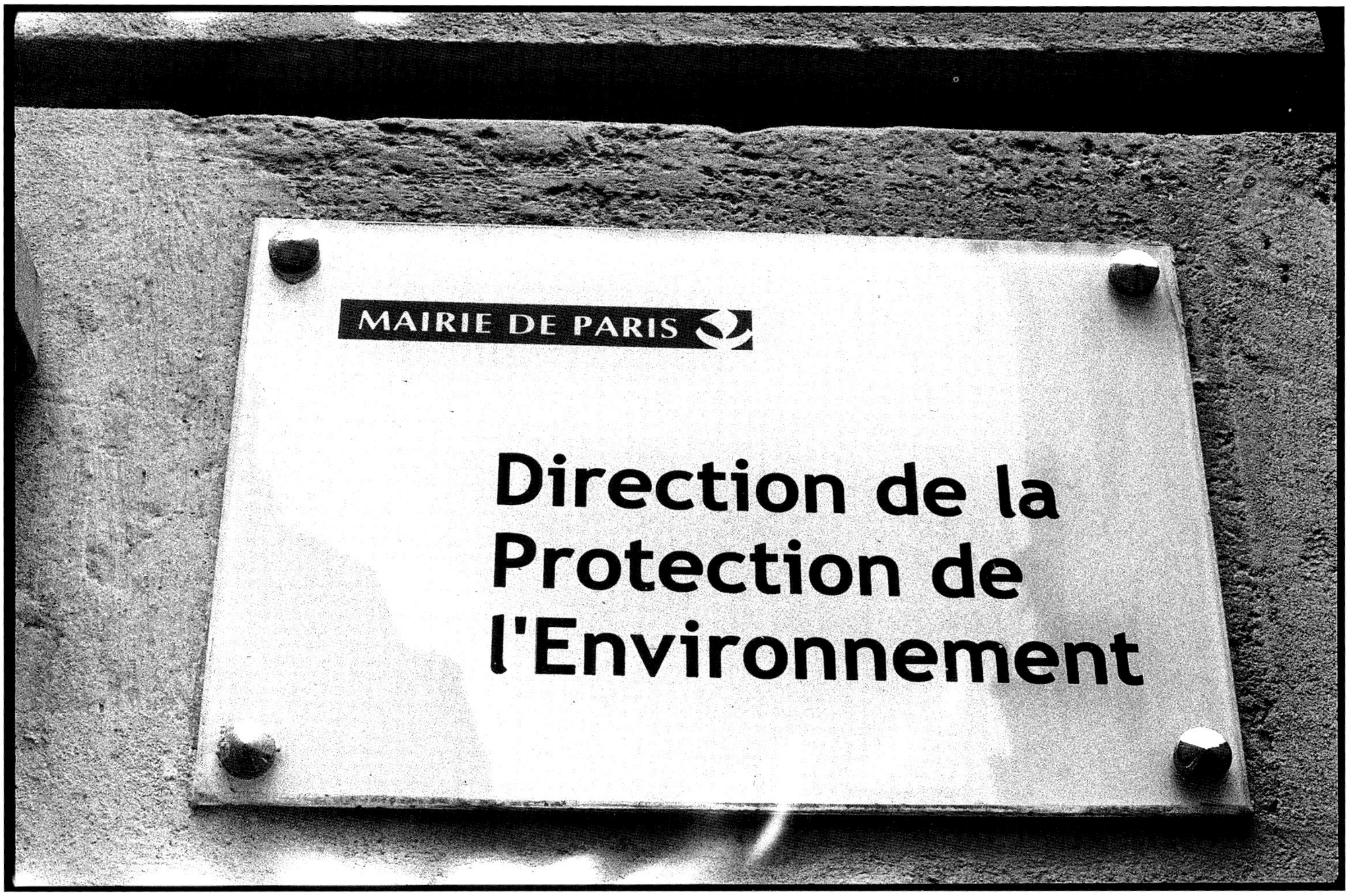

Protect Us, *Paris* series, 2006

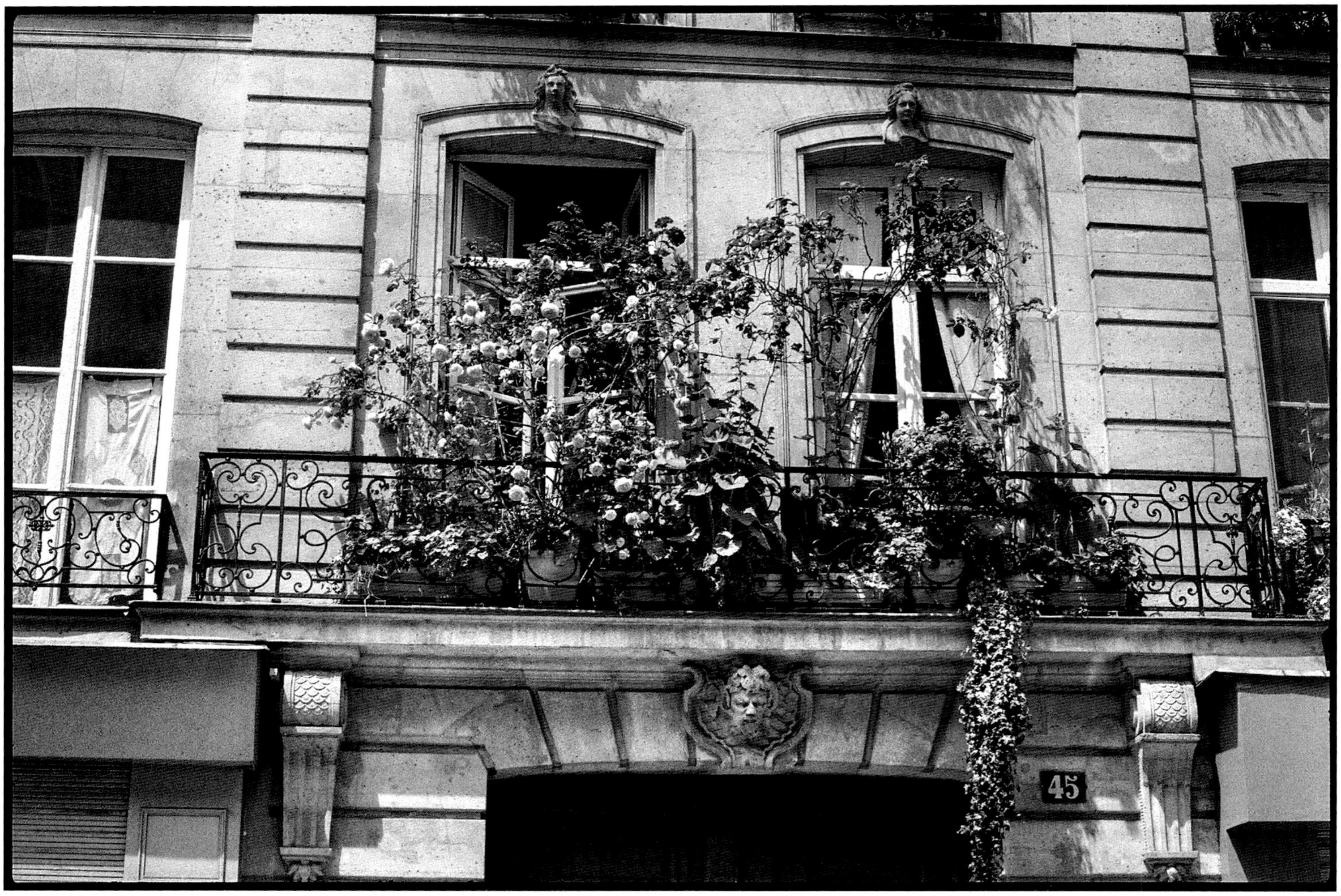

Paris Garden, *Paris* series, 2006

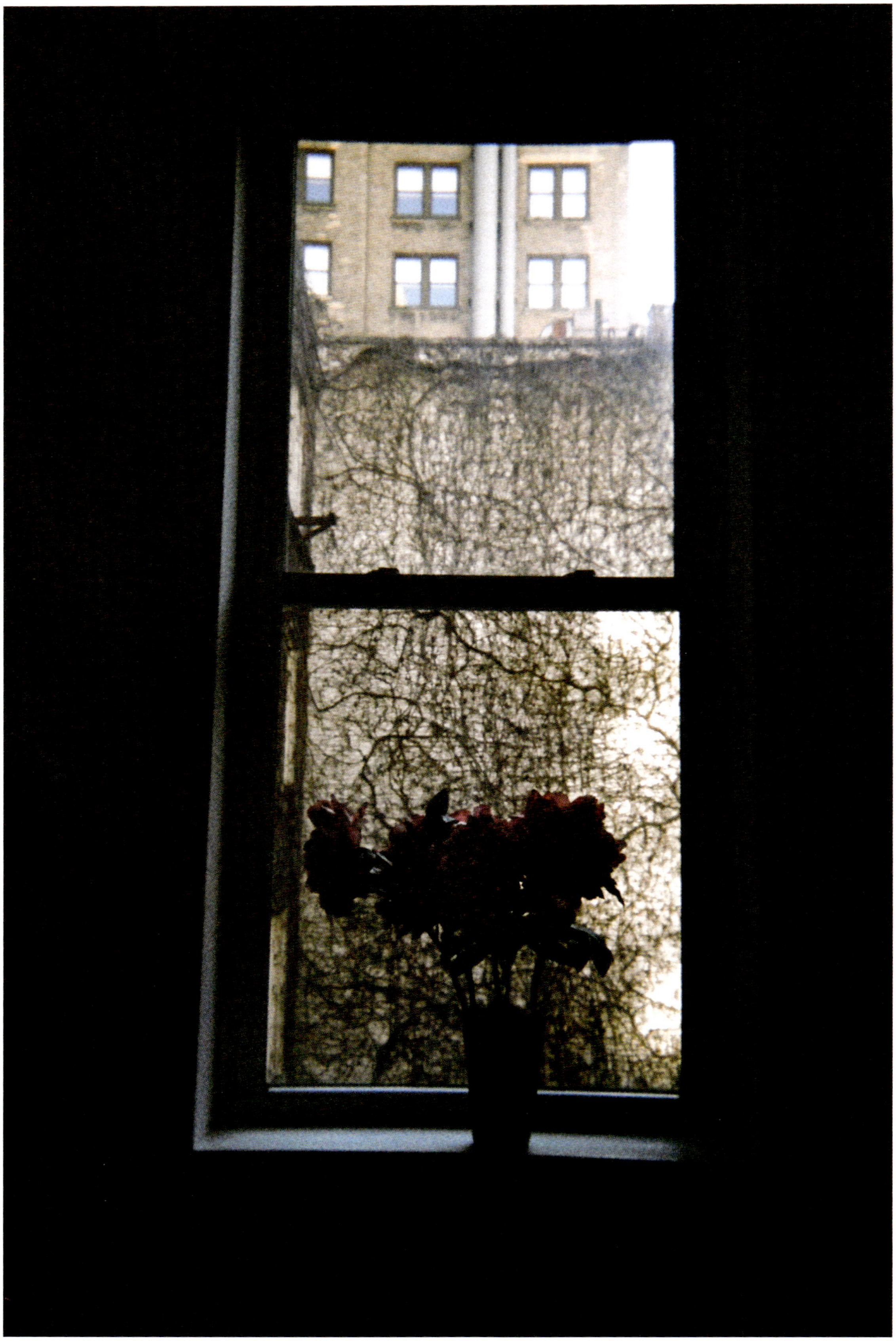

Upper East Side 1, *Manhattan* series, 2015–2021

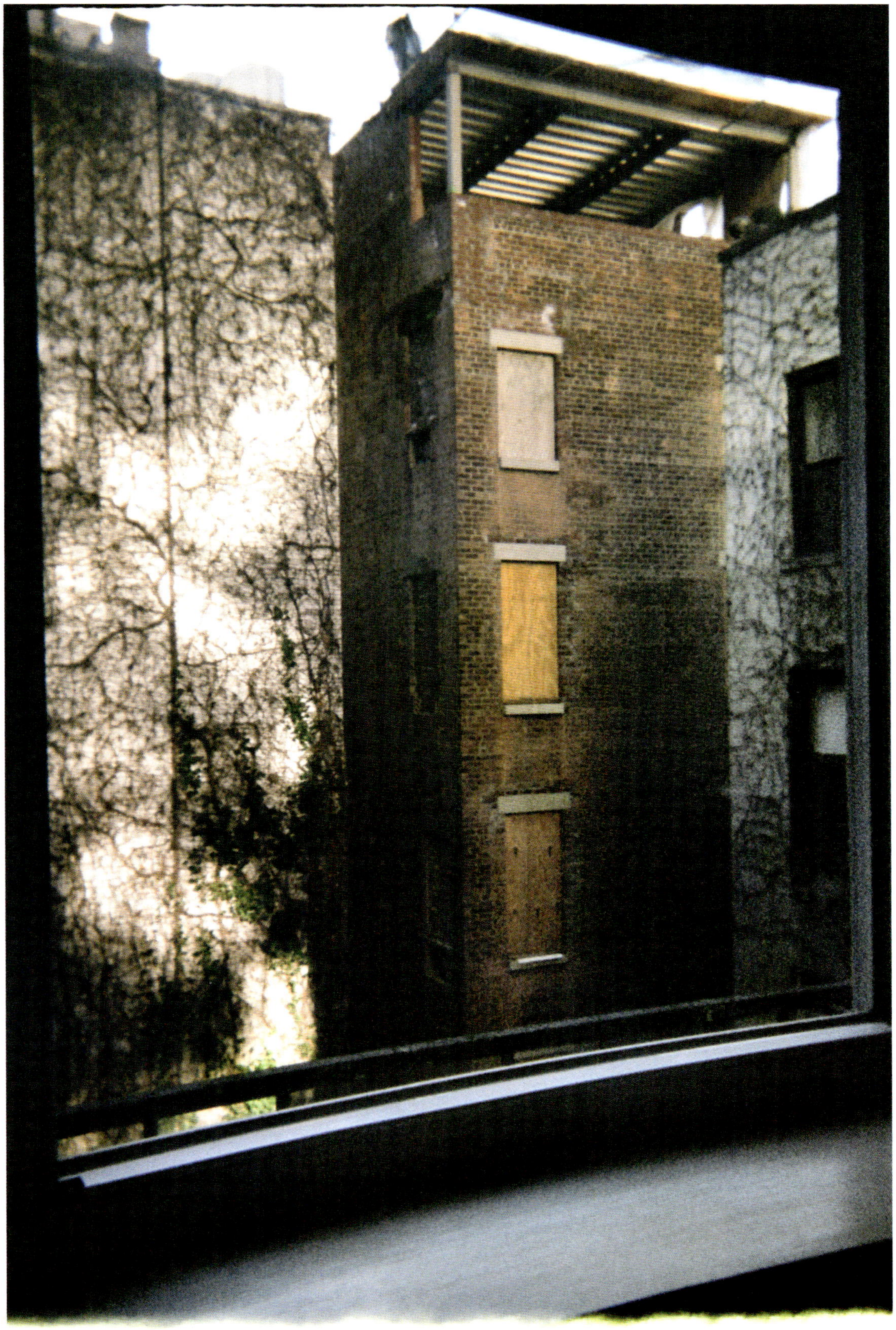

Upper East Side 2, *Manhattan* series, 2015–2021

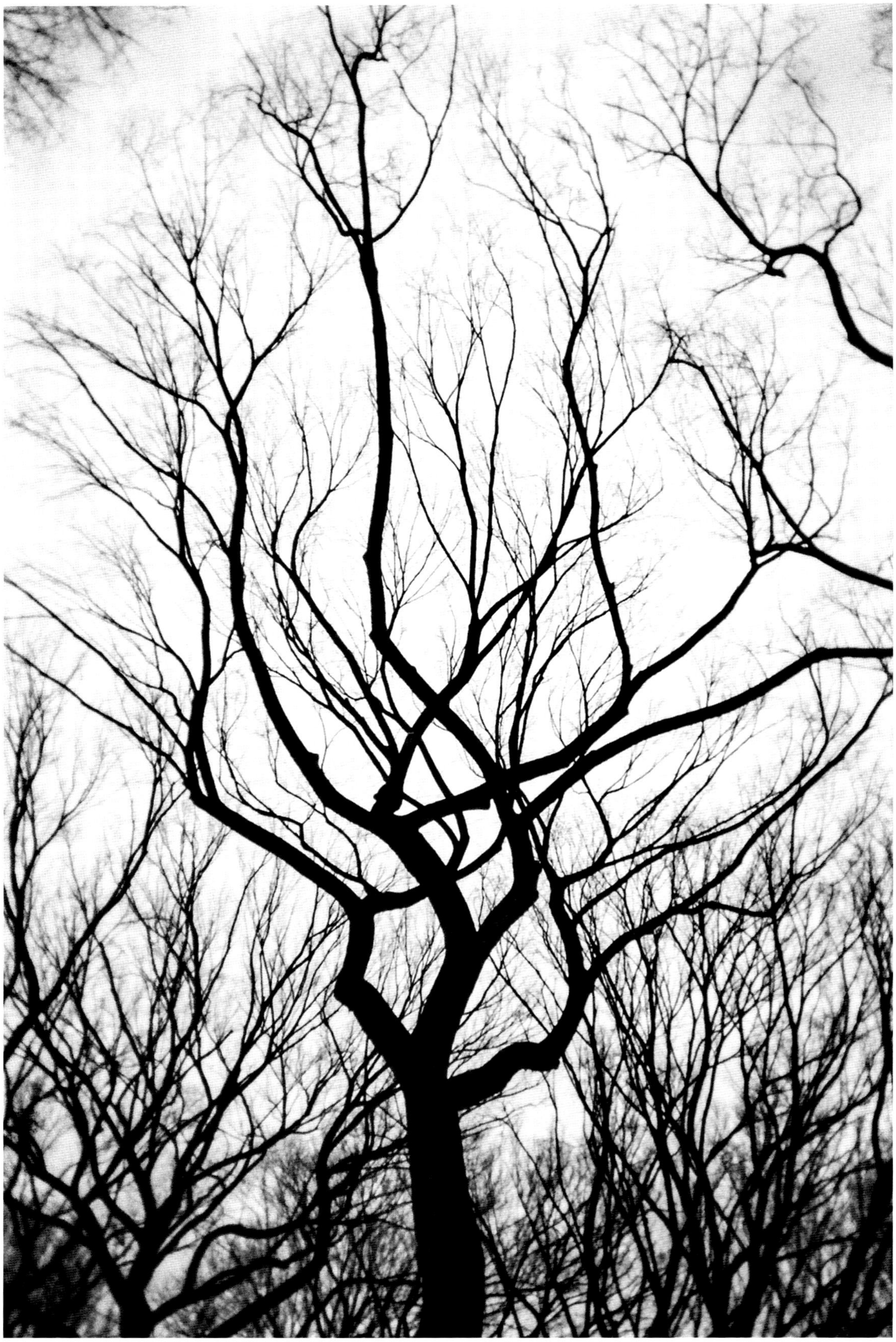

American Elm 1, *Manhattan* series, 2015–2021

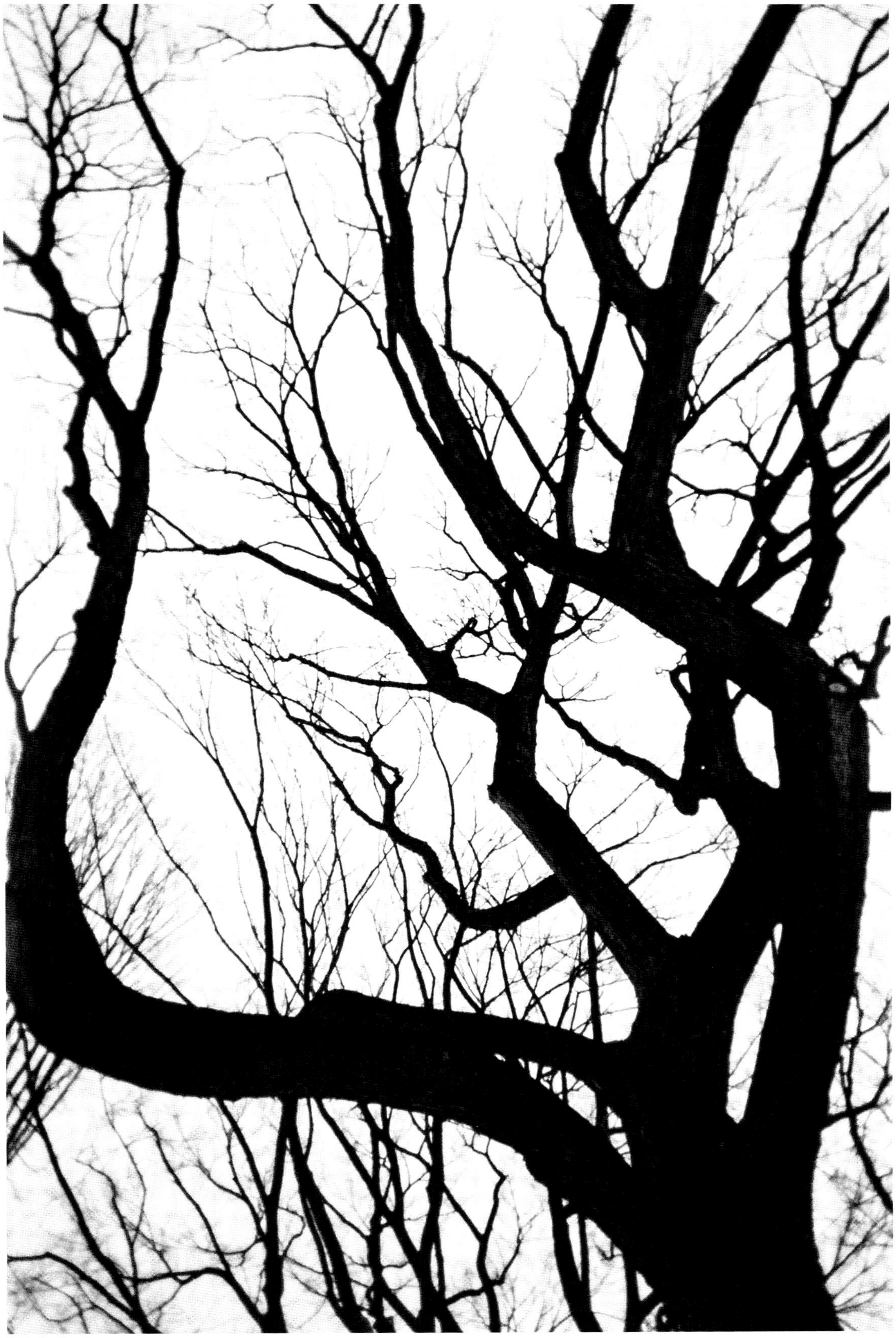

American Elm 2, *Manhattan* series, 2015–2021

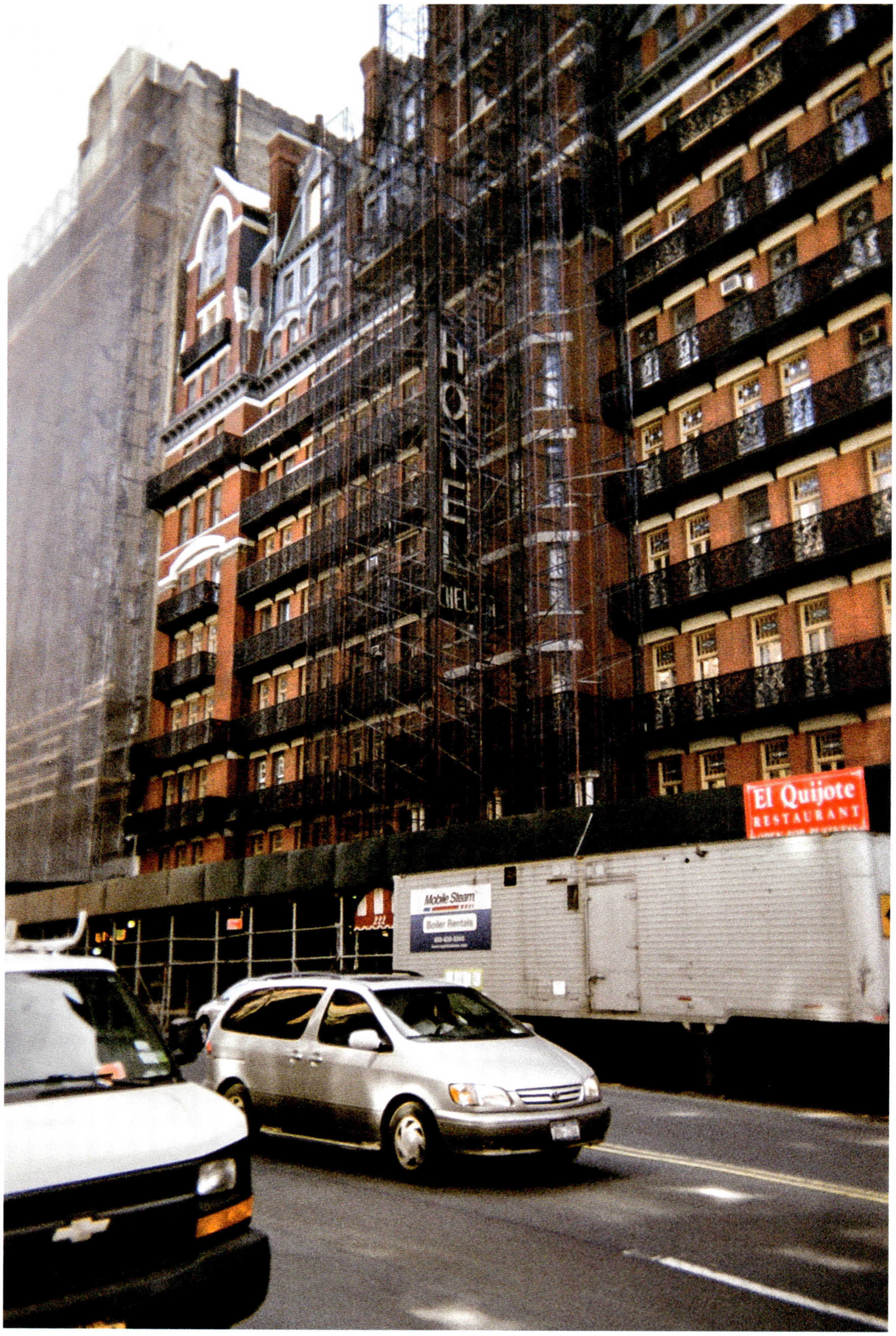

Chelsea Hotel, *Manhattan* series, 2015–2021

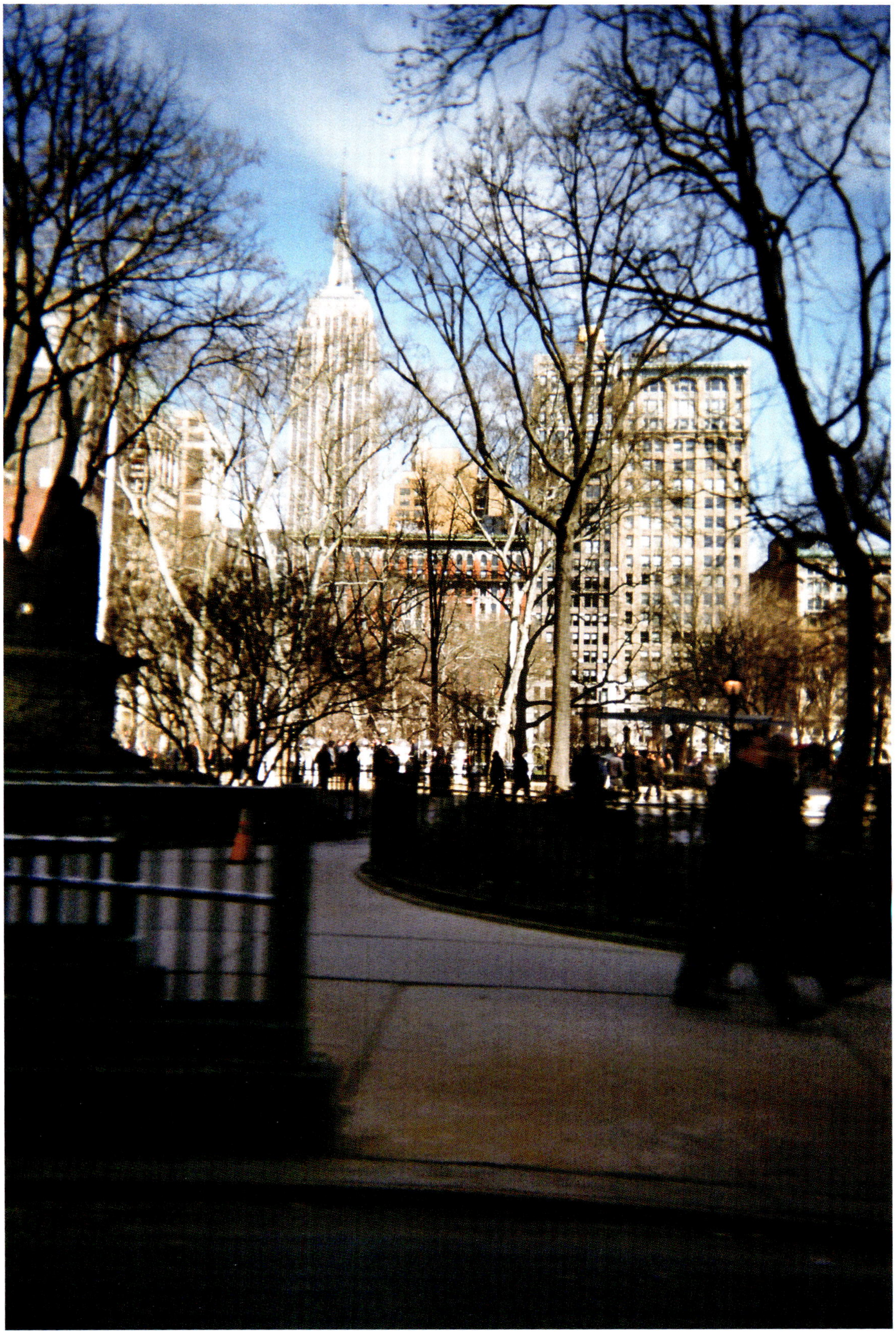

Empire State Building, *Manhattan* series, 2015–2021

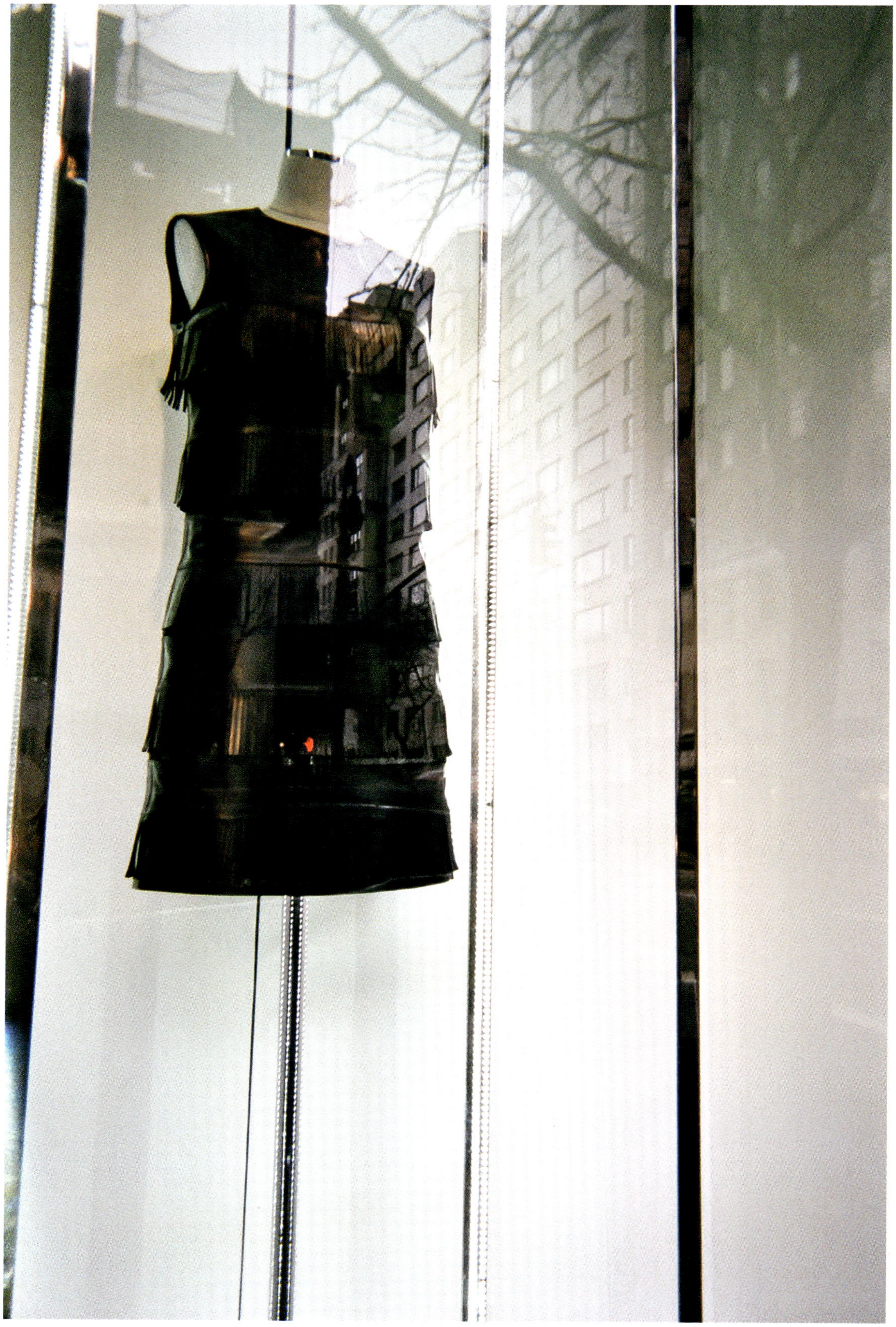

Black Fringe 1, *Manhattan* series, 2015–2021

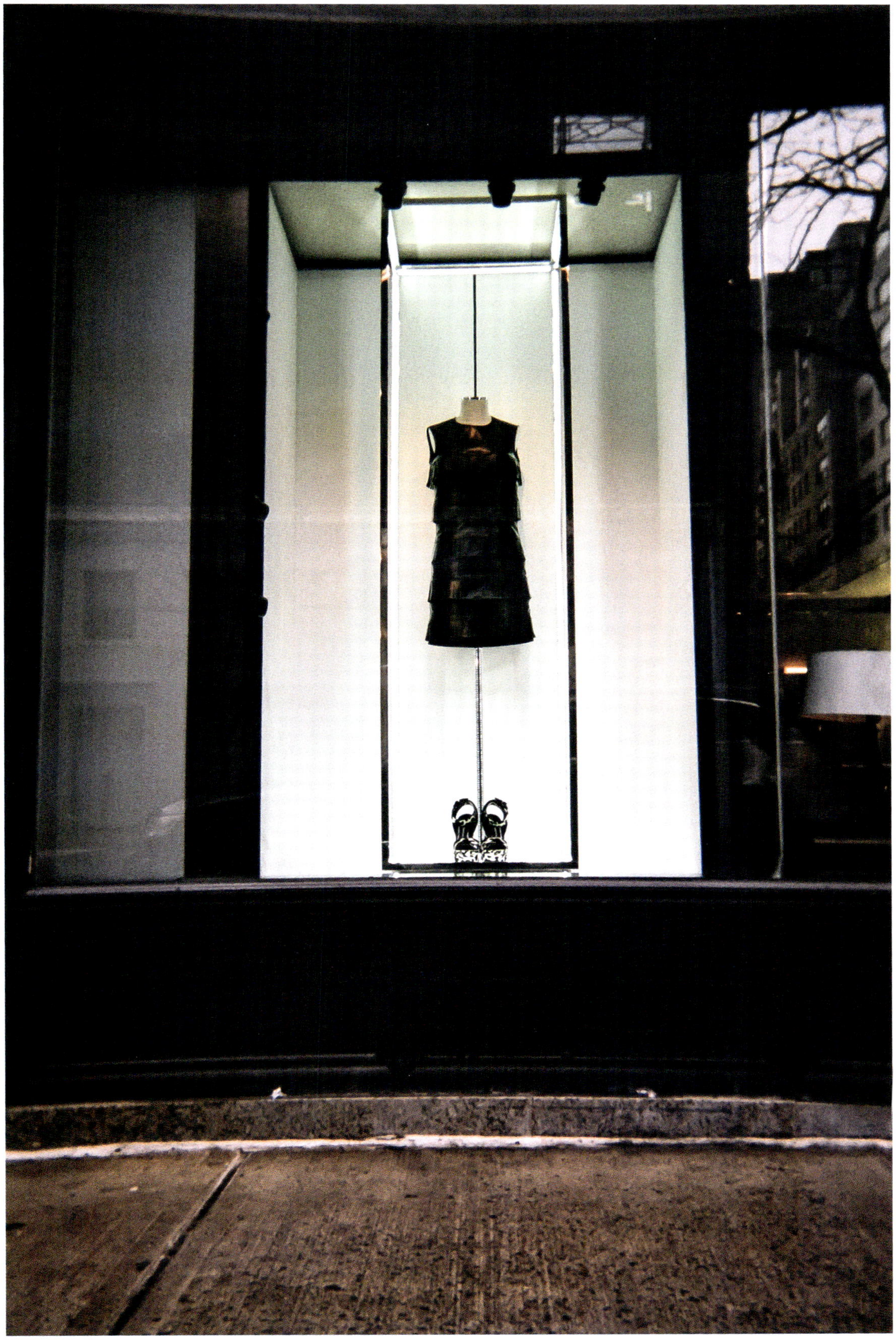

Black Fringe 2, *Manhattan* series, 2015–2021

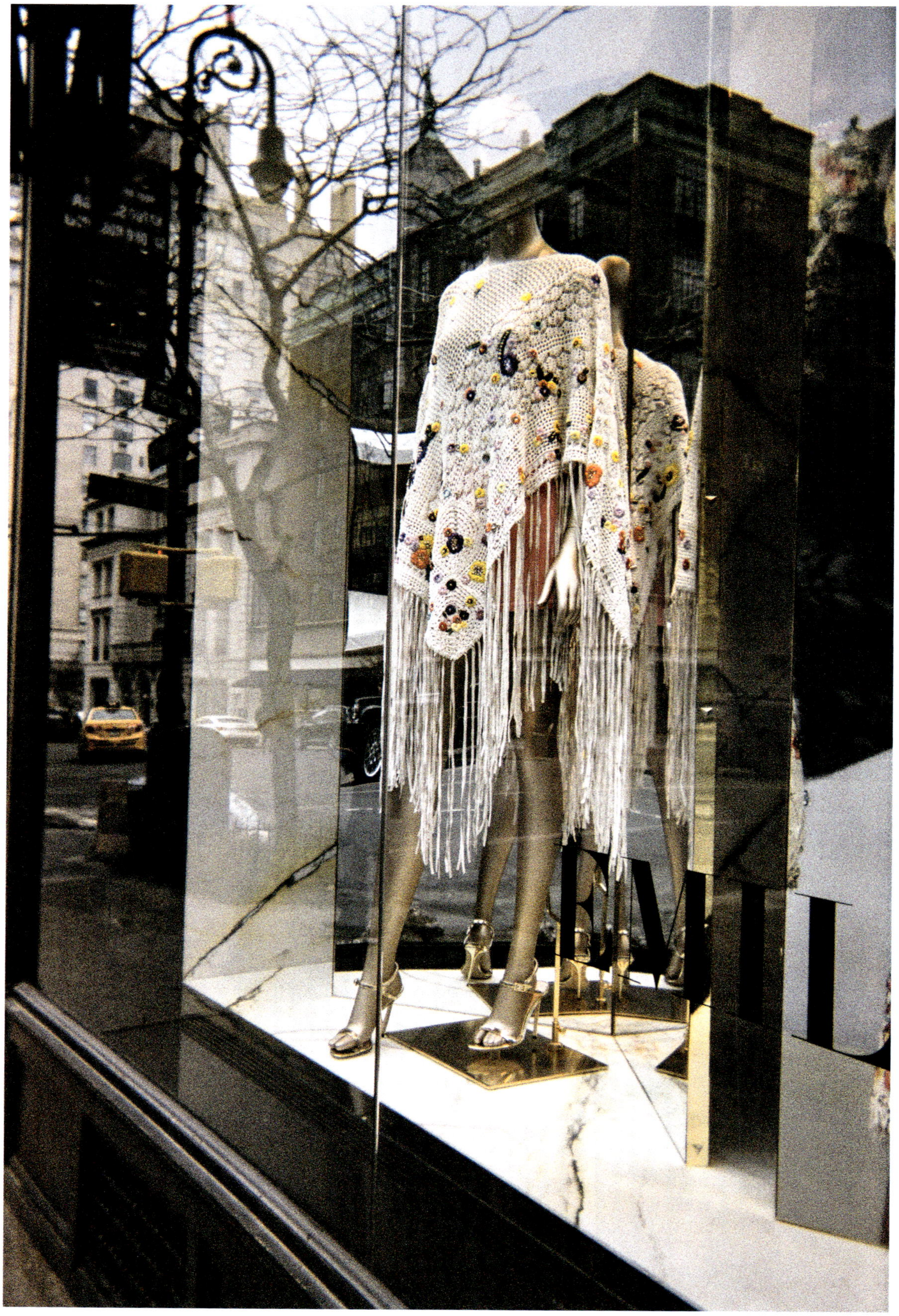

Fringe 1, *Manhattan* series, 2015–2021

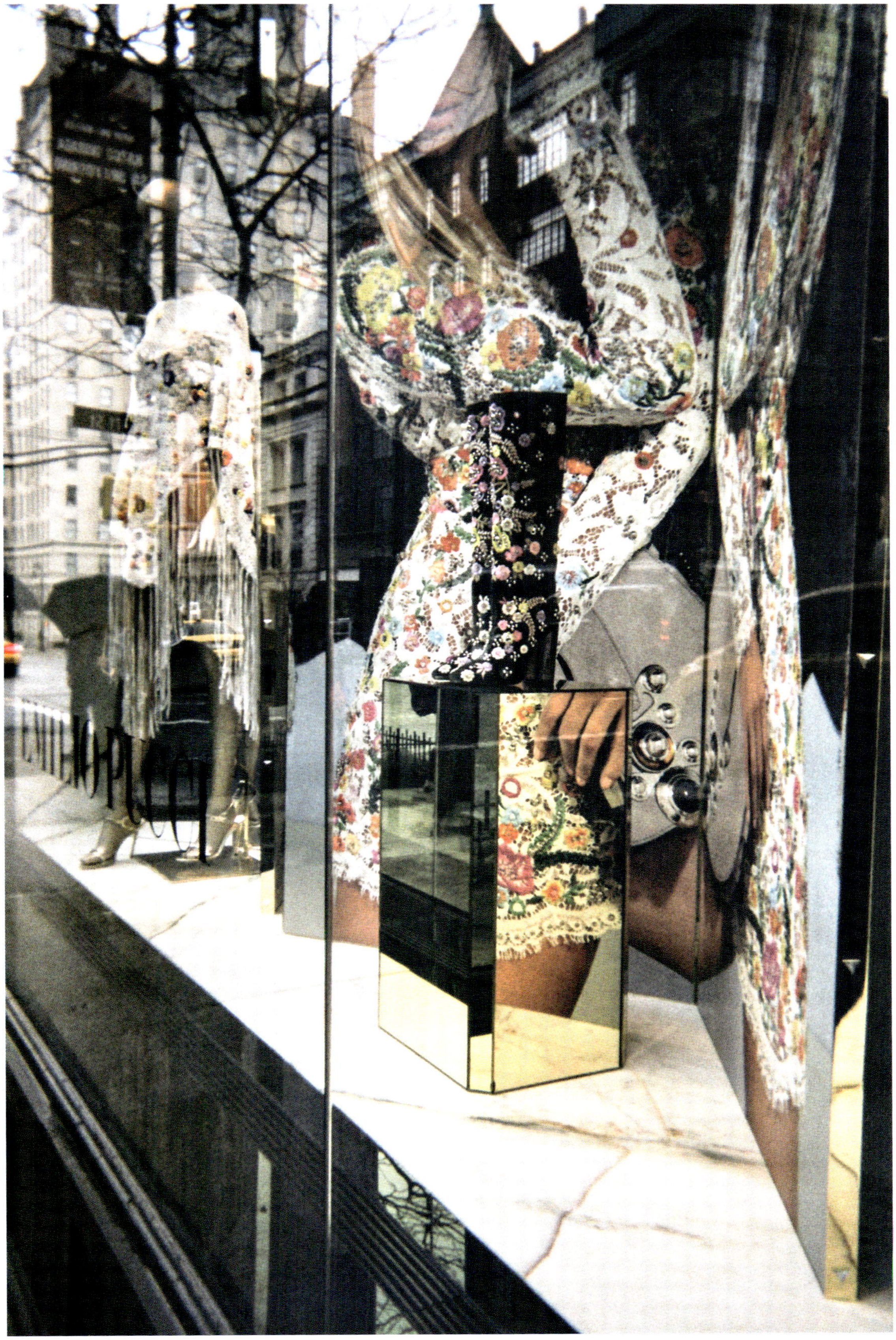

Fringe 2, *Manhattan* series, 2015–2021

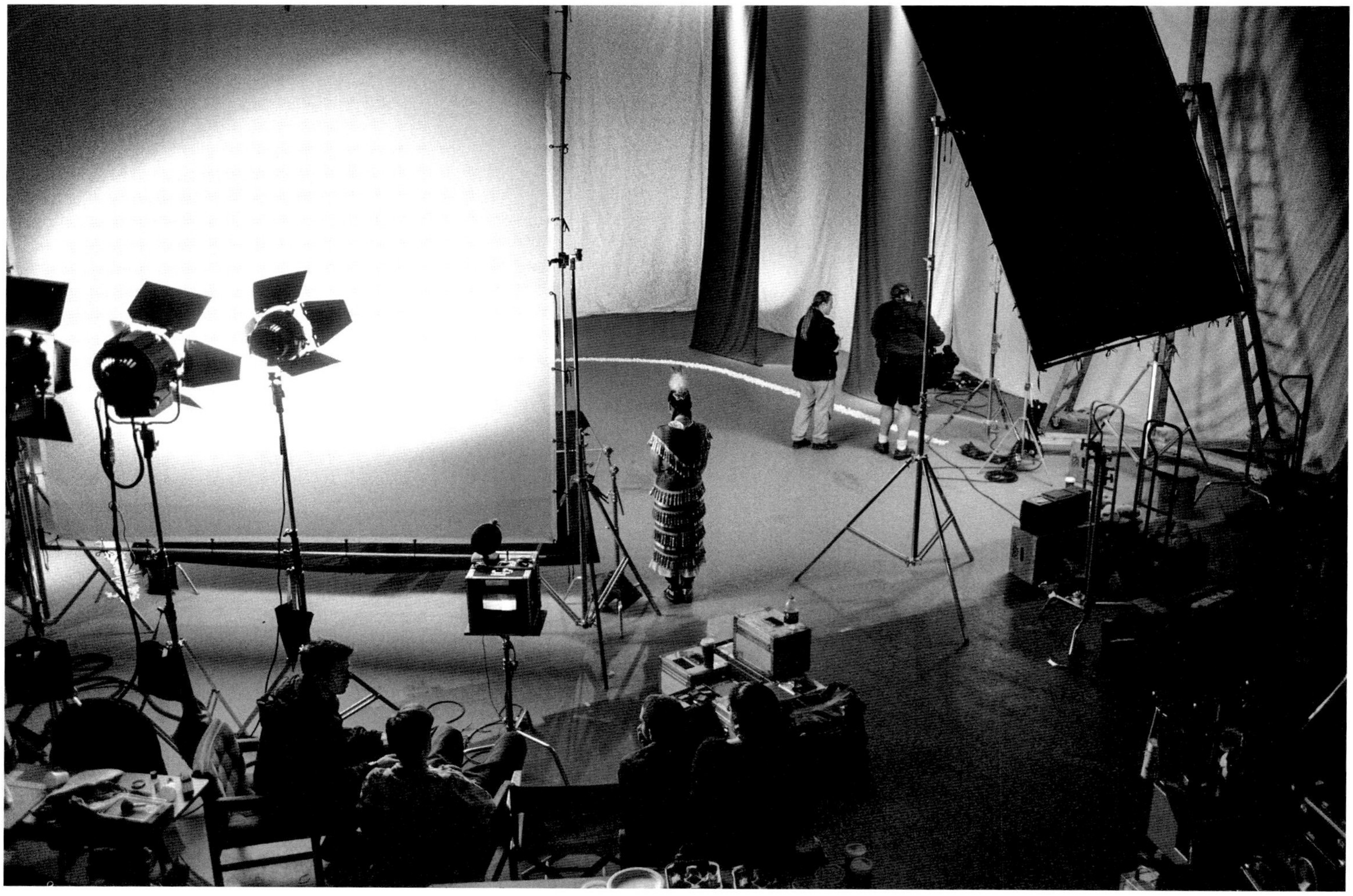

Jingle Dress 1, 1998–2011

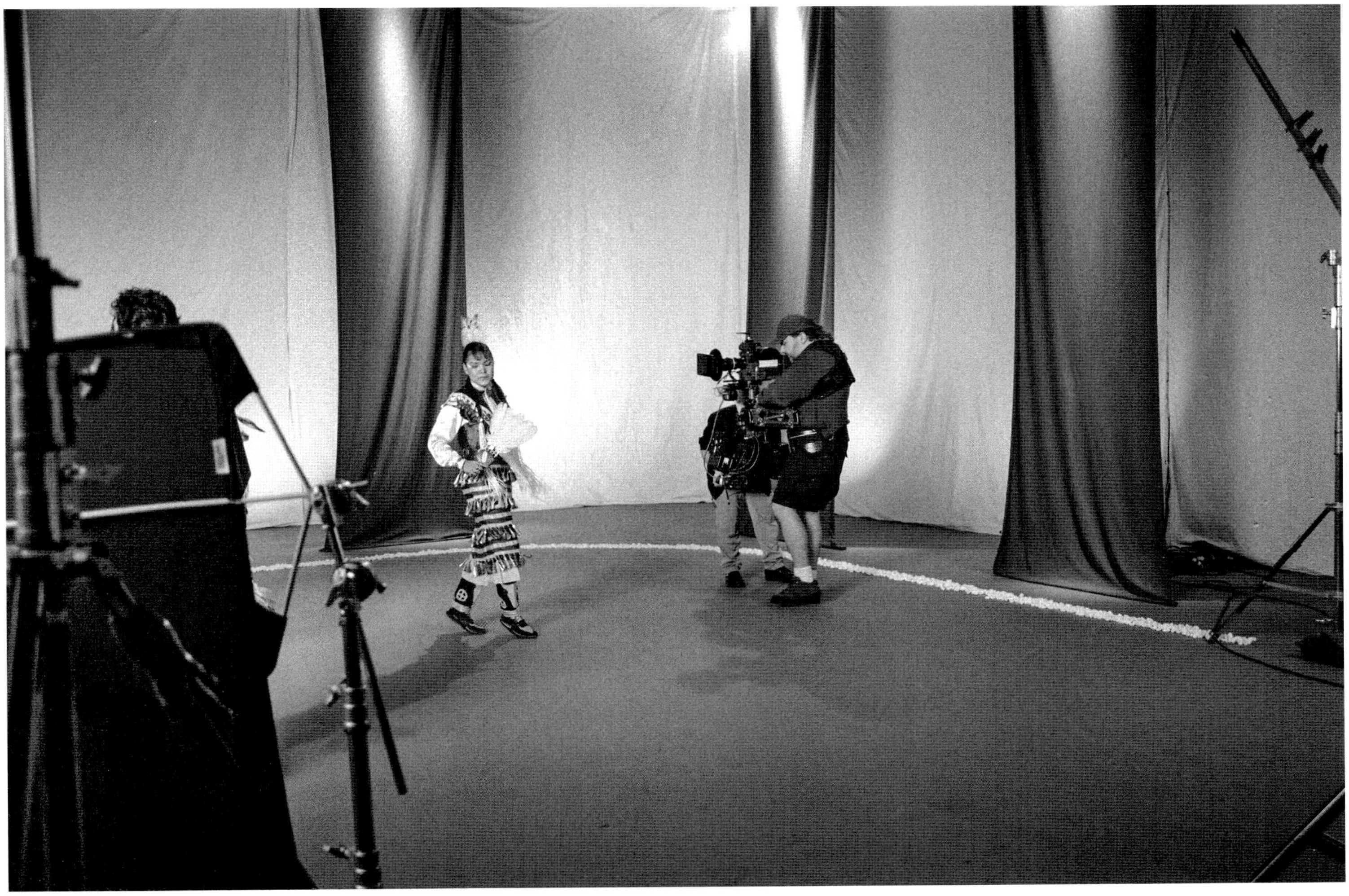

Jingle Dress 2, 1998–2011

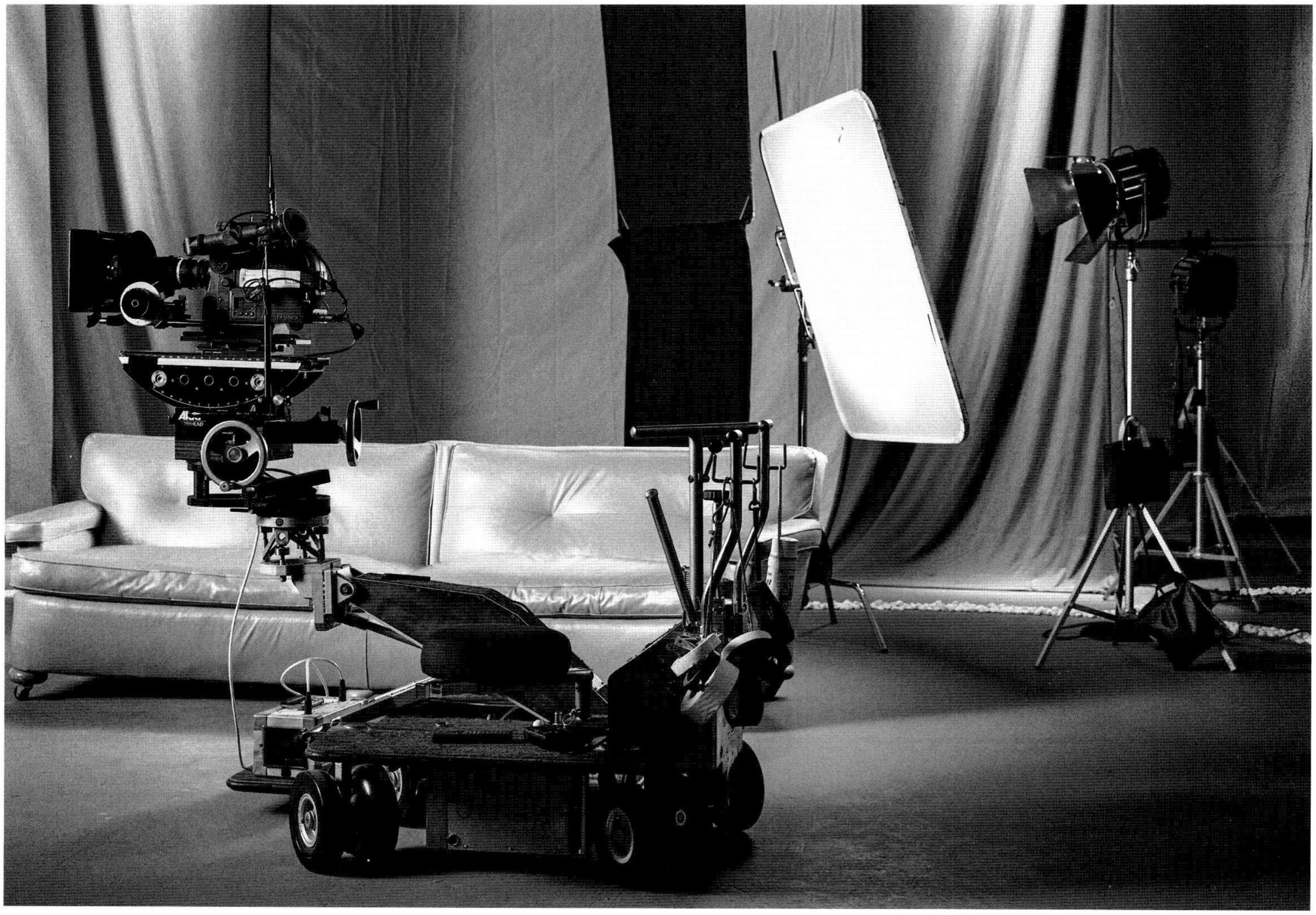

The People Dance (The Camera), 1998–2011

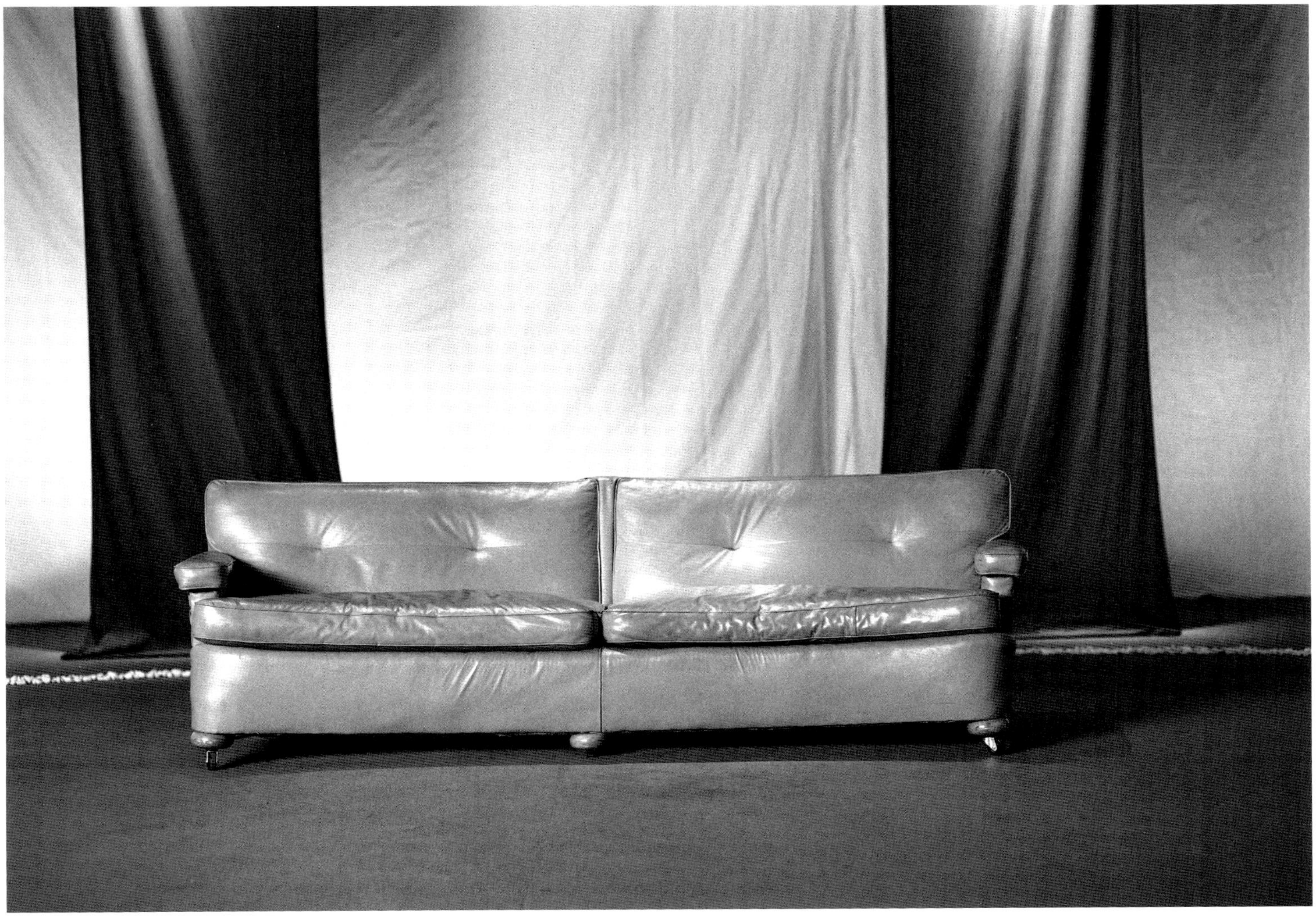

The People Dance (The Couch), 1998–2011

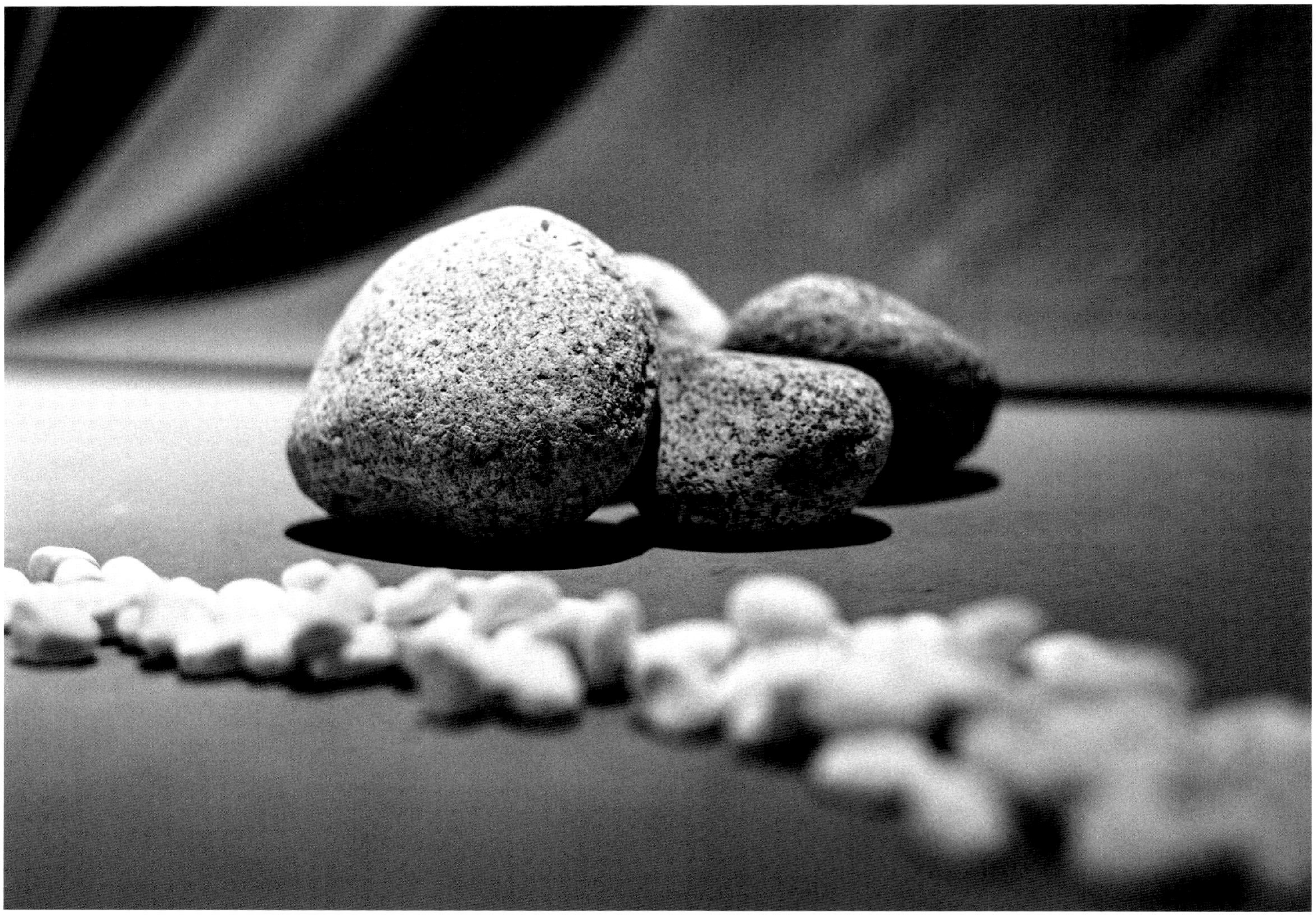

The People Dance (The Stone), 1998–2011

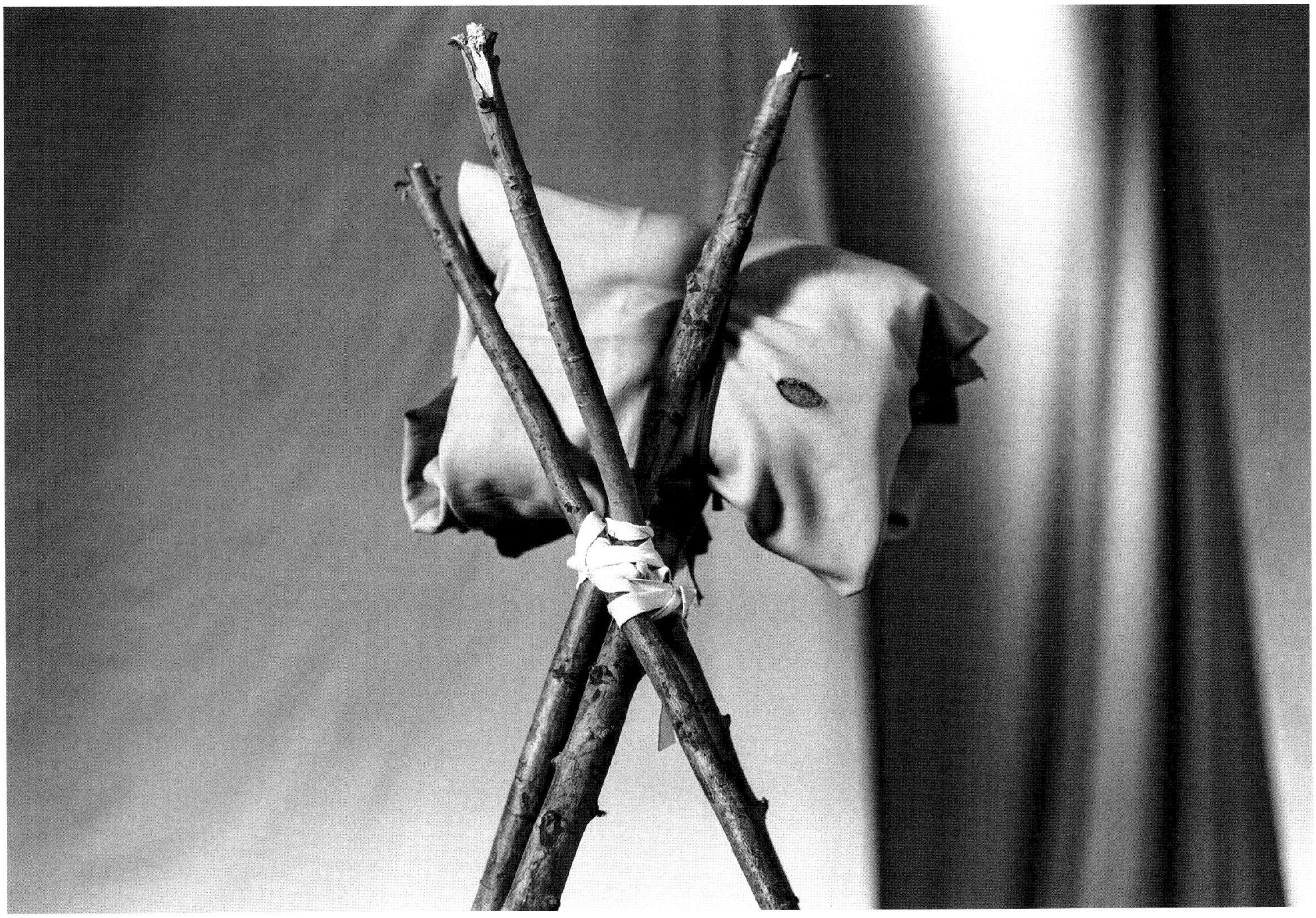

The People Dance (The Bundle), 1998–2011

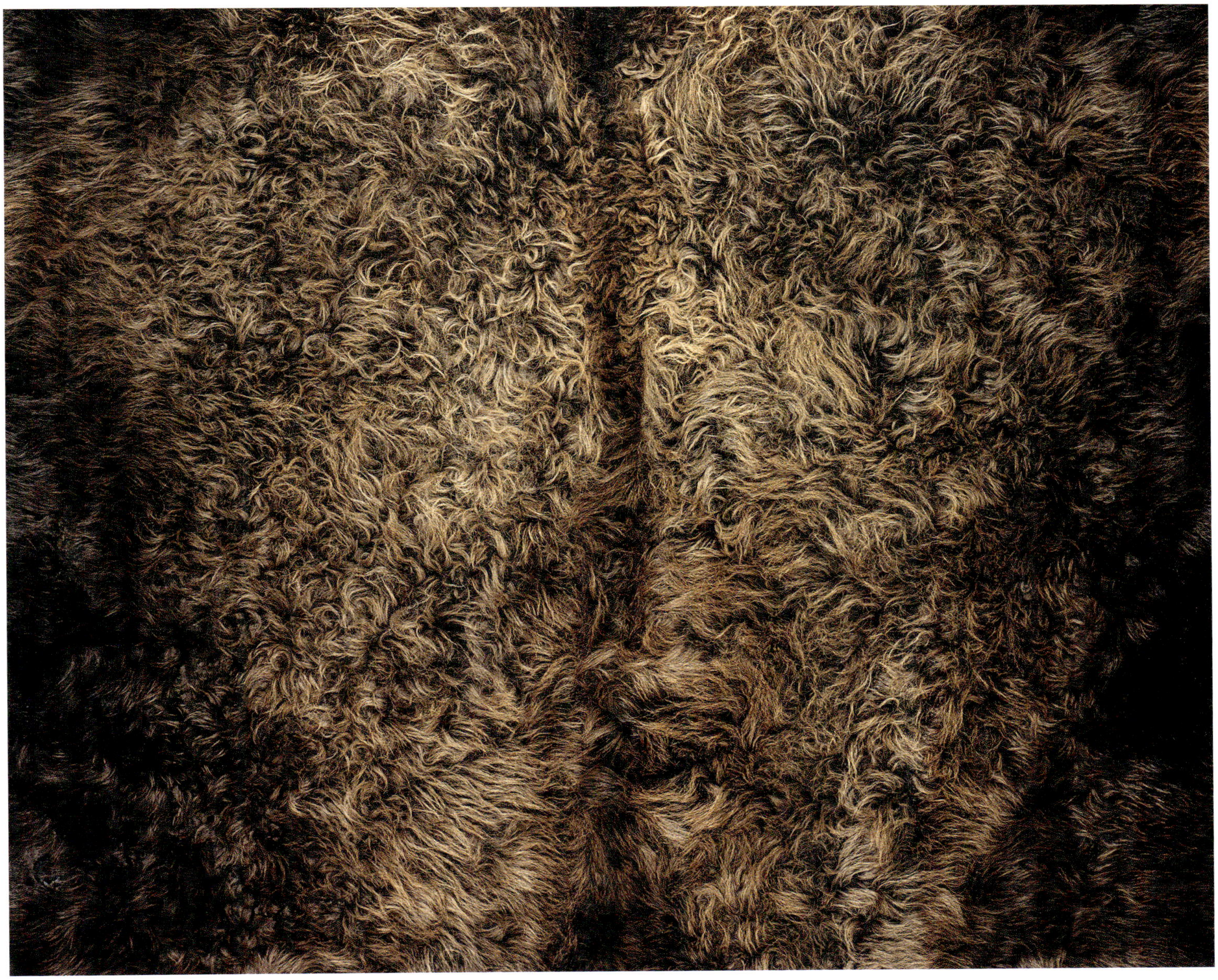

Tatanka Wanbli Chekpa Wicincala (Robe), 2006

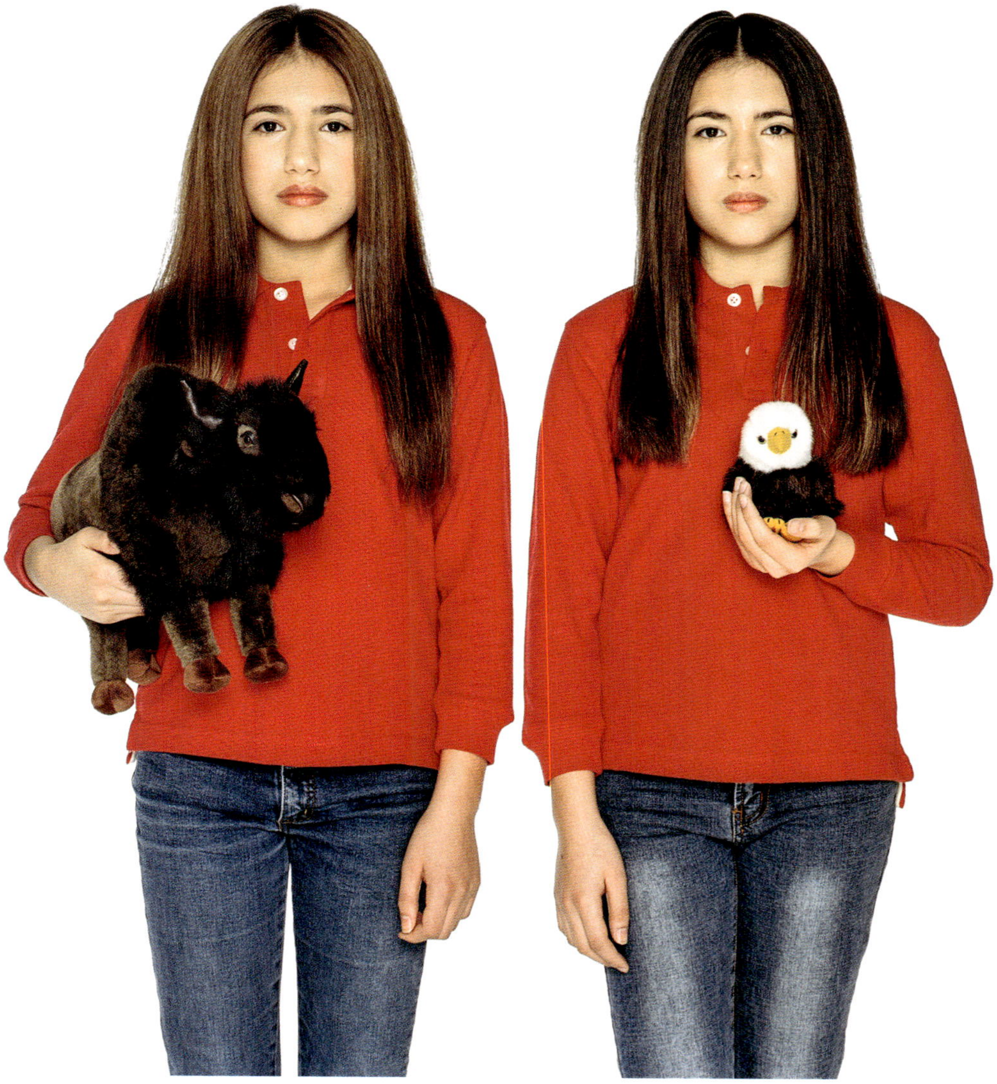

Tatanka Wanbli Chekpa Wicincala (Eyes Open), 2006

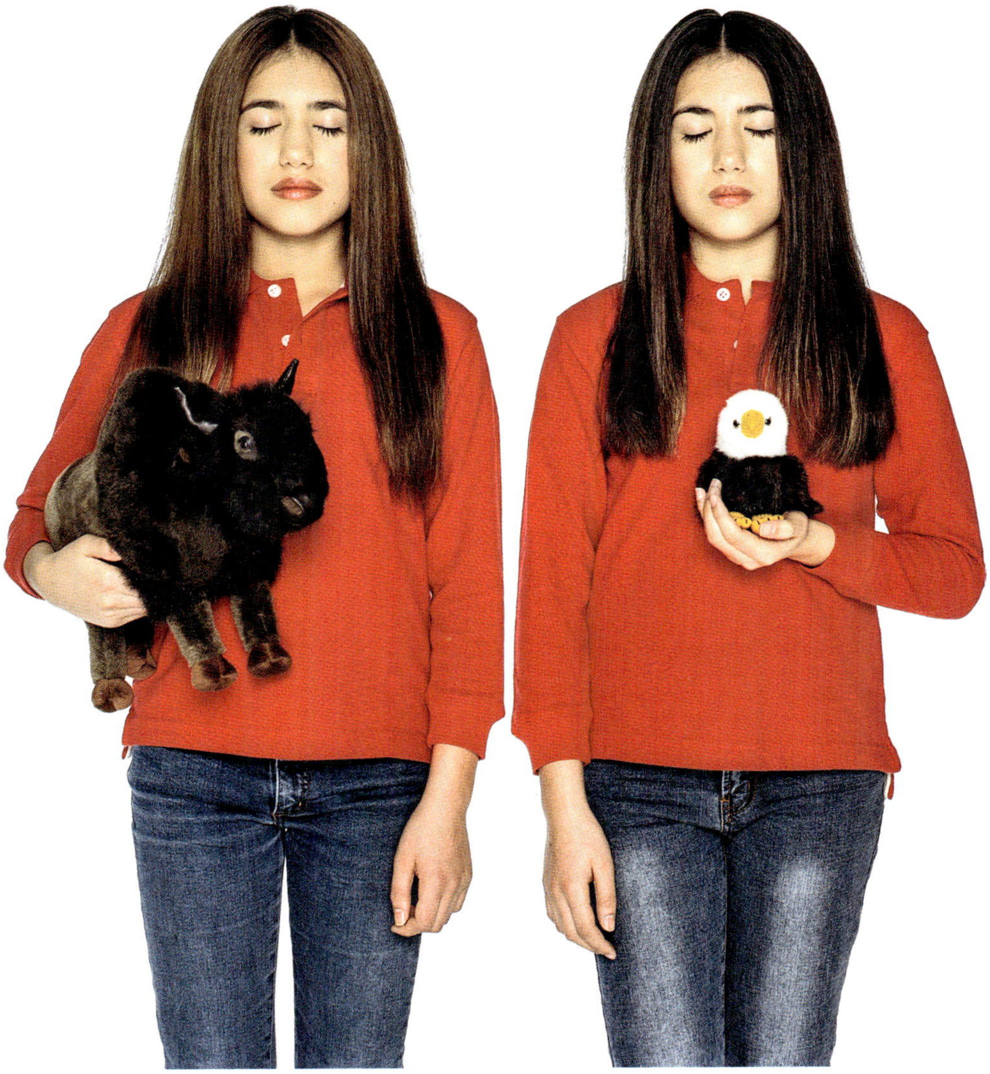

Tatanka Wanbli Chekpa Wicincala (Eyes Closed), 2006

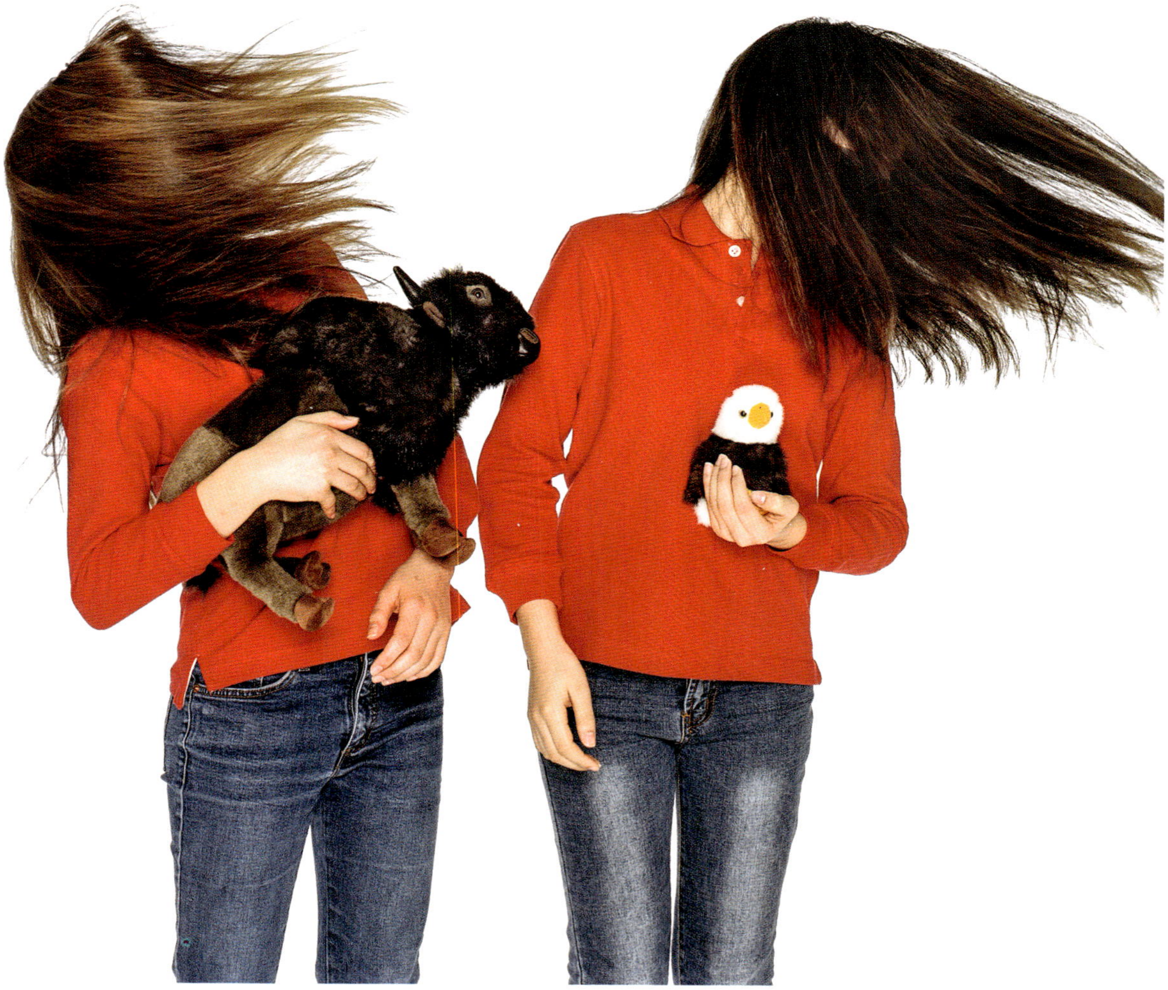

Tatanka Wanbli Chekpa Wicincala (Transformation), 2006

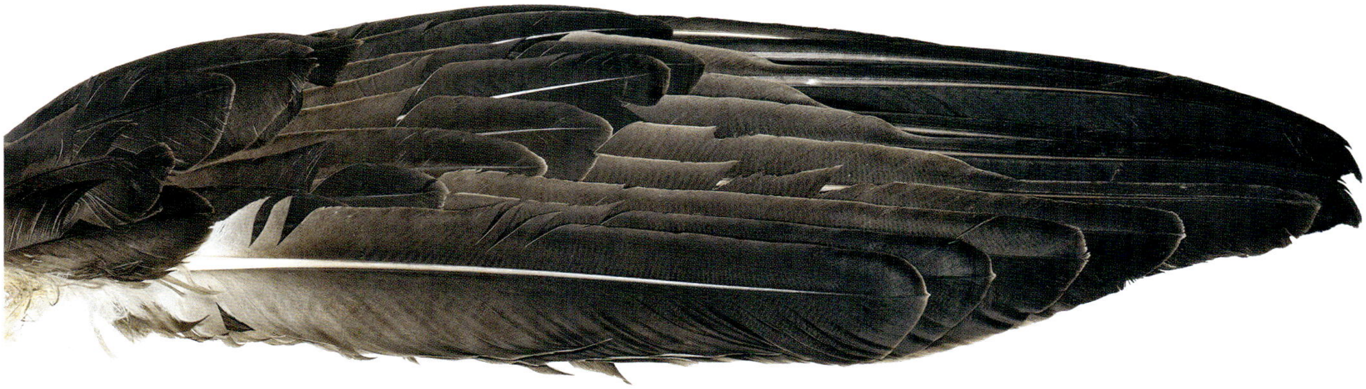

Tatanka Wanbli Chekpa Wicincala (Feather), 2006

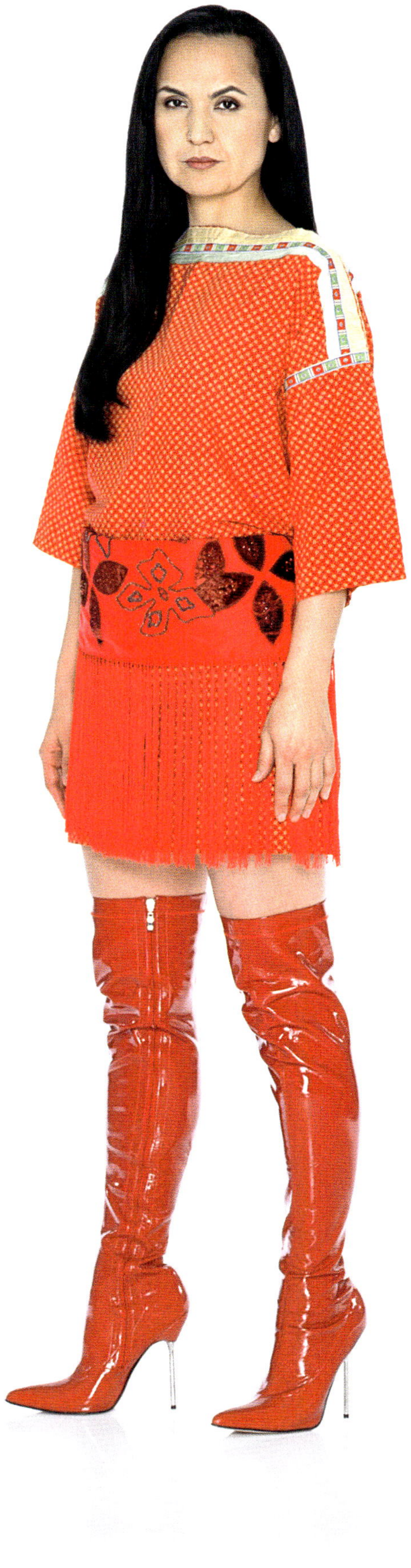

Onto the Red Road, 2006

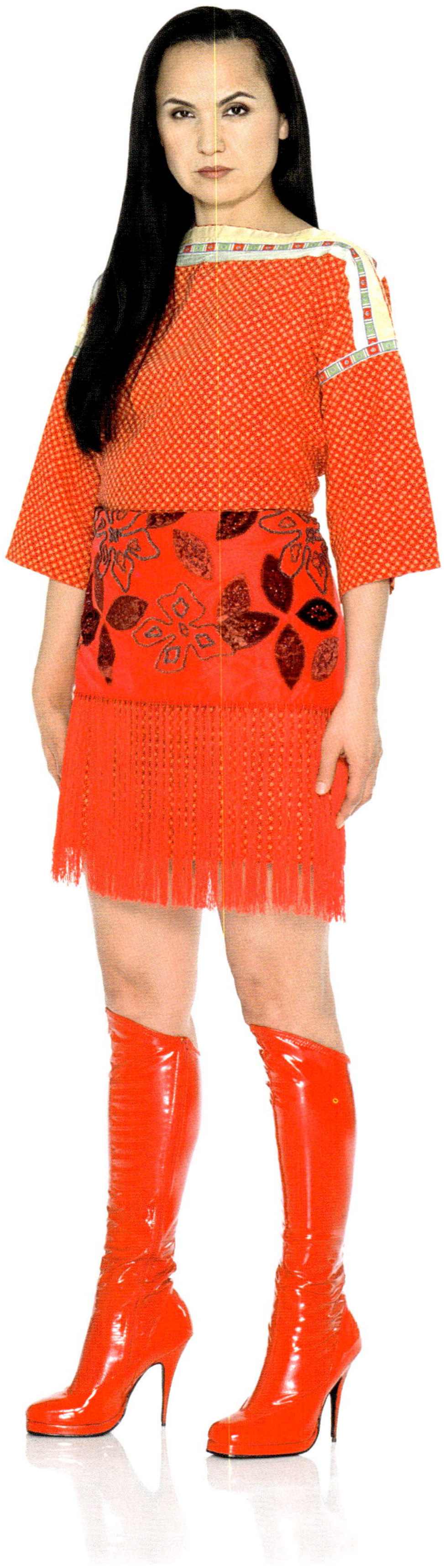

Onto the Red Road, 2006

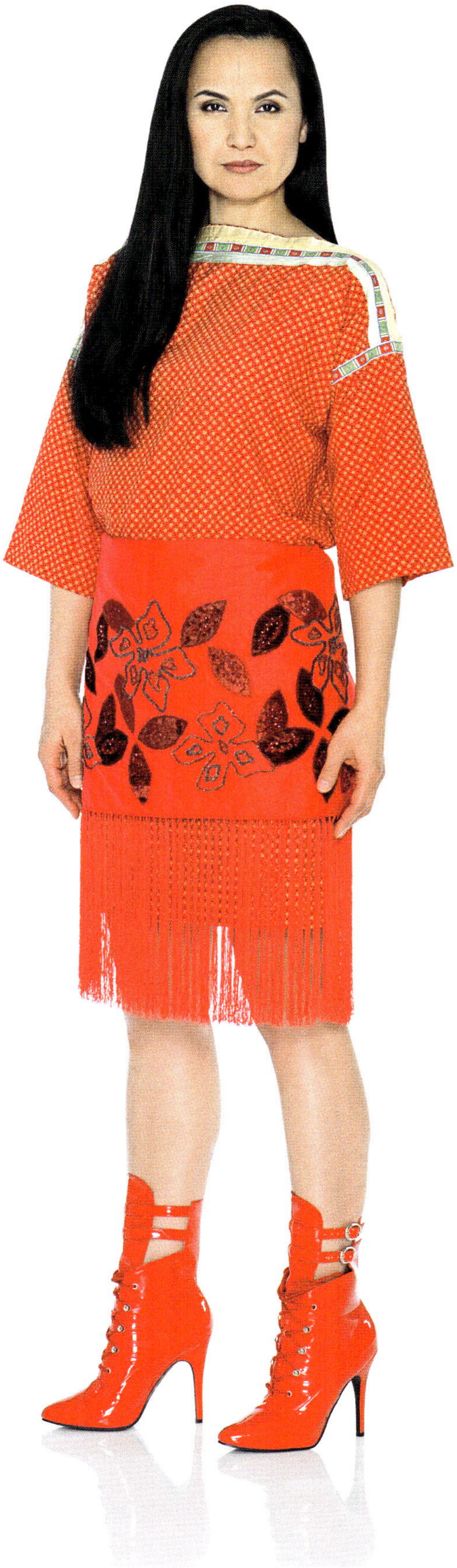

Onto the Red Road, 2006

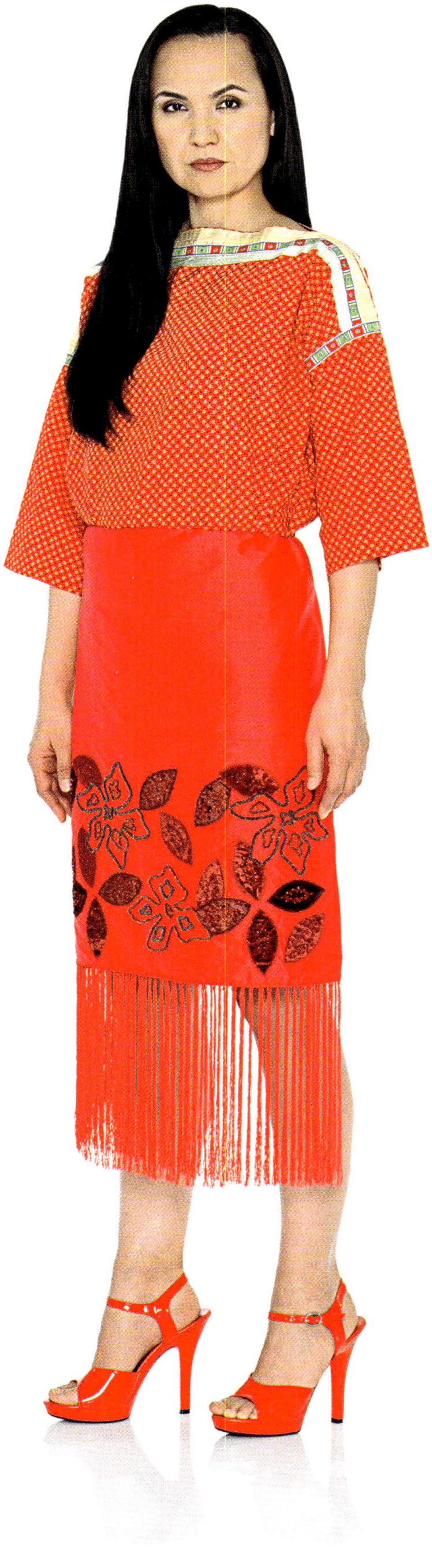

Onto the Red Road, 2006

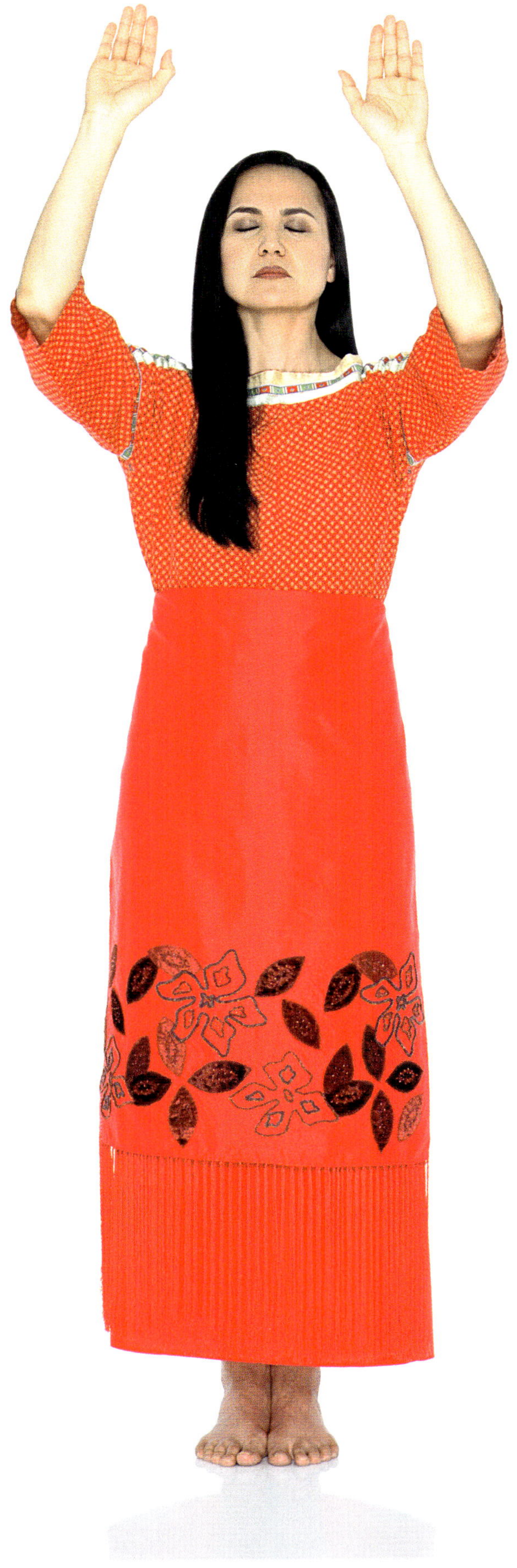

Onto the Red Road, 2006

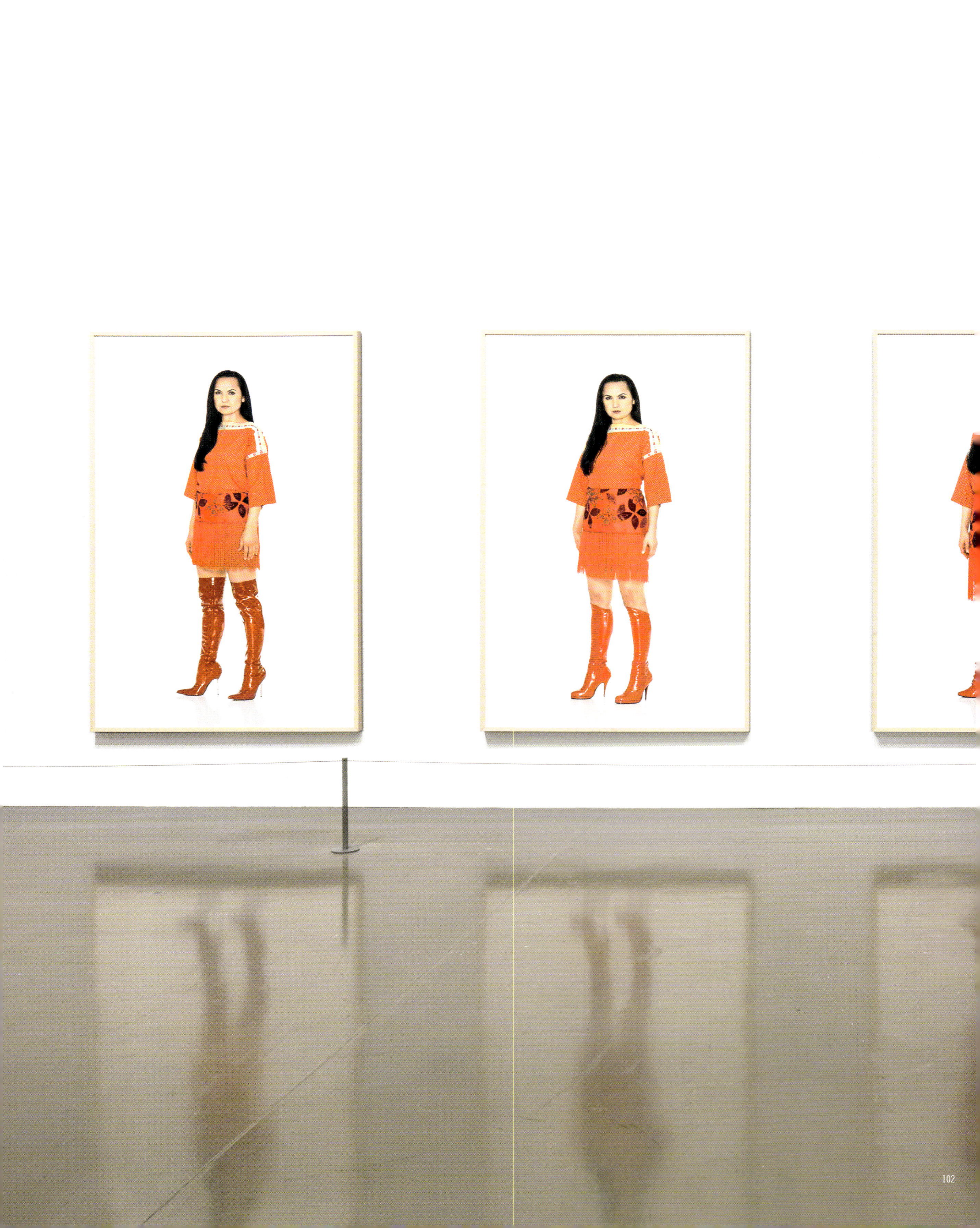

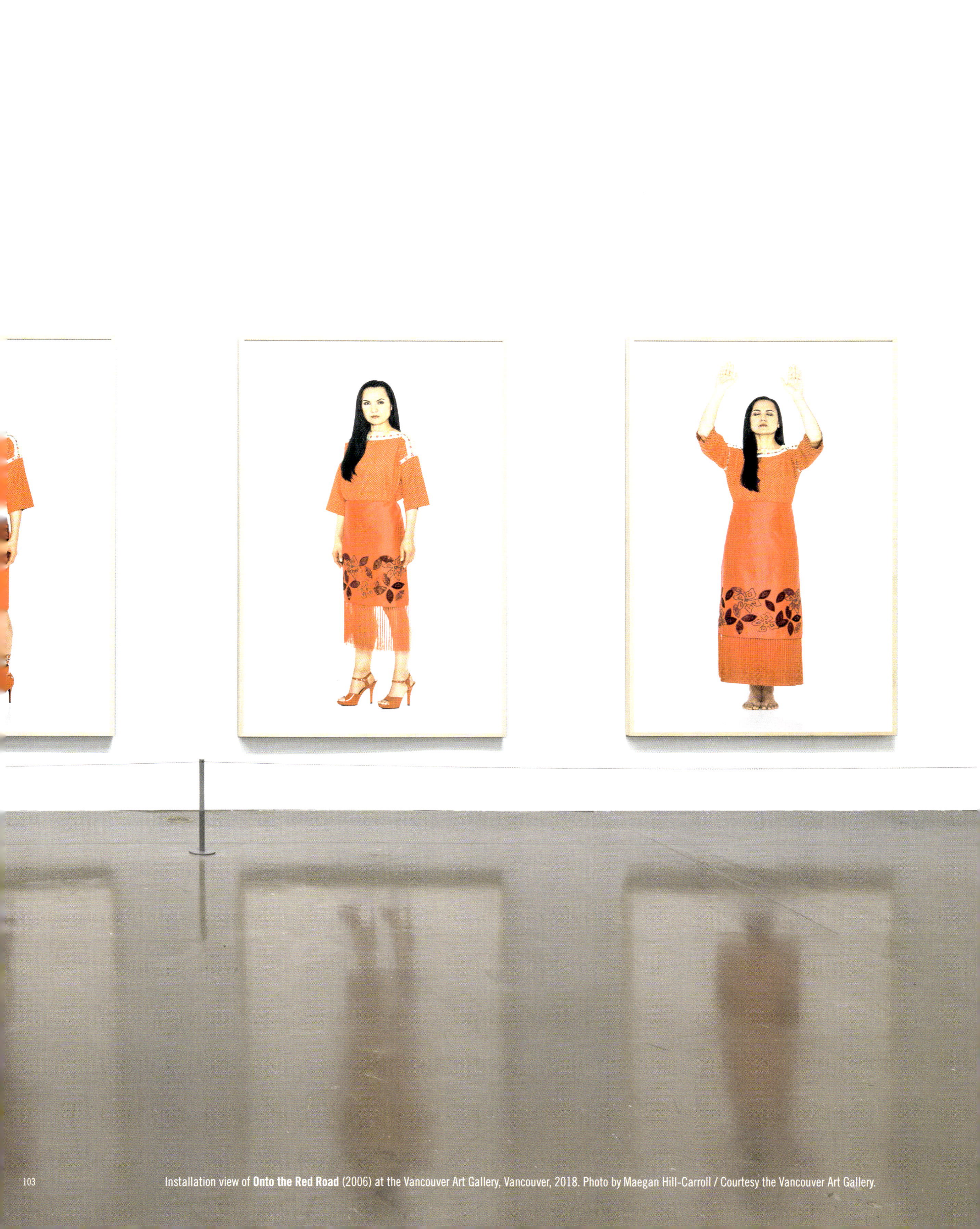

Installation view of **Onto the Red Road** (2006) at the Vancouver Art Gallery, Vancouver, 2018. Photo by Maegan Hill-Carroll / Courtesy the Vancouver Art Gallery.

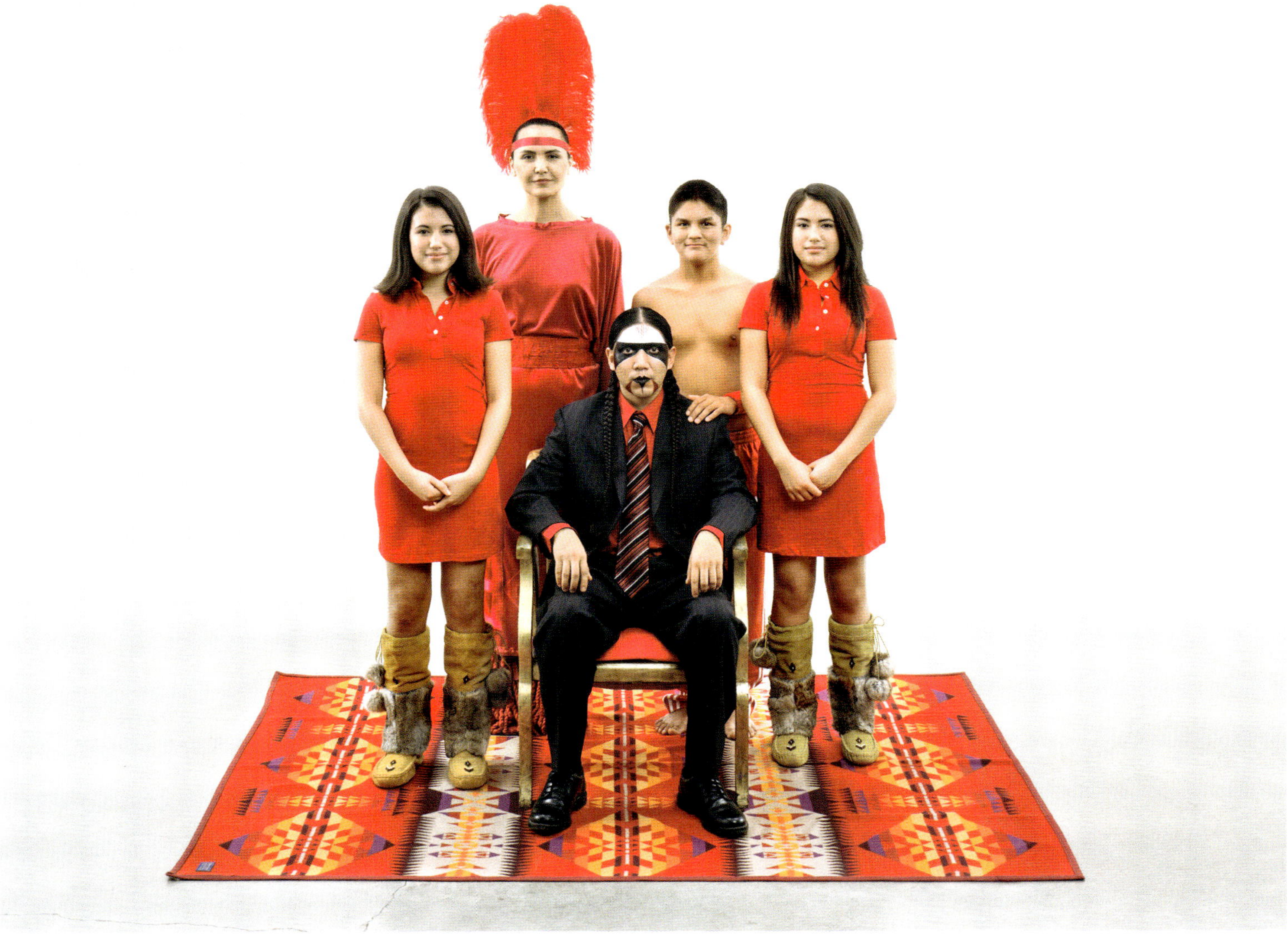

105 **The Mustang Suite: Family Portrait (Indians on a Blanket)**, 2008

107 **The Mustang Suite: Baby Boyz Gotta Indian Pony**, 2008

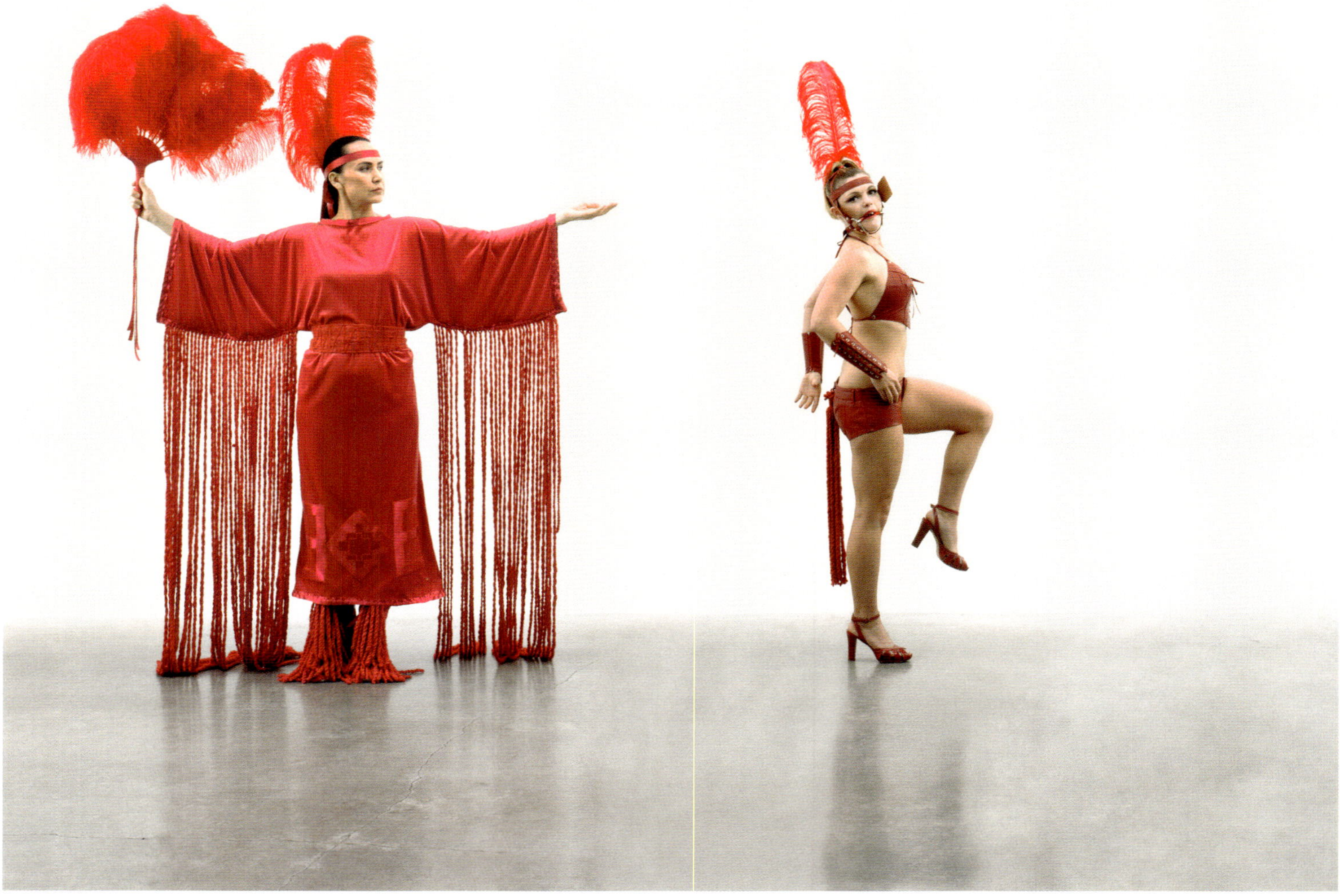

The Mustang Suite: Momma Has a Pony... (girl named History and sets her free), 2008

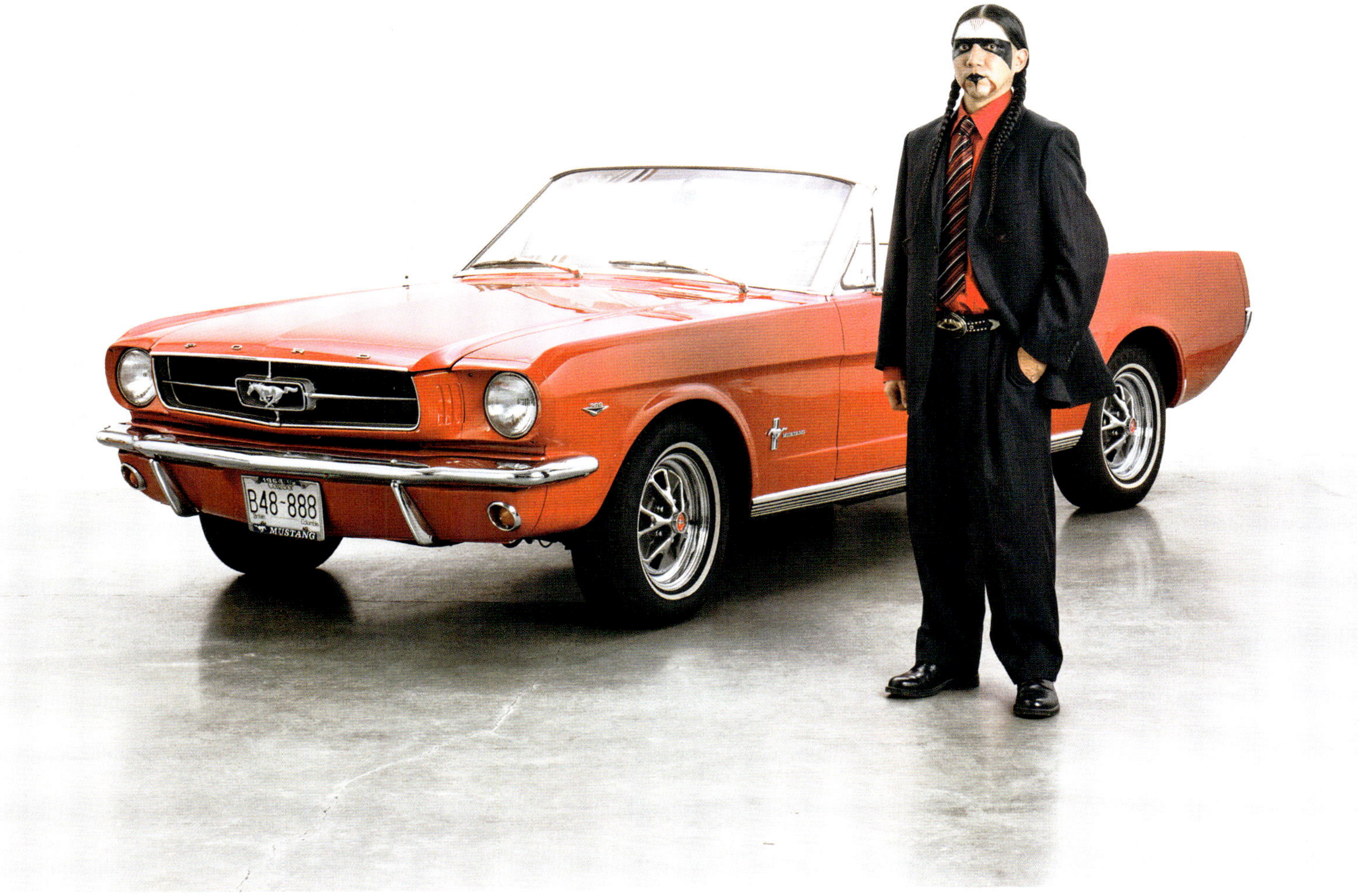

The Mustang Suite: Daddy's Gotta New Ride, 2008

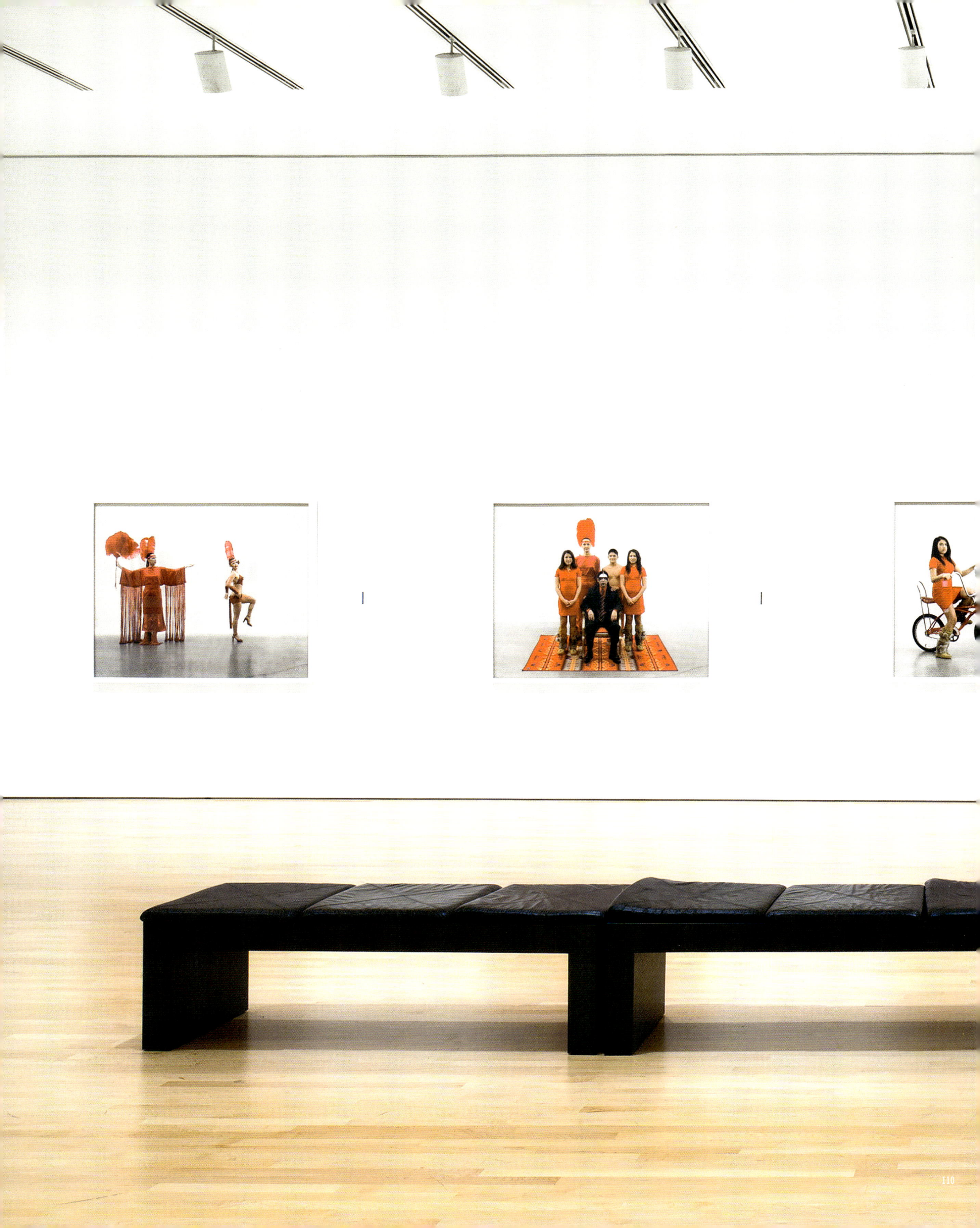

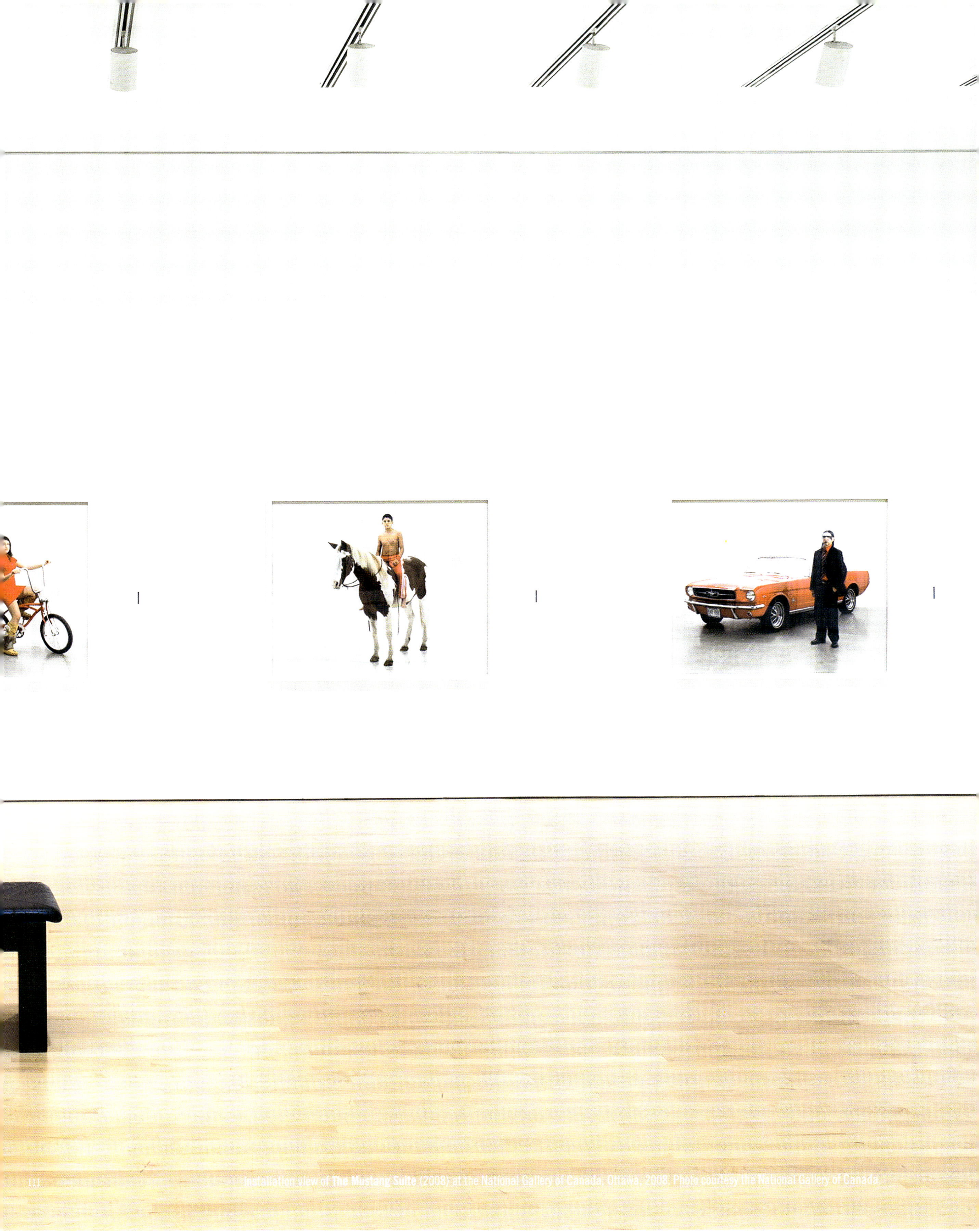

Installation view of **The Mustang Suite** (2008) at the National Gallery of Canada, Ottawa, 2008. Photo courtesy the National Gallery of Canada.

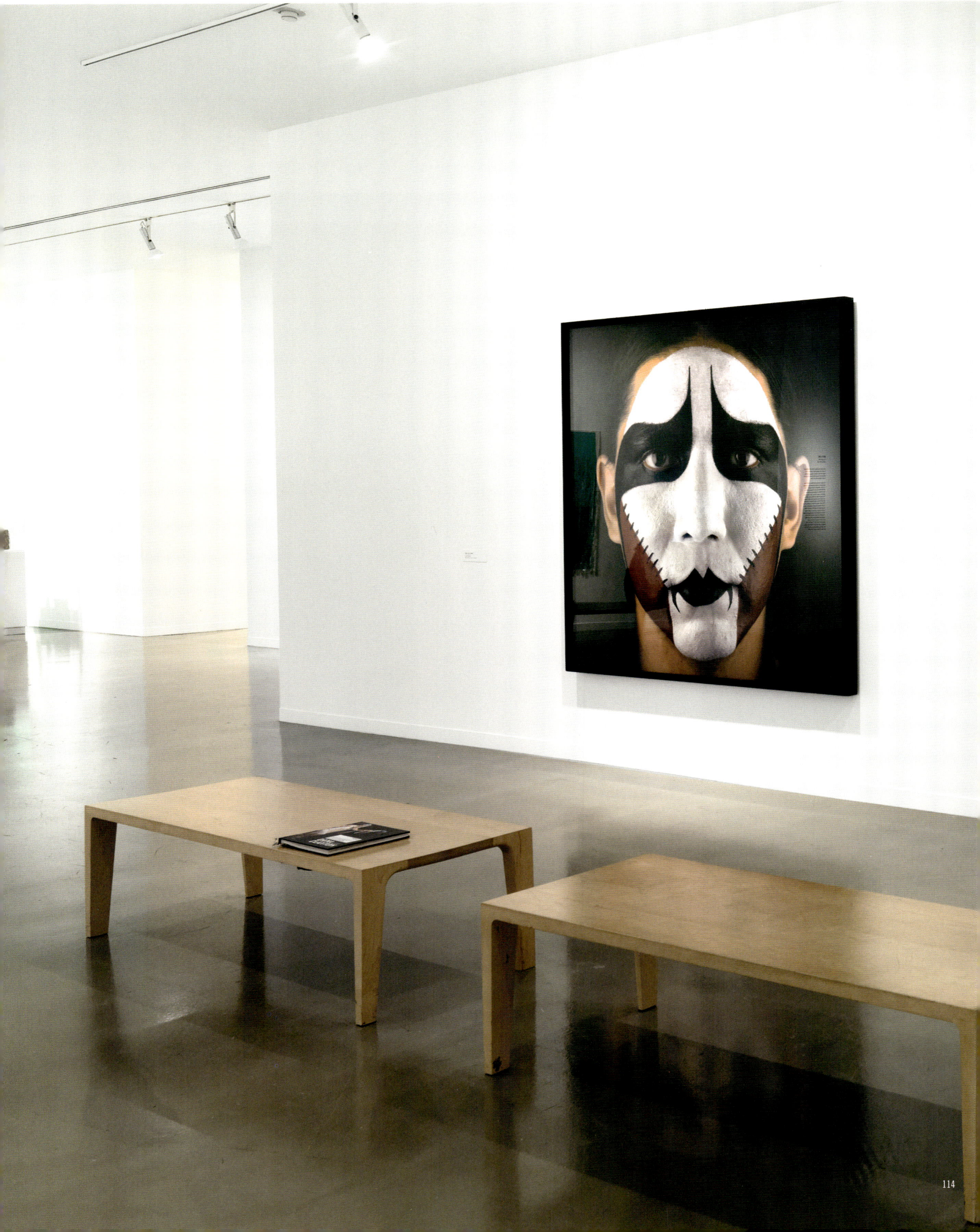

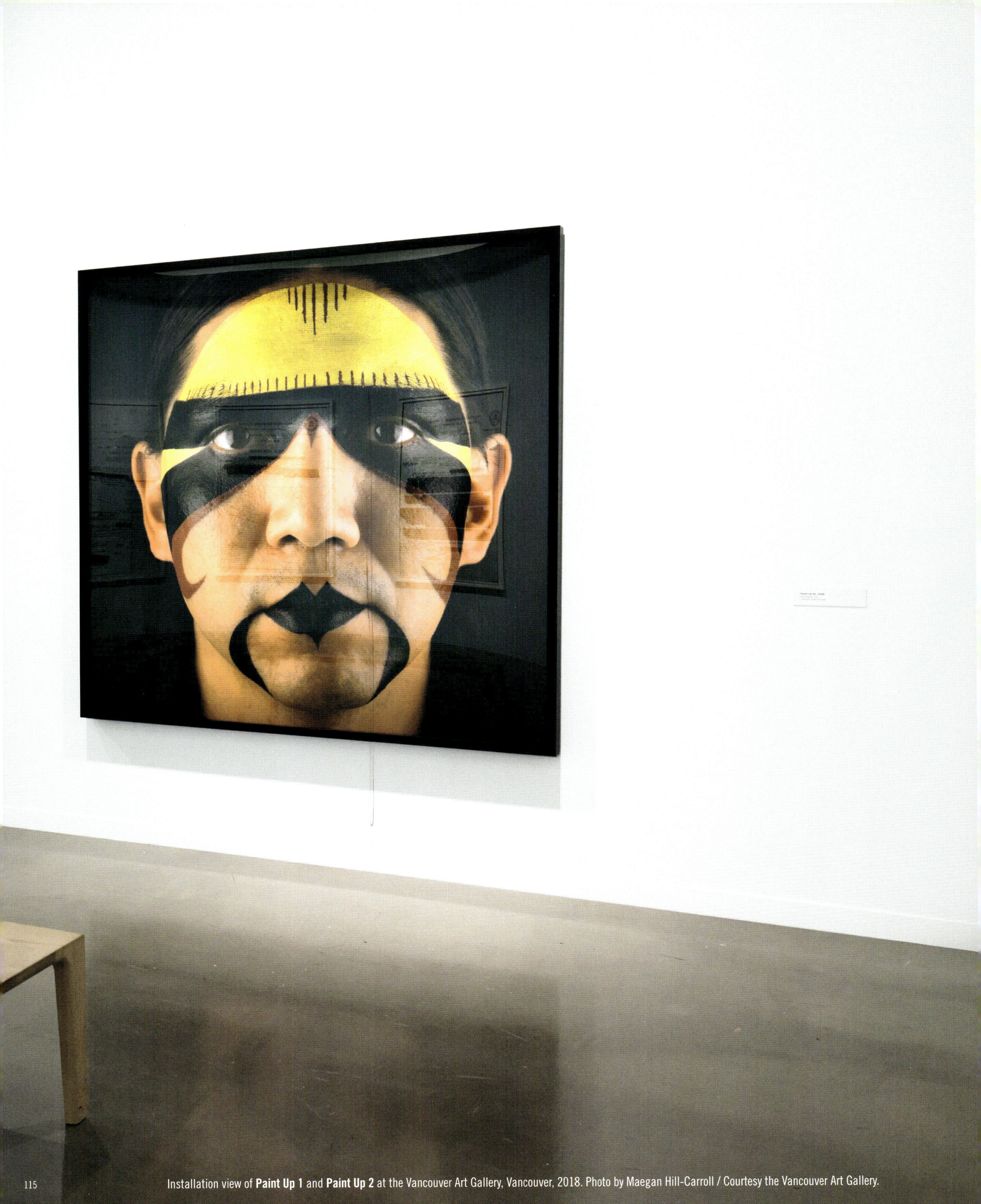

Installation view of **Paint Up 1** and **Paint Up 2** at the Vancouver Art Gallery, Vancouver, 2018. Photo by Maegan Hill-Carroll / Courtesy the Vancouver Art Gallery.

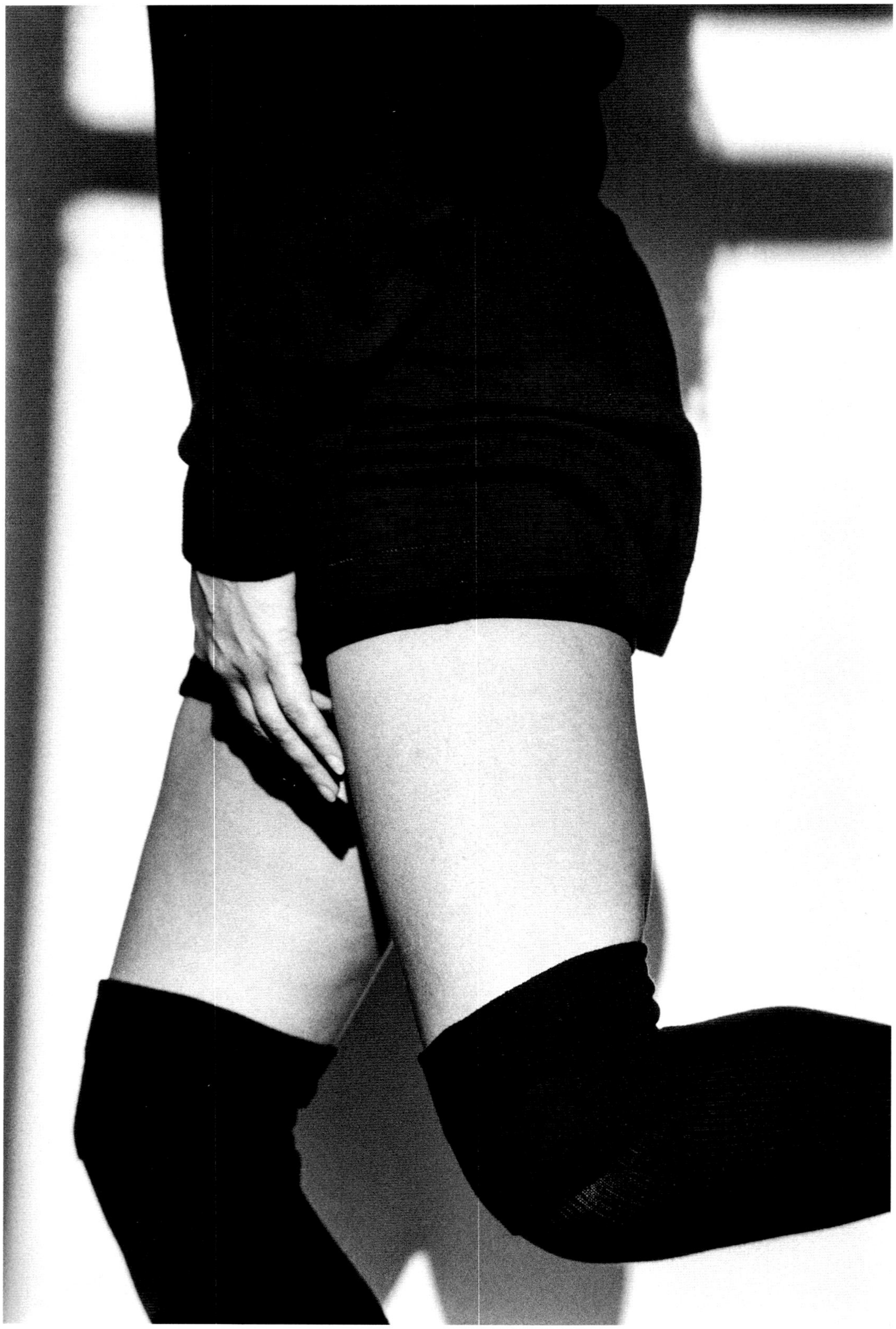
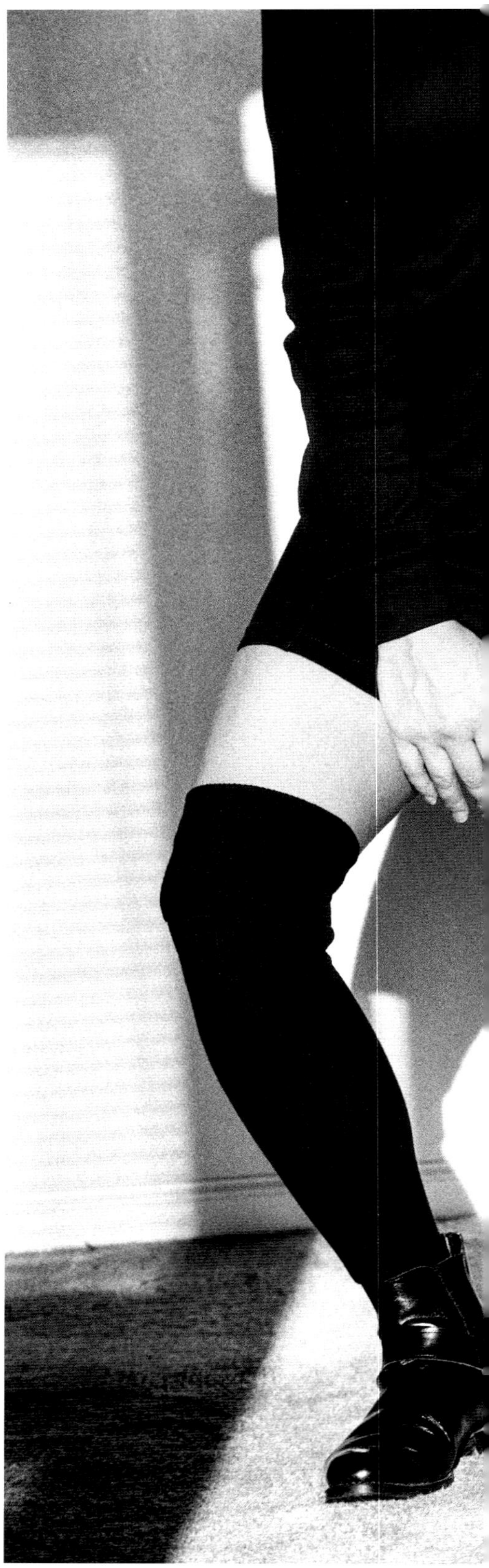

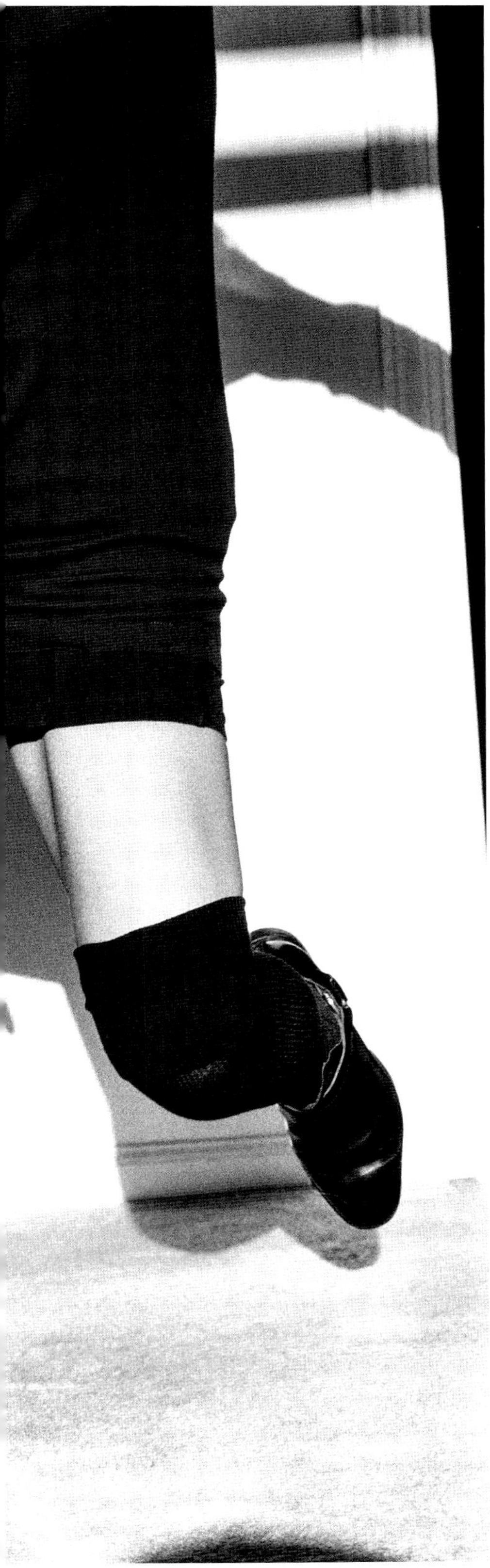

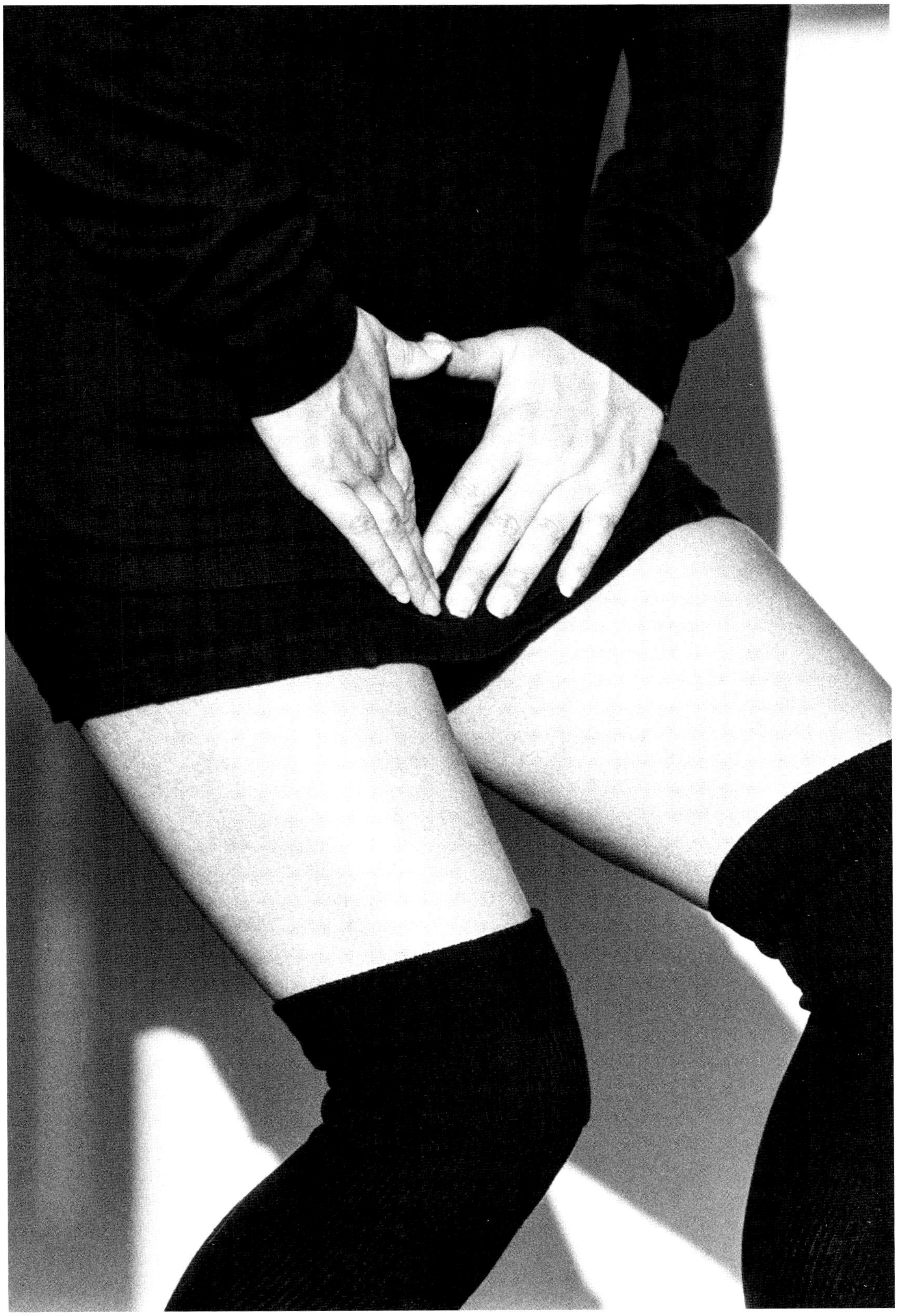

Untitled 1–3, 1992–2018

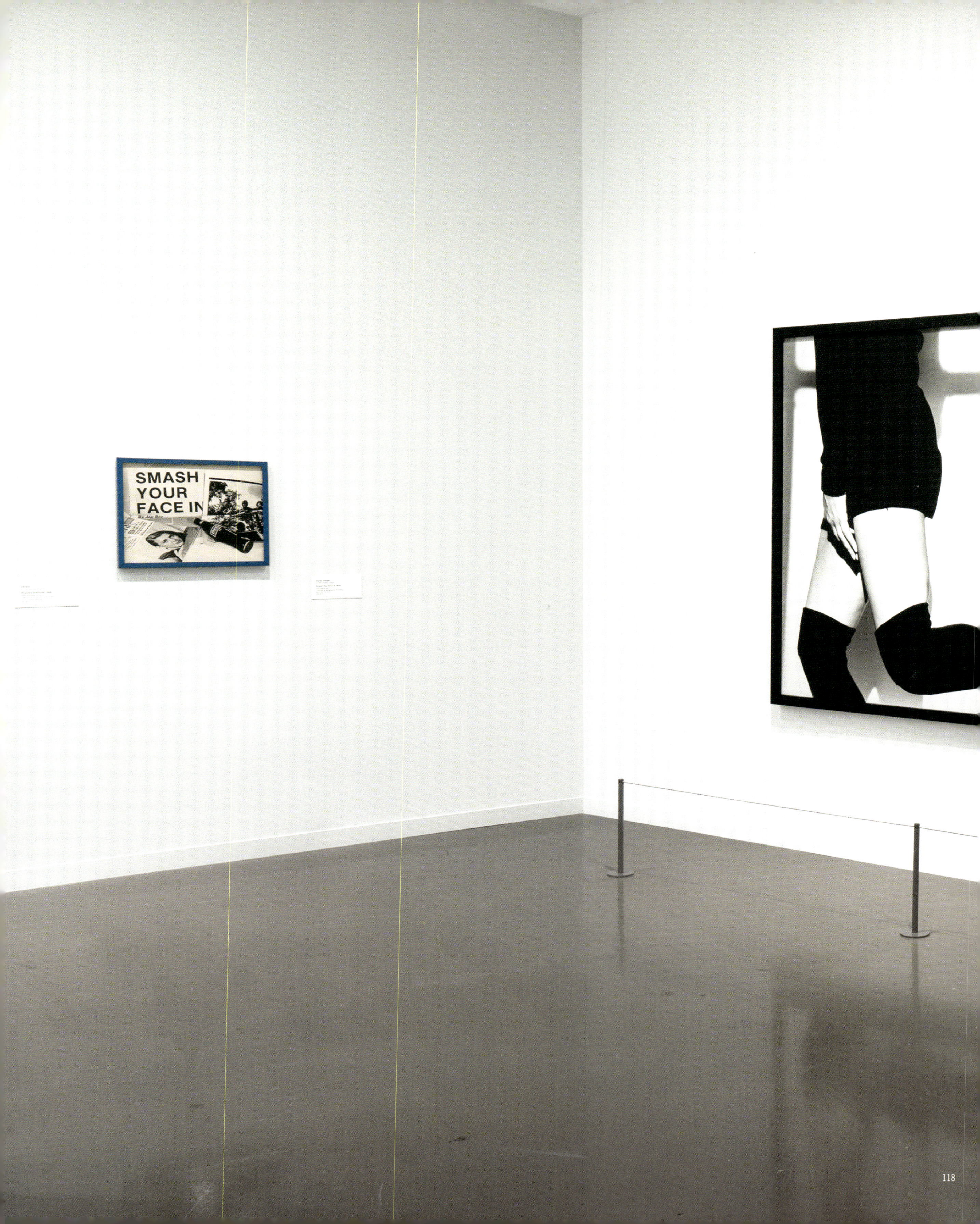
SMASH
YOUR
FACE IN

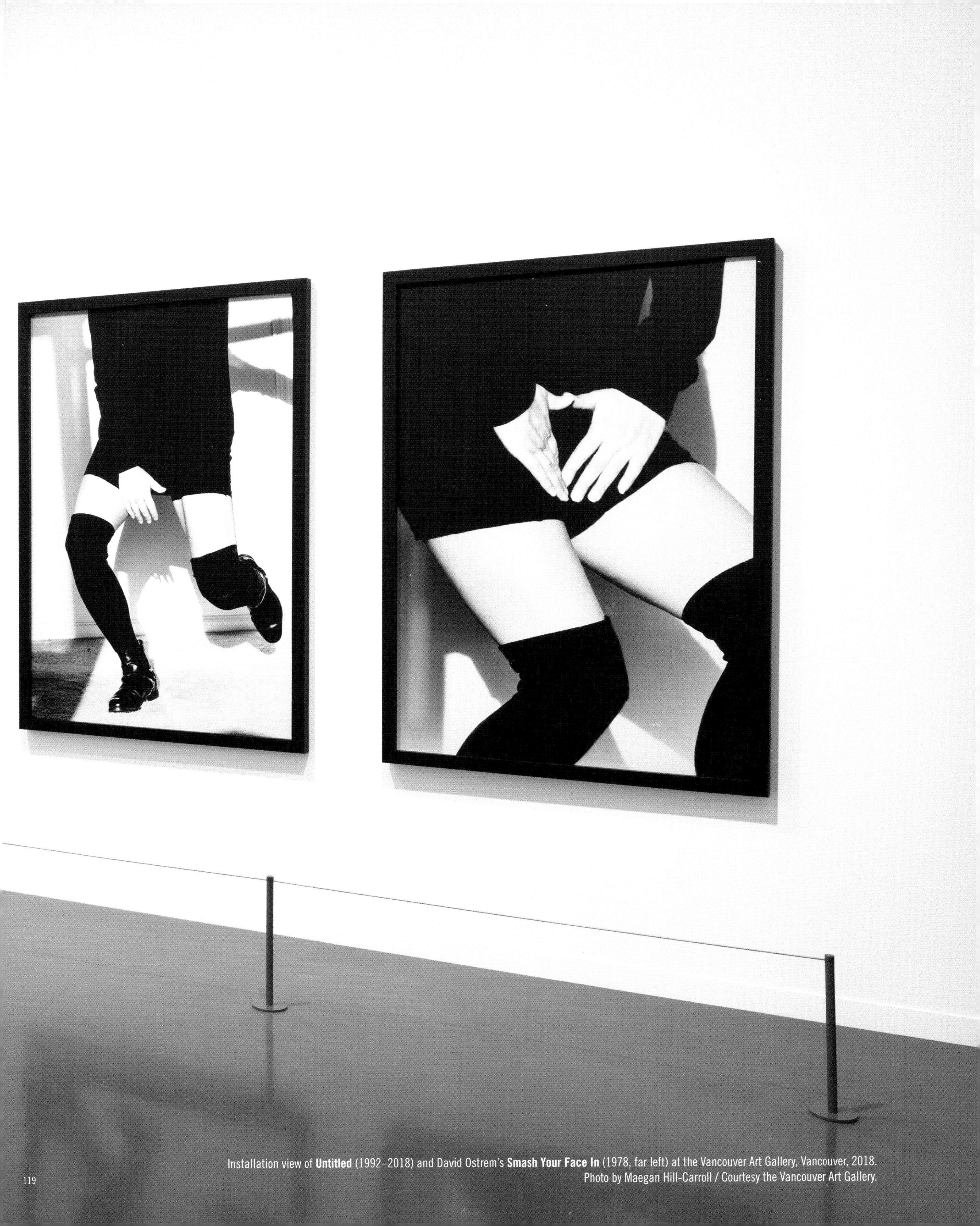

Installation view of **Untitled** (1992–2018) and David Ostrem's **Smash Your Face In** (1978, far left) at the Vancouver Art Gallery, Vancouver, 2018.
Photo by Maegan Hill-Carroll / Courtesy the Vancouver Art Gallery.

CONFIDENTIAL

AMERICAN INDIAN MOVEMENT

[redacted]

This document contains neither recommendations nor conclusions of the FBI. It is the property of the FBI and is loaned to your agency; it and its contents are not to be distributed outside your agency nor duplicated within your agency.

CONFIDENTIAL

- 4 -

UNITED STATES DEPARTMENT OF JUSTICE

FEDERAL BUREAU OF INVESTIGATION

In Reply, Please Refer to File No.

Denver, Colorado 80203
December 7, 1972

CONFIDENTIAL

ALL INFORMATION CONTAINED HEREIN IS UNCLASSIFIED DATE 12-29-83 SP5RJG/

AMERICAN INDIAN MOVEMENT
EXTREMIST MATTERS -
AMERICAN INDIAN AFFAIRS

[redacted] a source, with whom contact has been insufficient to determine reliability, advised [redacted]

MEMBER OF SUBJECT ORGANIZATION

CONFIDENTIAL

DECLASSIFIED BY 5886
ON 8/15/77

Classified by [redacted]
Exempt from General Declassification
Schedule of Executive Order 11652
Exemption Category Number 2
Automatically Declassified On Indefinite

100-462483-89

ENCLOSURE

UNITED STATES DEPARTMENT OF JUSTICE

FEDERAL BUREAU OF INVESTIGATION

In Reply, Please Refer to File No.

San Francisco, California

July 19, 1973

AMERICAN INDIAN MOVEMENT

[redacted] unidentified American Indian Movement (AIM) members were among approximately two hundred persons who attended a social gathering in San Francisco June 16, 1973. [redacted] No specific information regarding the type of action or the dates was discussed.

American Indian Movement is self-described as the shock troops of Indian sovereignty that intends to raise questions in the minds of Indians and non-Indians alike regarding Indian sovereignty, land and culture.

ALL INFORMATION CONTAINED HEREIN IS UNCLASSIFIED DATE 1-20-84 BY SP5RJG/gab

- 1* -

This document contains neither recommendations nor conclusions of the FBI. It is the property of the FBI and is loaned to your agency; it and its contents are not to be distributed outside your agency.

ENCLOSURE

100-462483- 859

FBI

Date: 12/8/72

Transmit the following in (Type in plaintext or code)

AIRTEL AIRMAIL (Priority)

TO: ACTING DIRECTOR, FBI ATTN: DID

FROM: SAC, LOS ANGELES (157-8224) (P)

SUBJECT: AMERICAN INDIAN MOVEMENT (AIM)
EM - AMERICAN INDIAN AFFAIRS

Re Los Angeles teletype to Bureau dated 12/1/72, captioned, "AMERICAN INDIAN MOVEMENT, IS - INDIAN MATTERS."

On 12/8/72, [redacted] Bureau of Indian Affairs (BIA), Los Angeles, California, provided the names of the following AIM national leaders and their residences:

RUSSELL MEANS
Cleveland, Ohio

VERNON BELLECOURT
Denver, Colorado

CLYDE BELLECOURT
Minneapolis, Minnesota

DENNIS BANKS
Minneapolis, Minnesota

CALIF

ALL INFORMATION CONTAINED HEREIN IS UNCLASSIFIED DATE 12-29-83 BY SP5RJG/PMC

On 12/8/72, [redacted] Los Angeles County Sheriff's Office, Intelligence Division, Los Angeles, California requested descriptive and background data concerning above individuals in order that they may be promptly identified in future visits to Los Angeles.

3 - Bureau (AM) (RM)
2 - Cleveland (AM) (RM)
2 - Denver (AM) (RM)
2 - Minneapolis (AM) (RM)
2 - Los Angeles

[redacted] dmg
(11)

REC-70

EX-101

100-462483-8

DEC 13 1972

[redacted]

DEC 21 1972

Approved: Special Agent in Charge Sent M Per

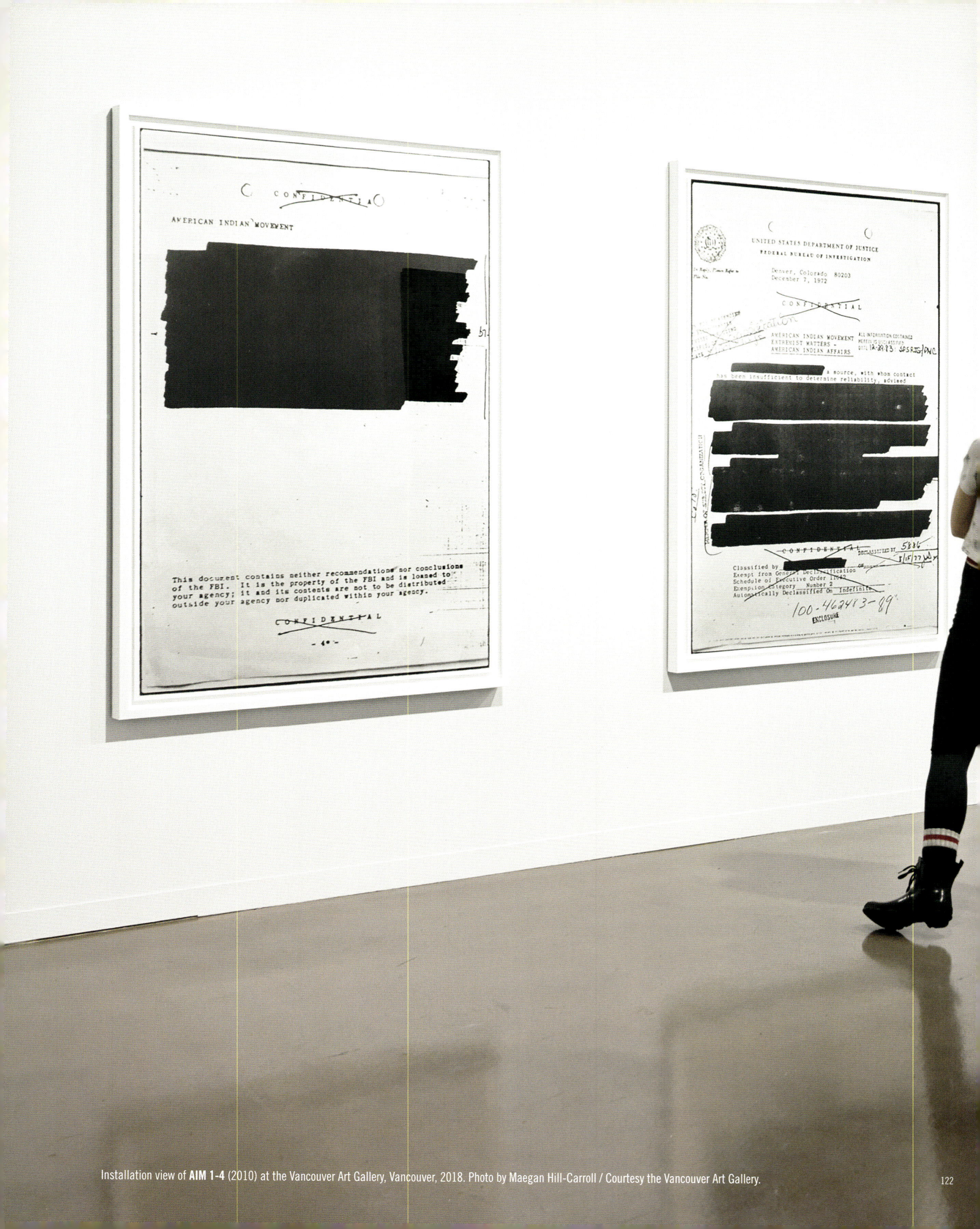

Installation view of **AIM 1-4** (2010) at the Vancouver Art Gallery, Vancouver, 2018. Photo by Maegan Hill-Carroll / Courtesy the Vancouver Art Gallery.

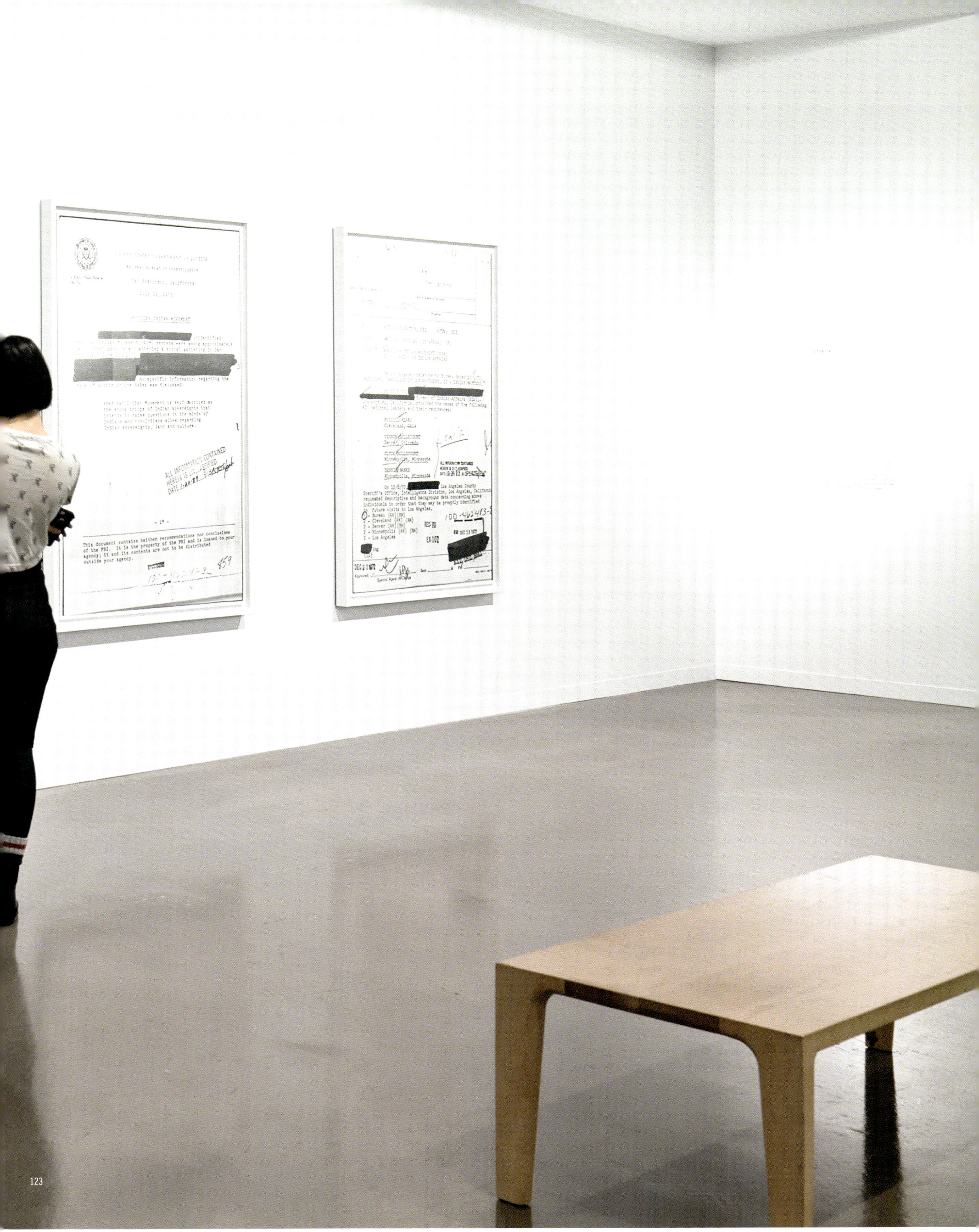
ALL INFORMATION CONTAINED
HEREIN IS UNCLASSIFIED
This document contains neither recommendations nor conclusions of the FBI. It is the property of the FBI and is loaned to your agency; it and its contents are not to be distributed outside your agency.

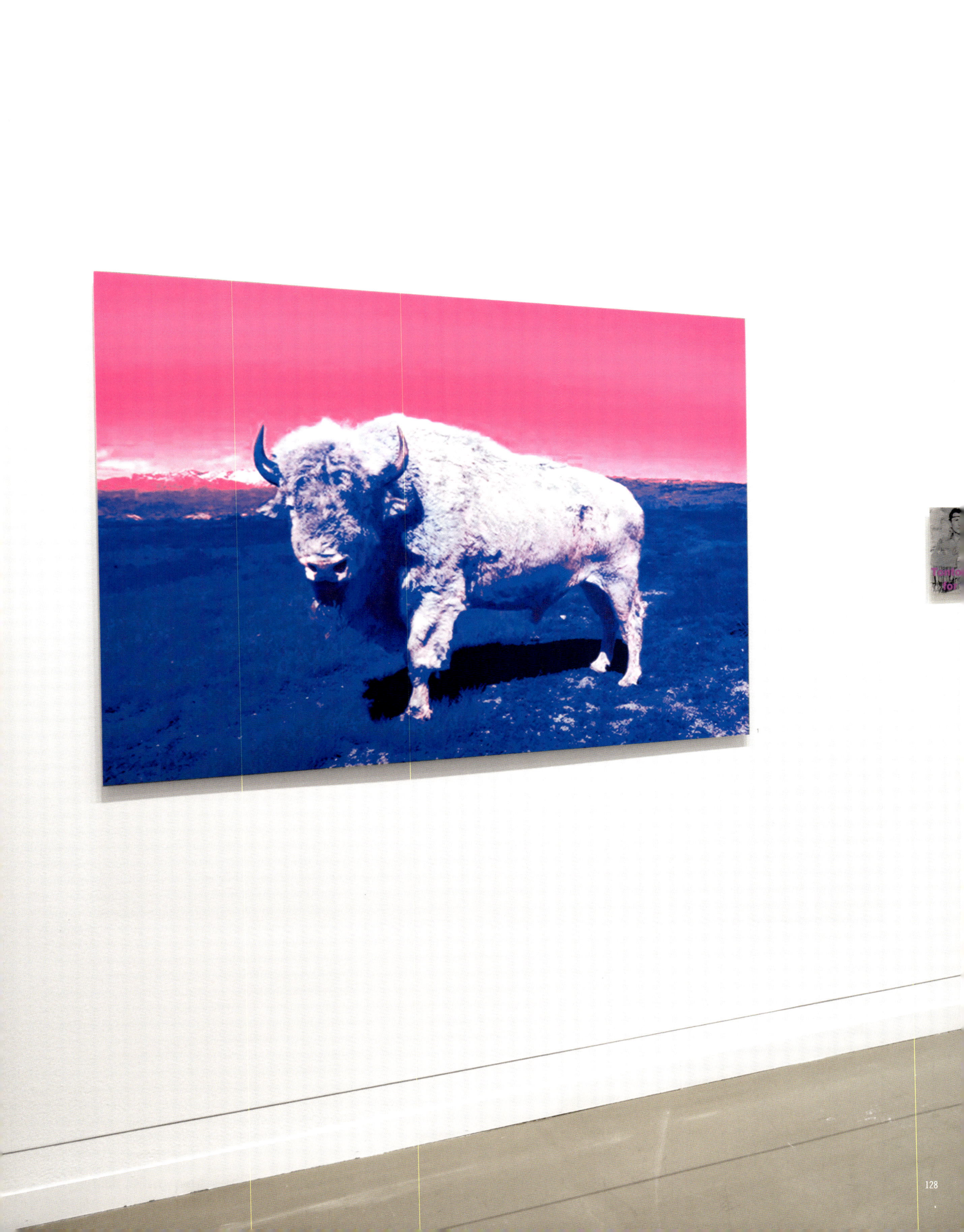

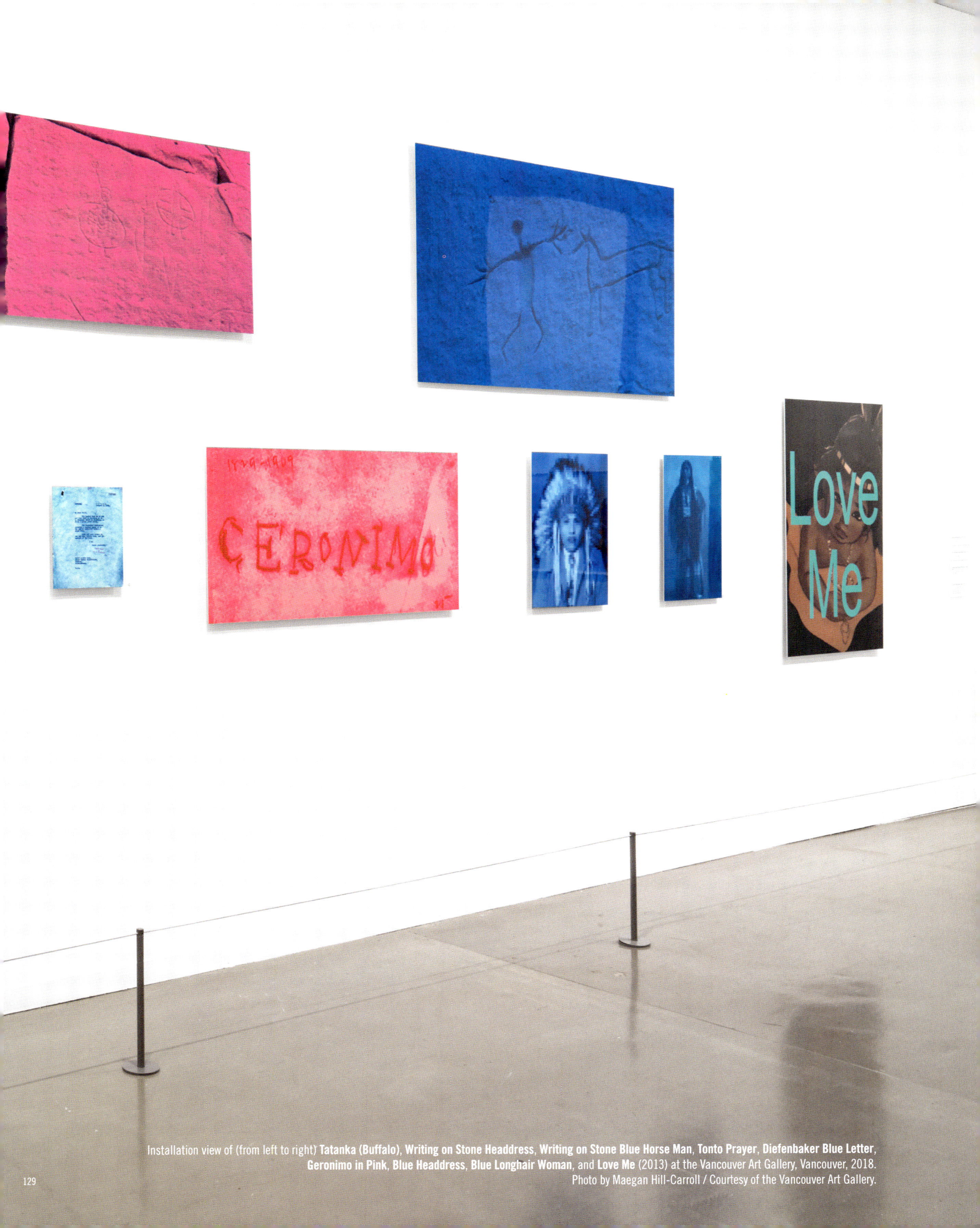

Installation view of (from left to right) **Tatanka (Buffalo)**, **Writing on Stone Headdress**, **Writing on Stone Blue Horse Man**, **Tonto Prayer**, **Diefenbaker Blue Letter**, **Geronimo in Pink**, **Blue Headdress**, **Blue Longhair Woman**, and **Love Me** (2013) at the Vancouver Art Gallery, Vancouver, 2018.
Photo by Maegan Hill-Carroll / Courtesy of the Vancouver Art Gallery.

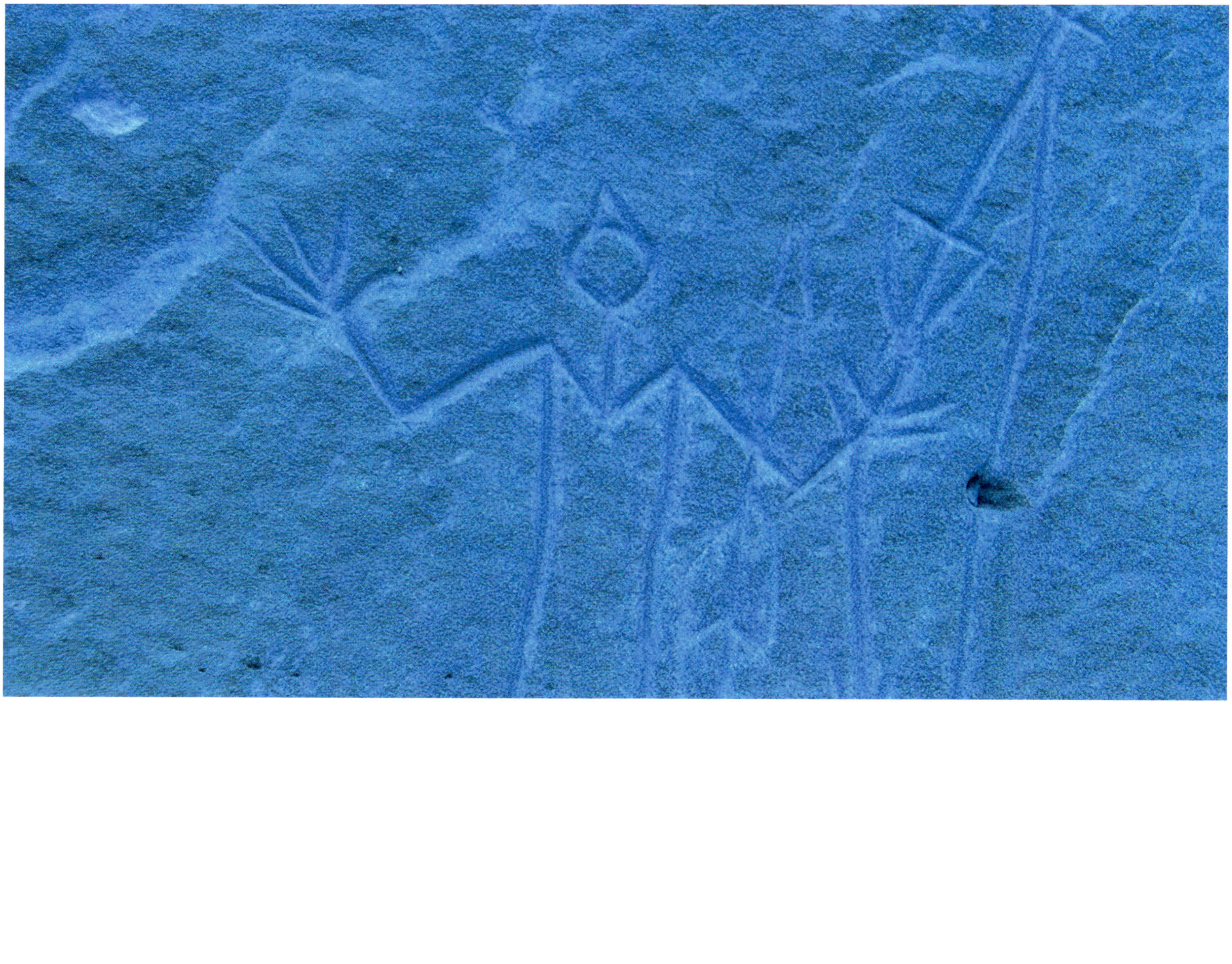

Indian Candy: Writing on Stone (Blue Hands), 2013

Indian Candy: Writing on Stone (Headdress), 2013

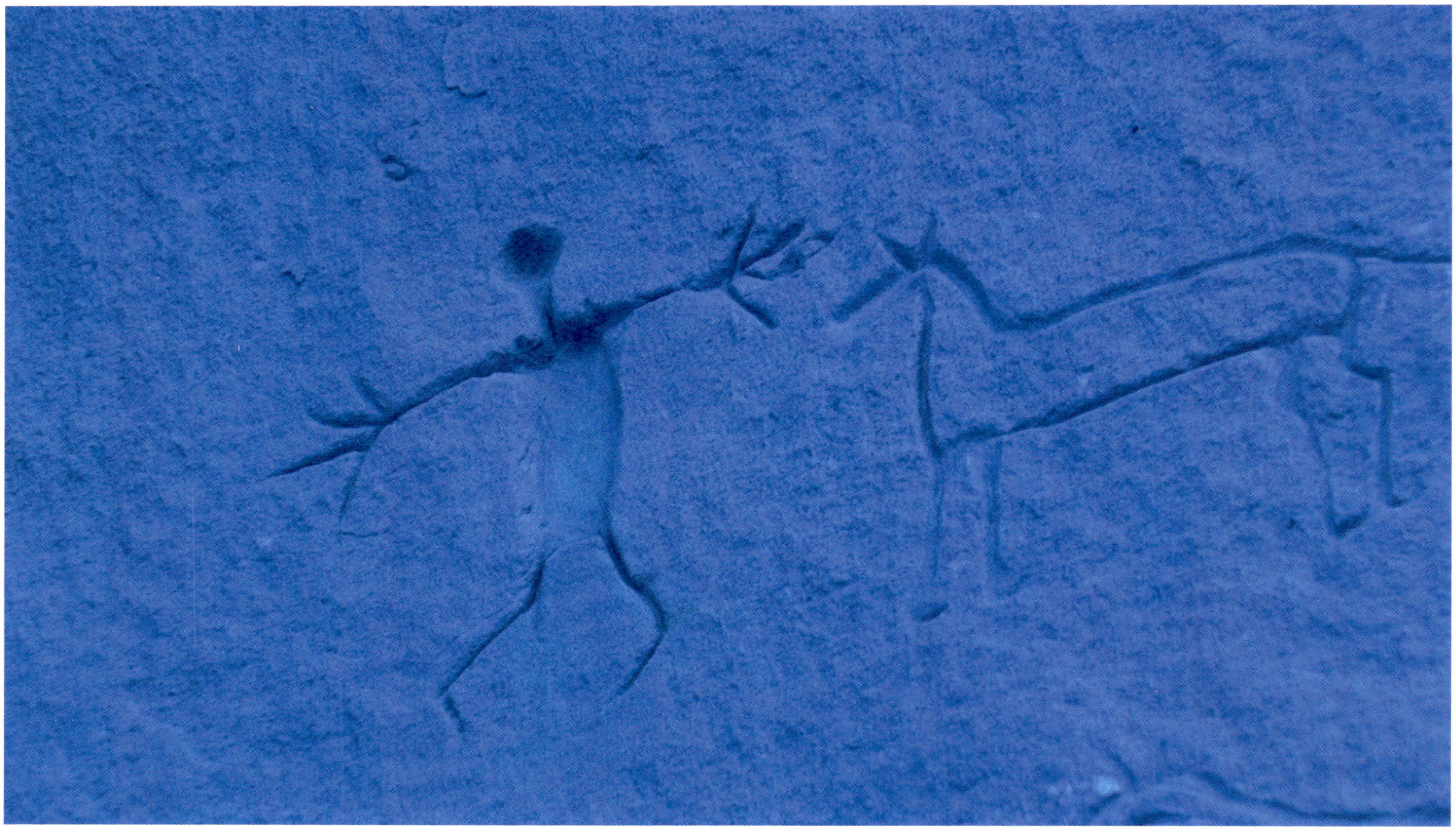

Indian Candy: Writing on Stone (Blue Horse Man), 2013

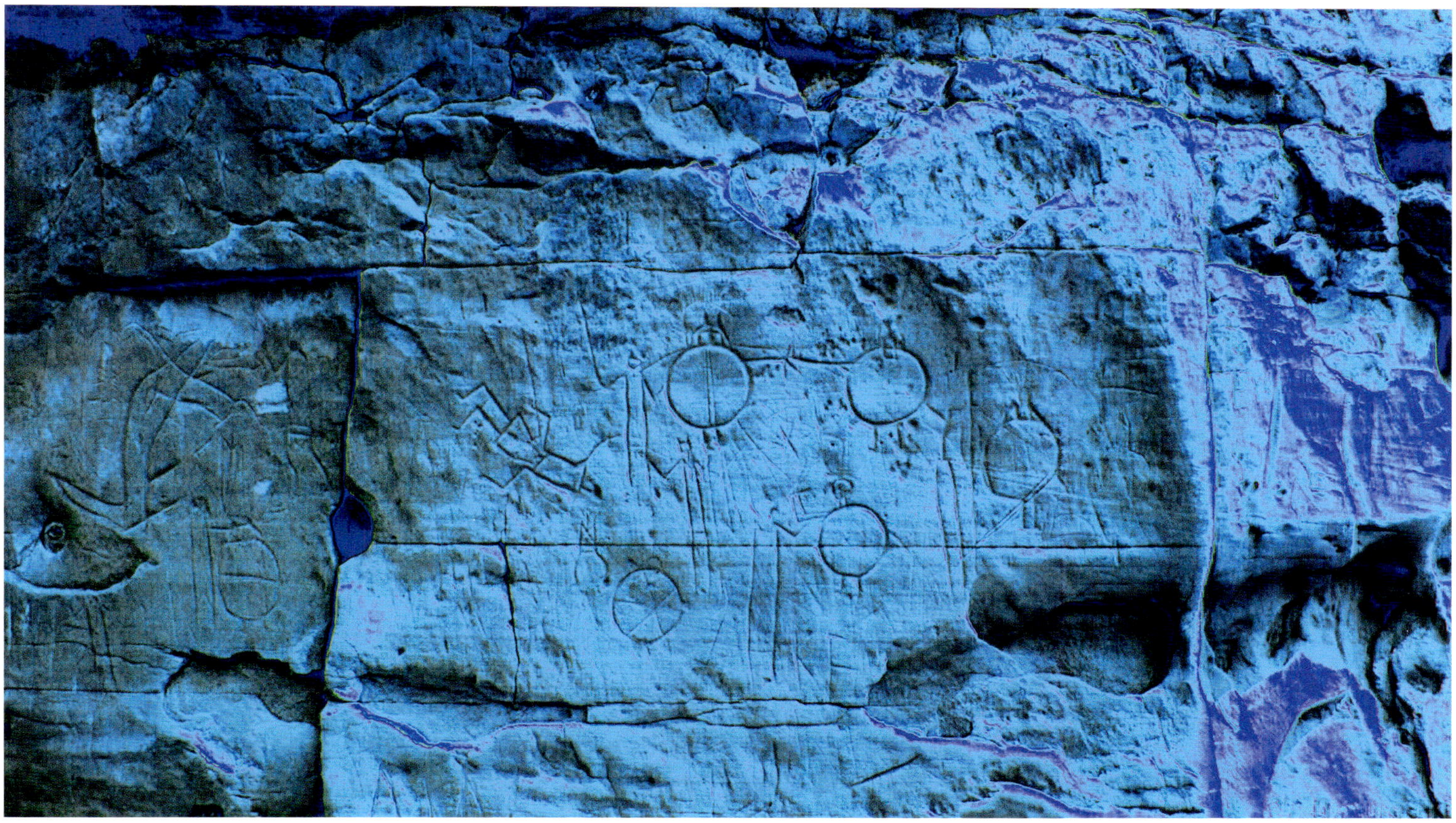

Indian Candy: Writing on Stone (Aqua Blue Wall), 2013

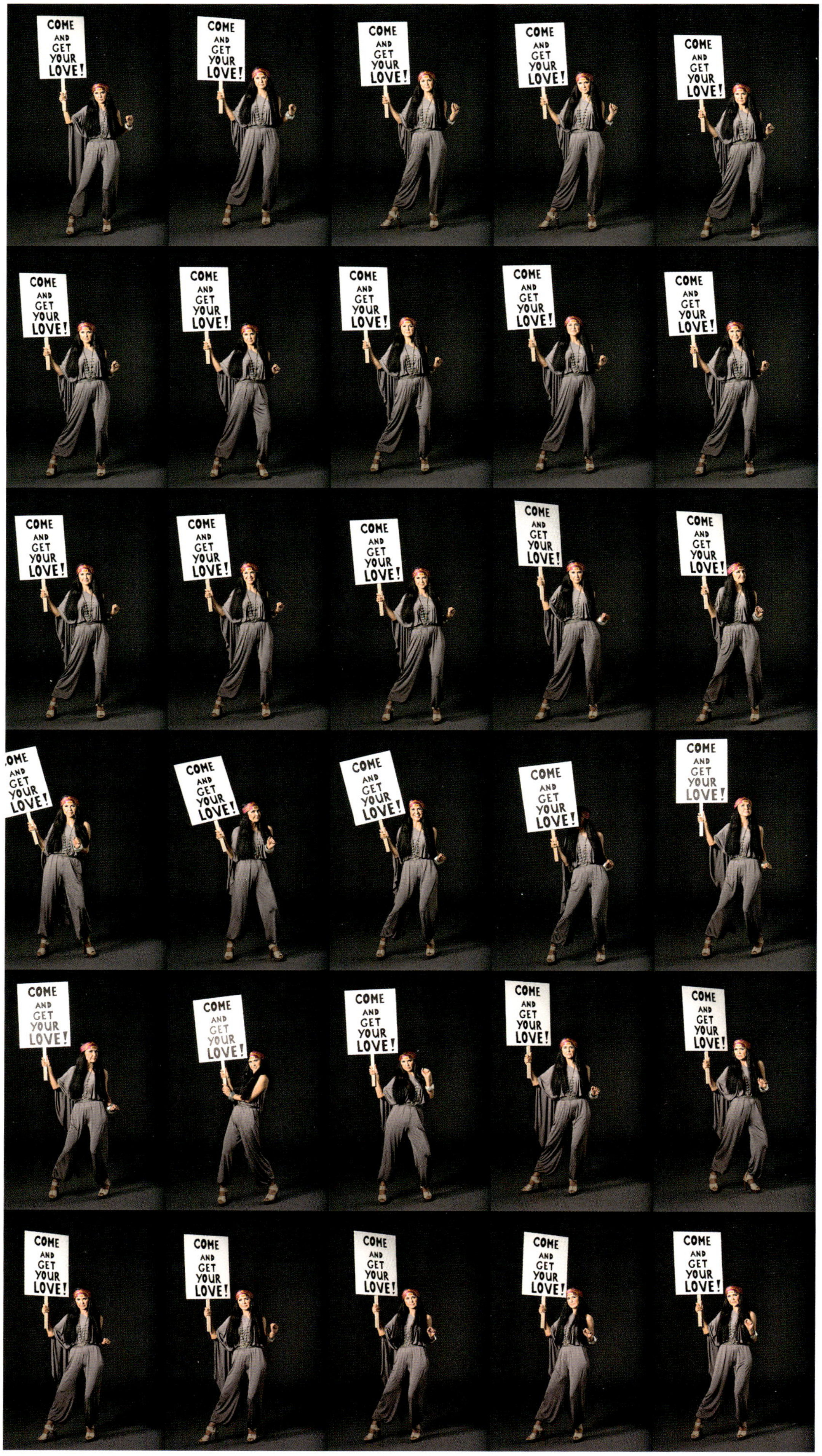

The Protector (Grid), 2020

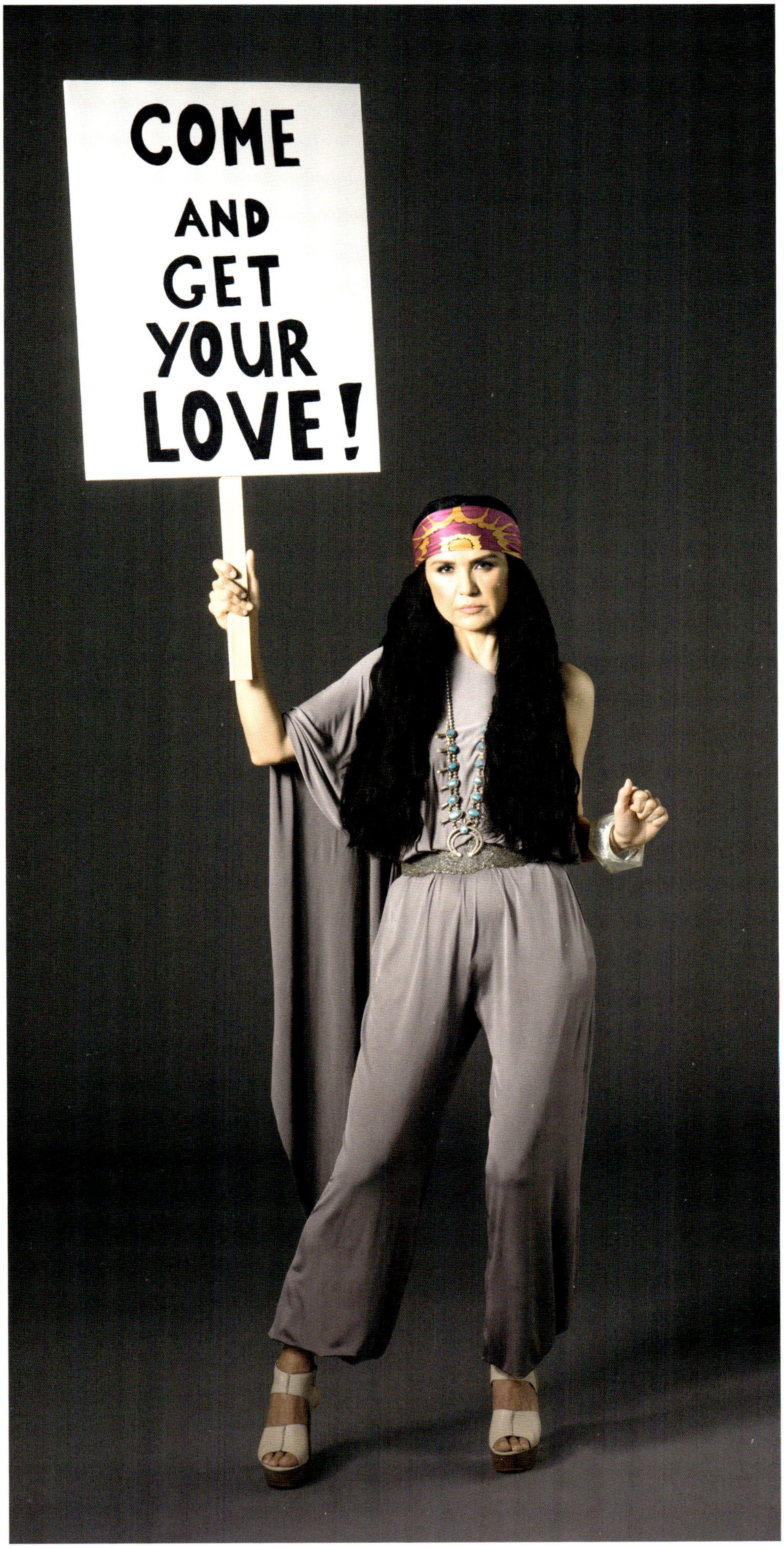

The Protector, 2017

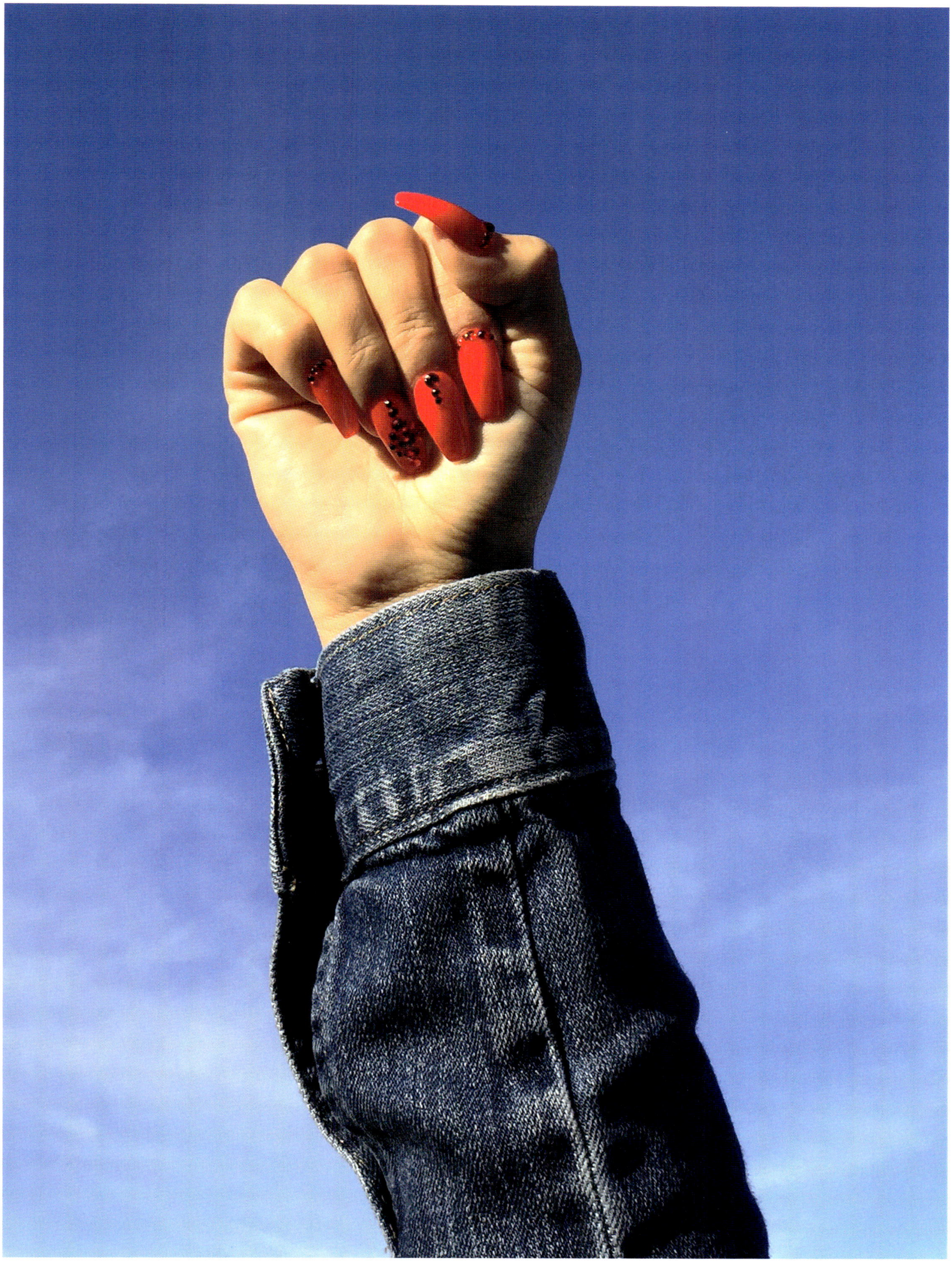

Defiance 1 (rezthetics for Skeena), 2021

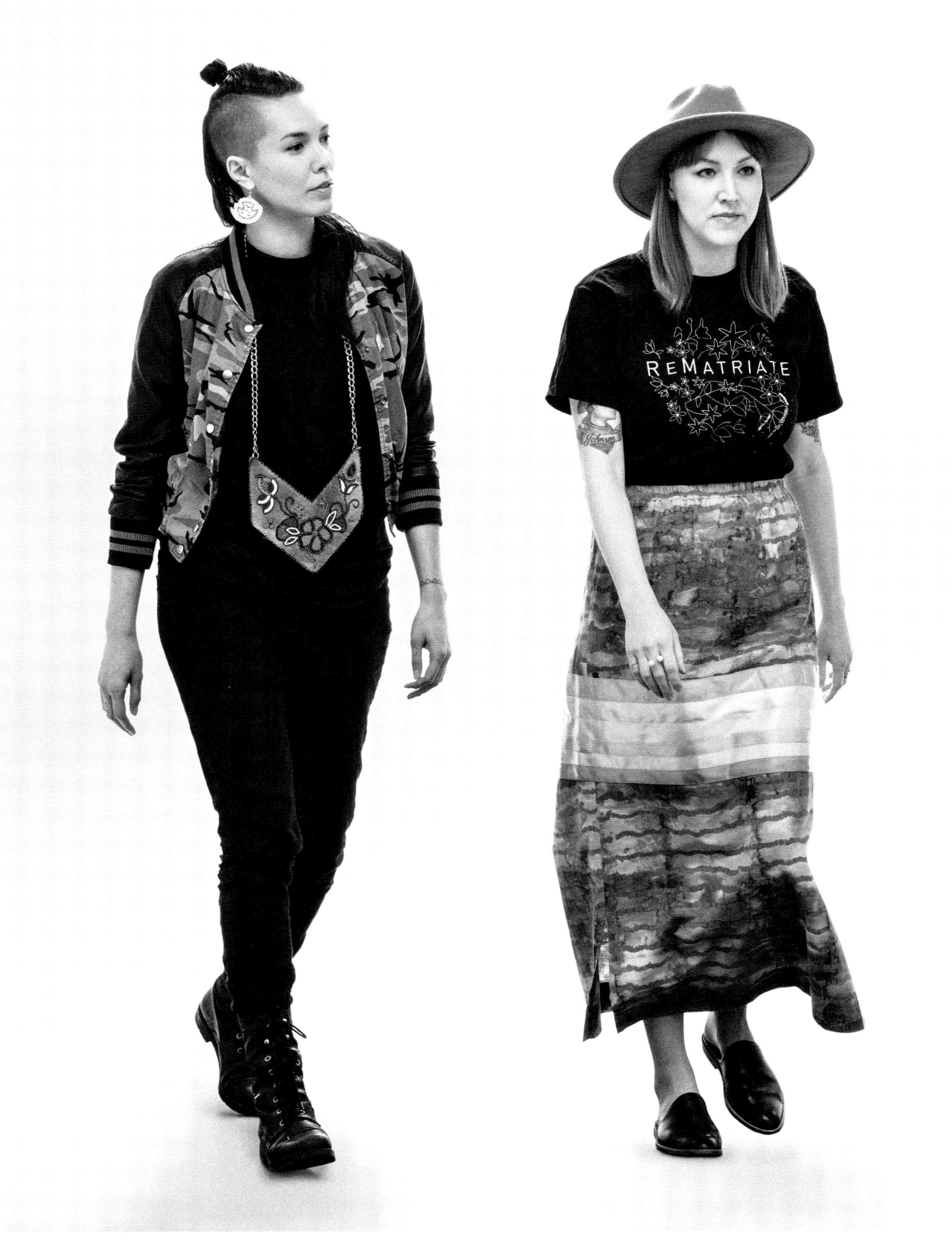

Study for a Protest 1, 2018

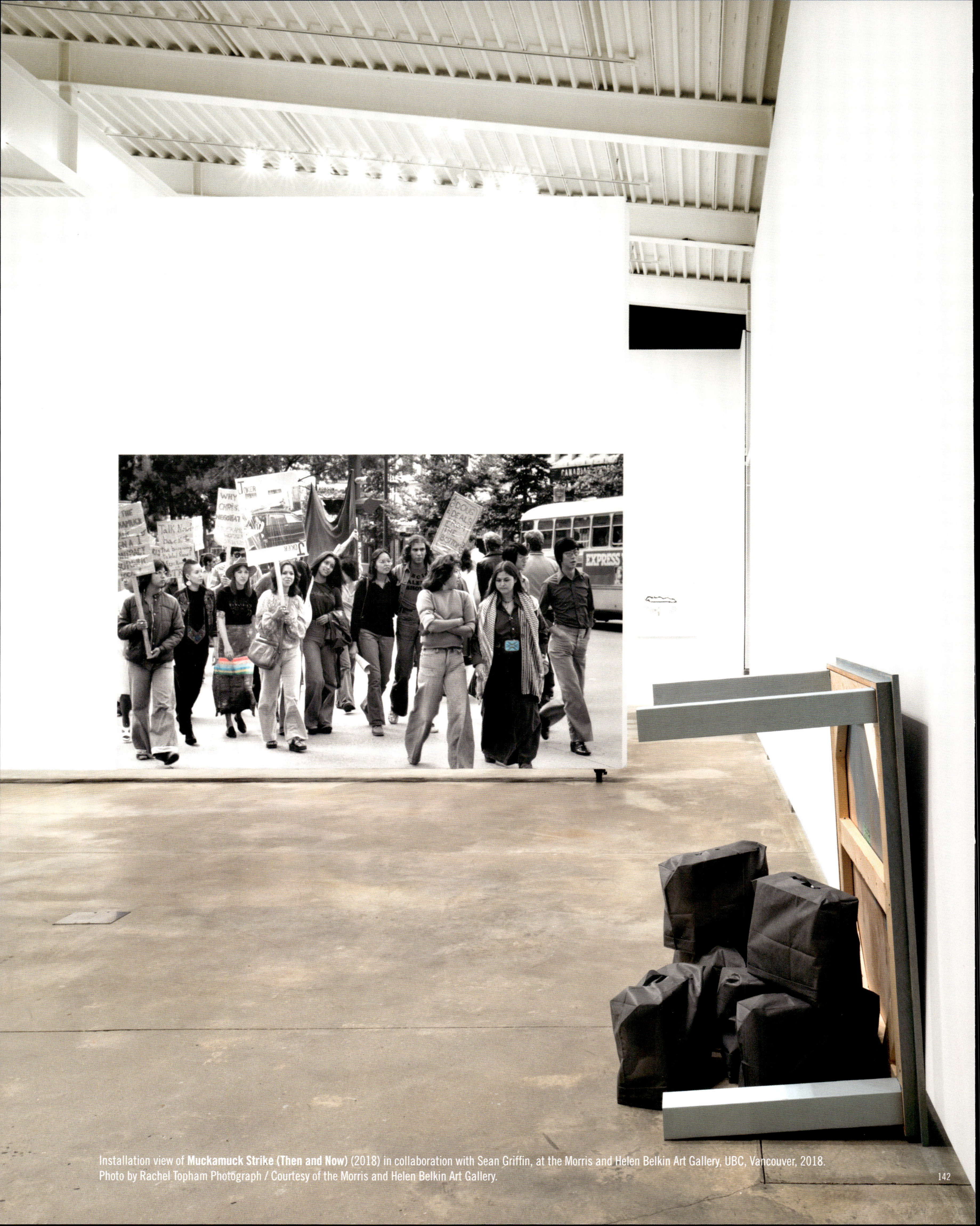

Installation view of **Muckamuck Strike (Then and Now)** (2018) in collaboration with Sean Griffin, at the Morris and Helen Belkin Art Gallery, UBC, Vancouver, 2018.
Photo by Rachel Topham Photograph / Courtesy of the Morris and Helen Belkin Art Gallery.

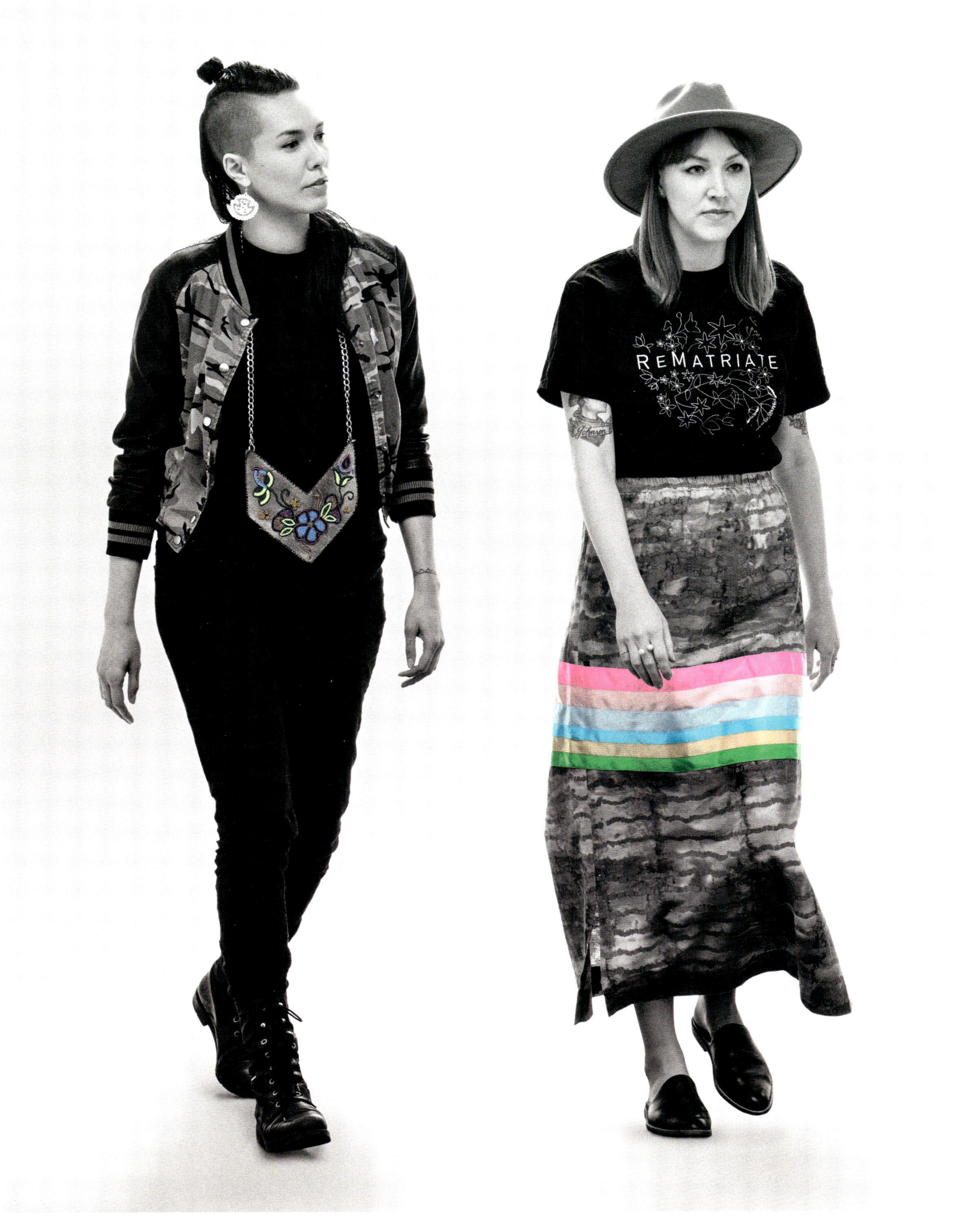

Study for a Protest 2, 2018

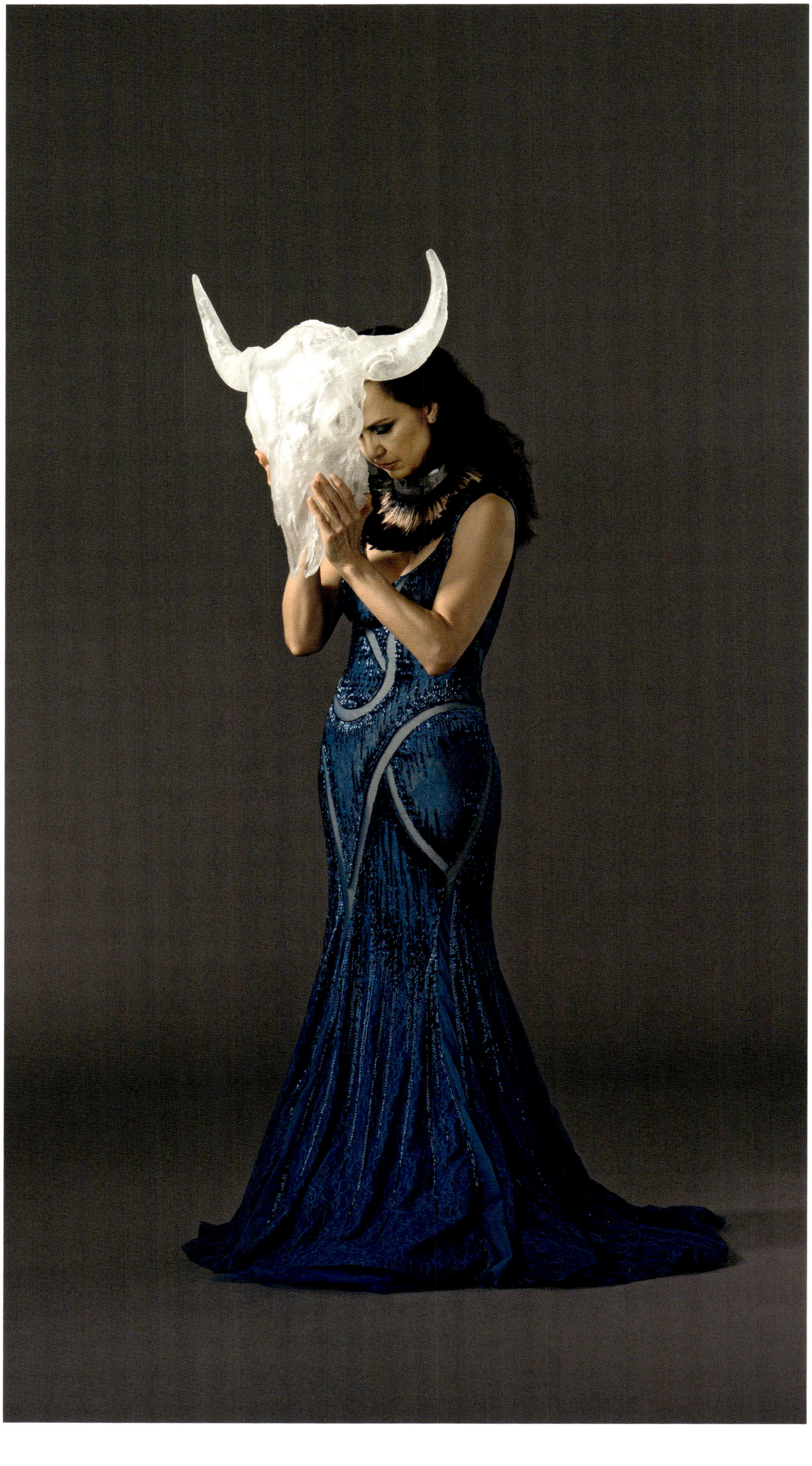

Buffalo Woman 1 (crystal skull resin by Kevin McKenzie), 2016

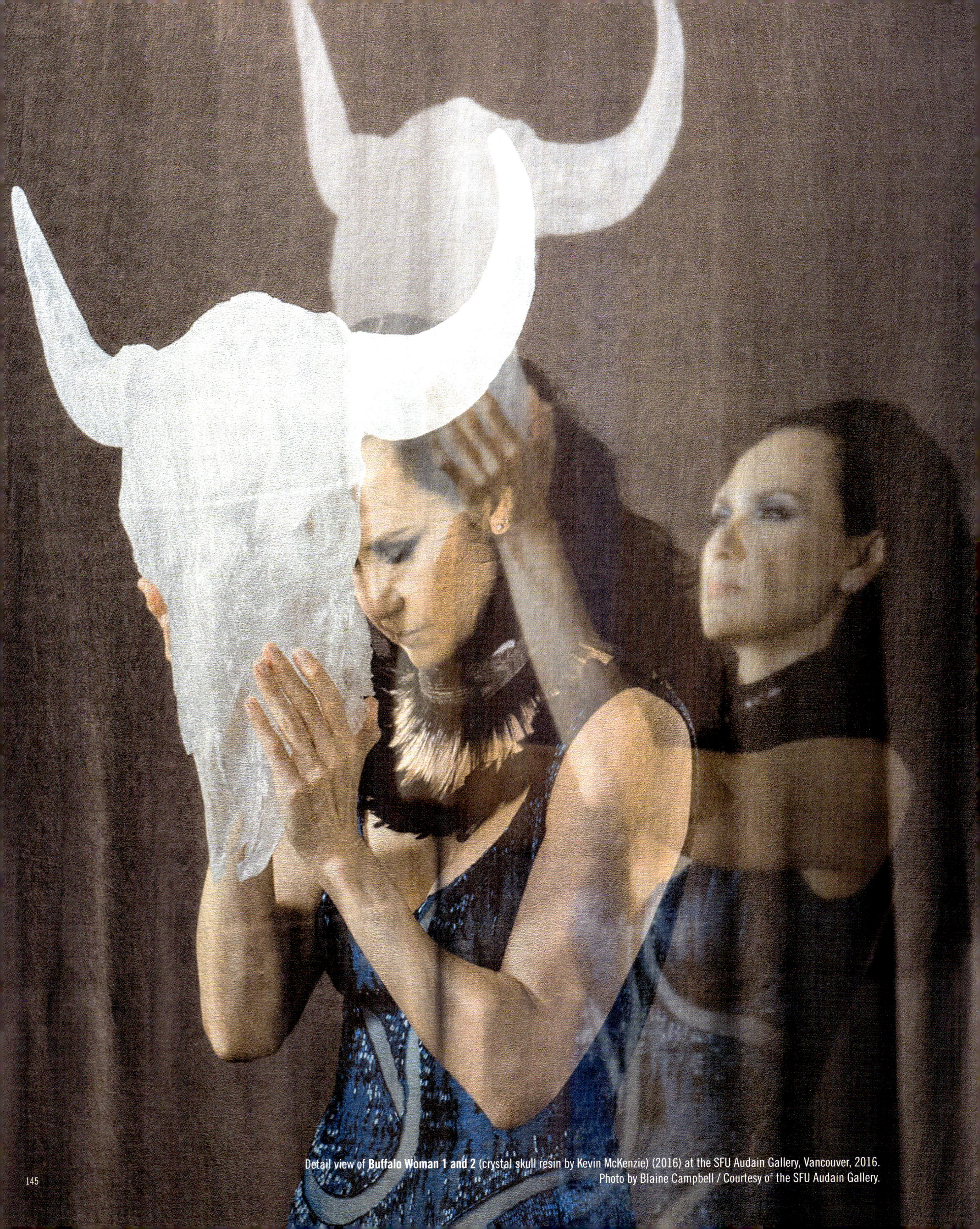

Detail view of **Buffalo Woman 1 and 2** (crystal skull resin by Kevin McKenzie) (2016) at the SFU Audain Gallery, Vancouver, 2016.
Photo by Blaine Campbell / Courtesy of the SFU Audain Gallery.

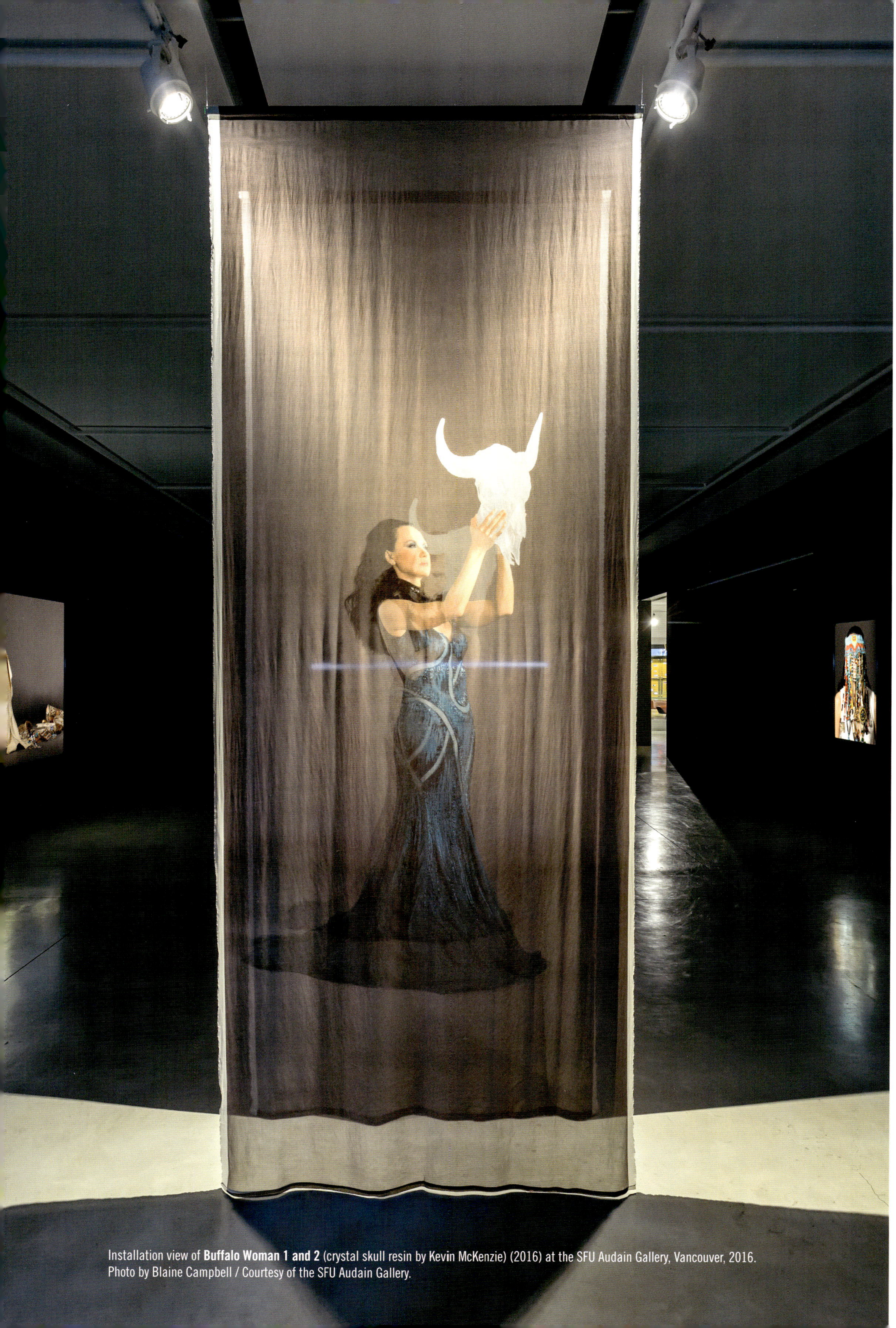

Installation view of **Buffalo Woman 1 and 2** (crystal skull resin by Kevin McKenzie) (2016) at the SFU Audain Gallery, Vancouver, 2016. Photo by Blaine Campbell / Courtesy of the SFU Audain Gallery.

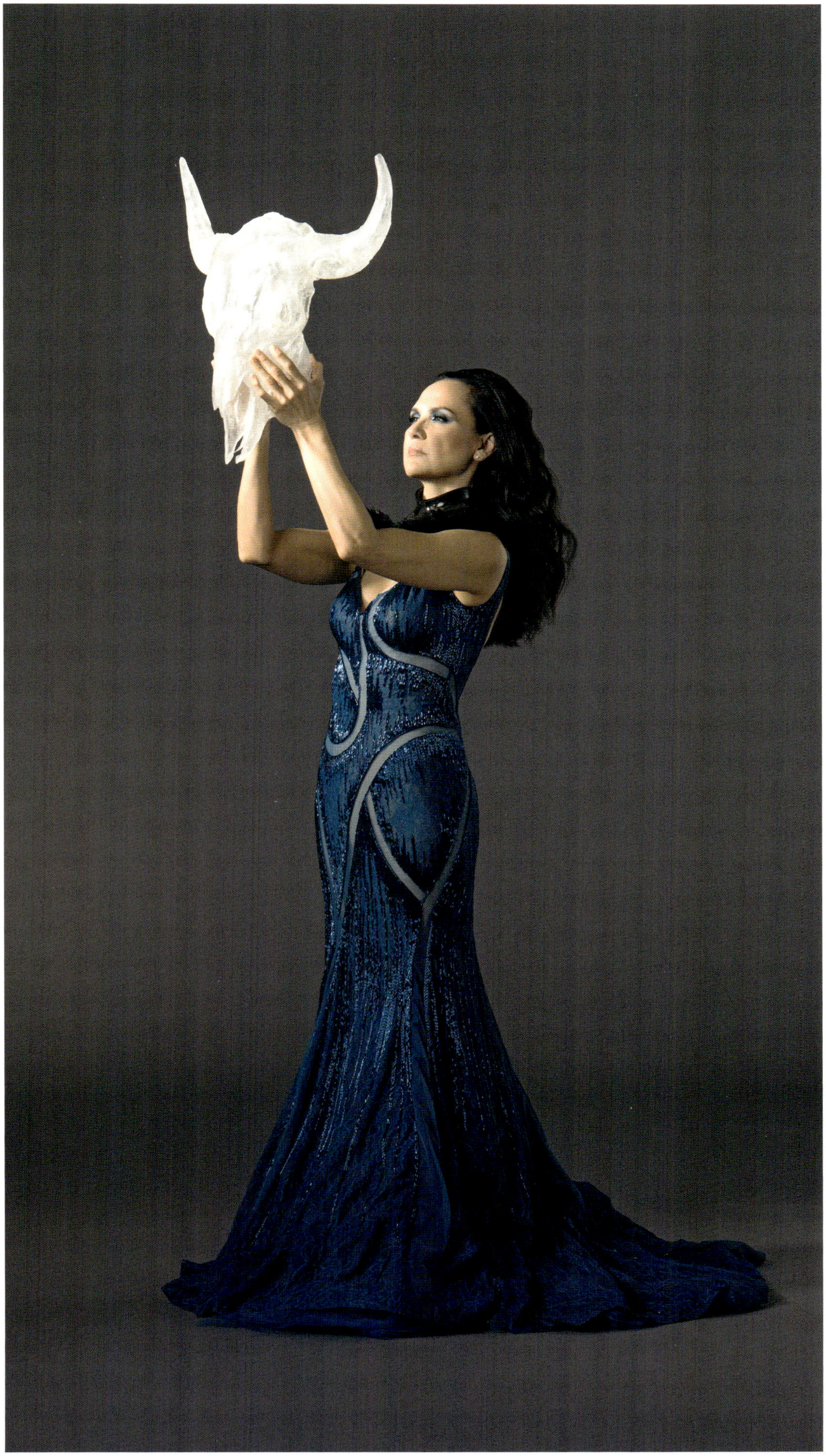

Buffalo Woman 2 (crystal skull resin by Kevin McKenzie), 2016

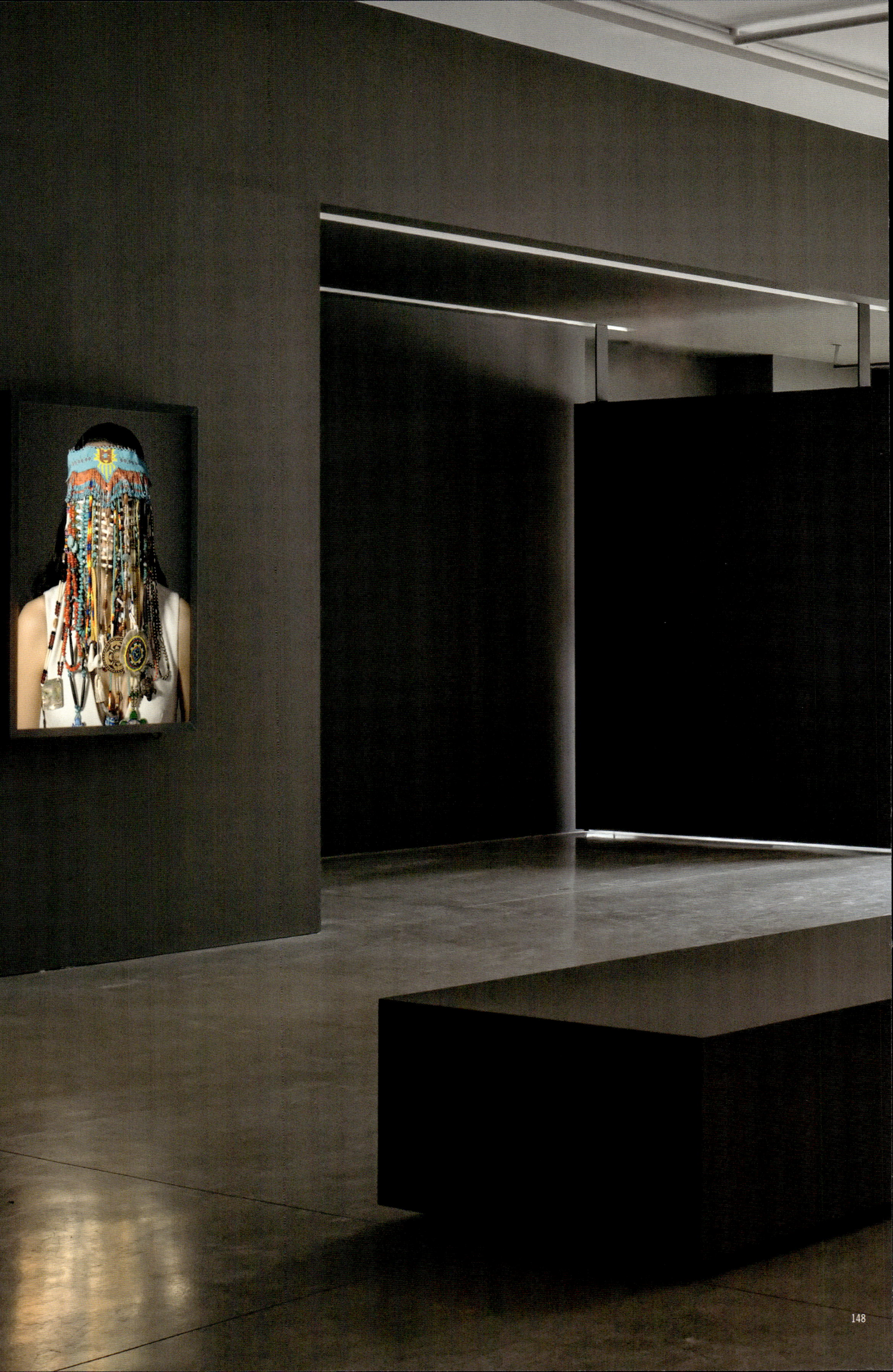

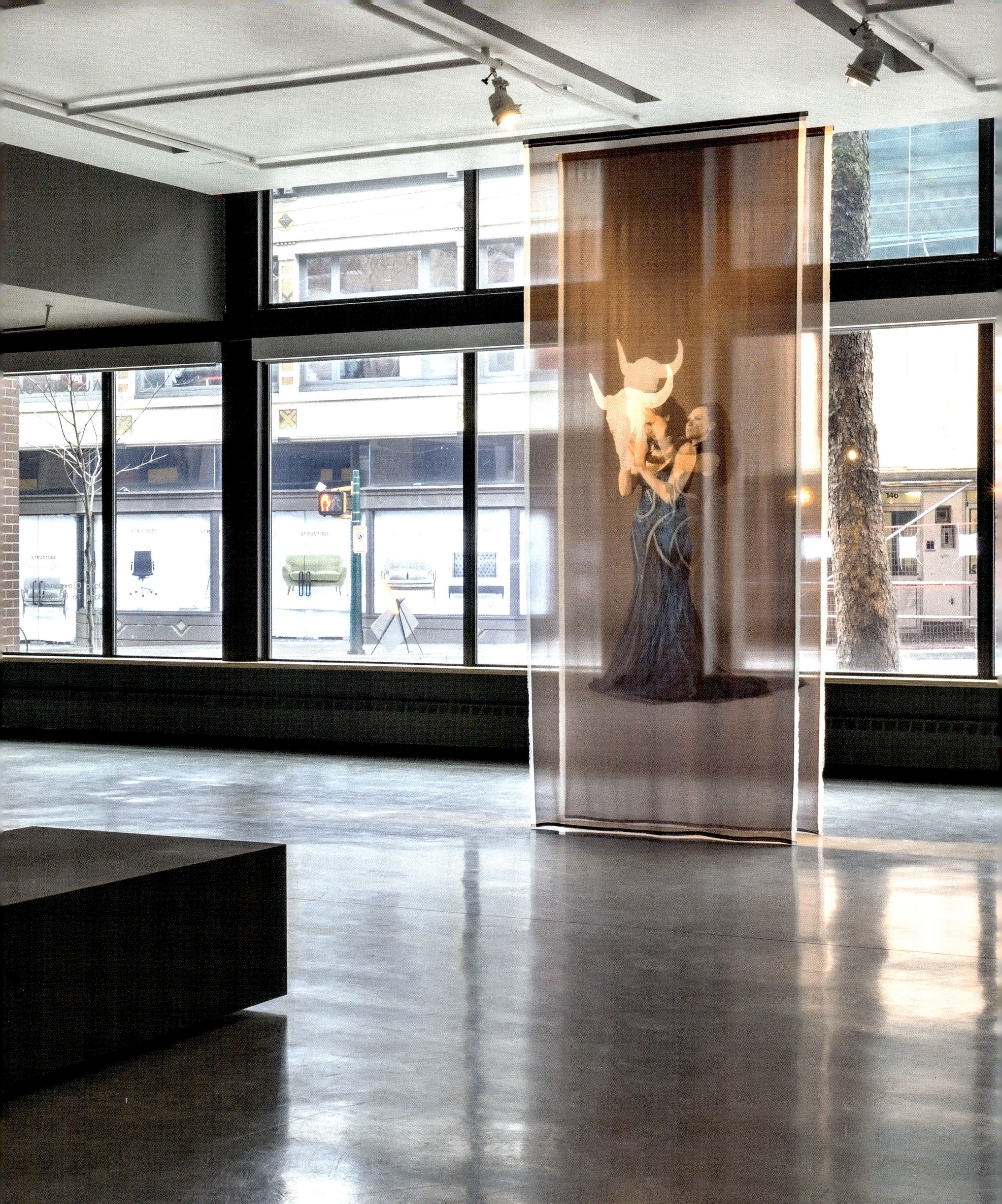

Installation view of **Headdress** and **Buffal**[illegible] **and 2** (2016) at the SFU Audain Gallery, Vancouver, 2016. Photo by Blaine Campbell / Courtesy of the SFU Audain Gallery.

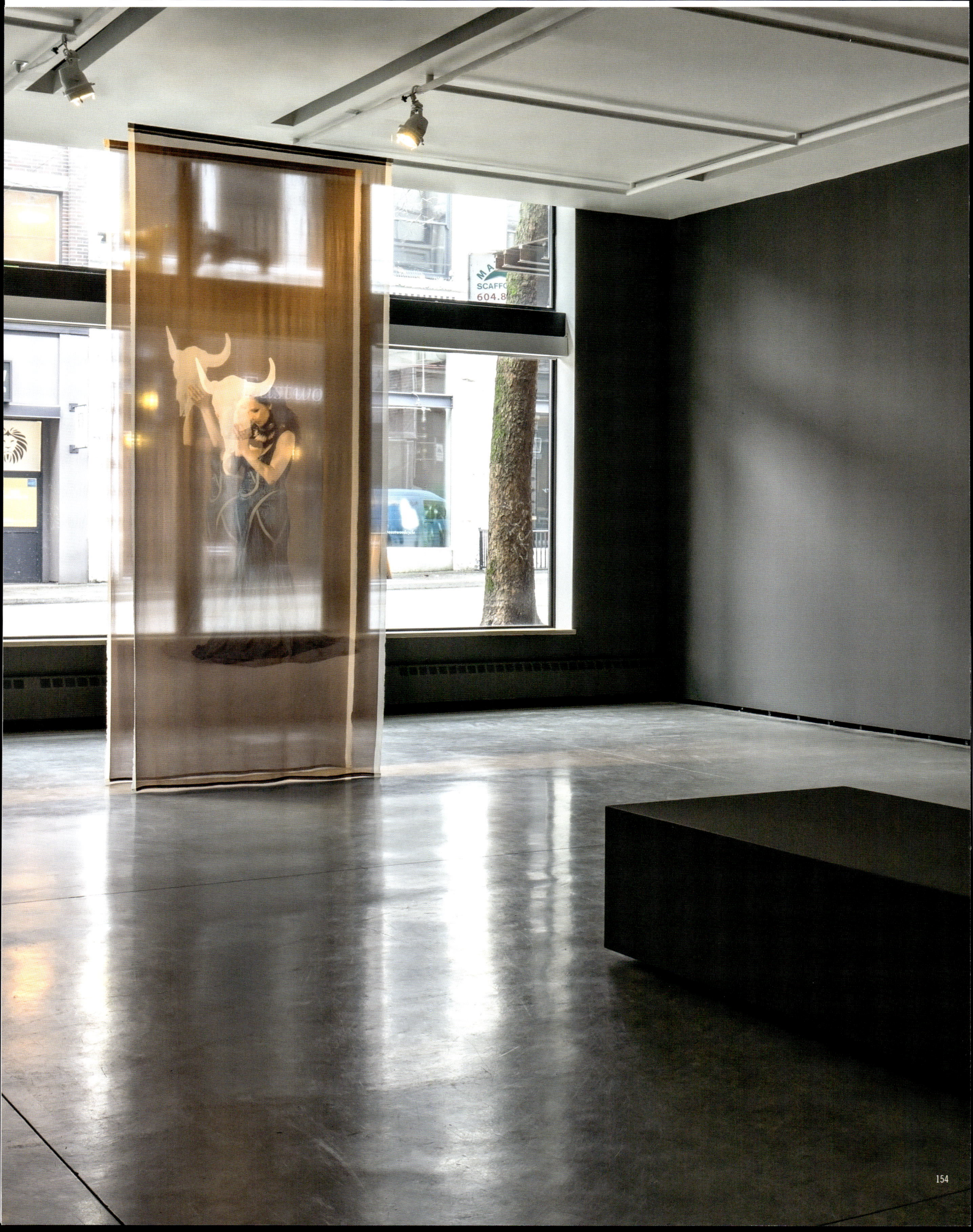

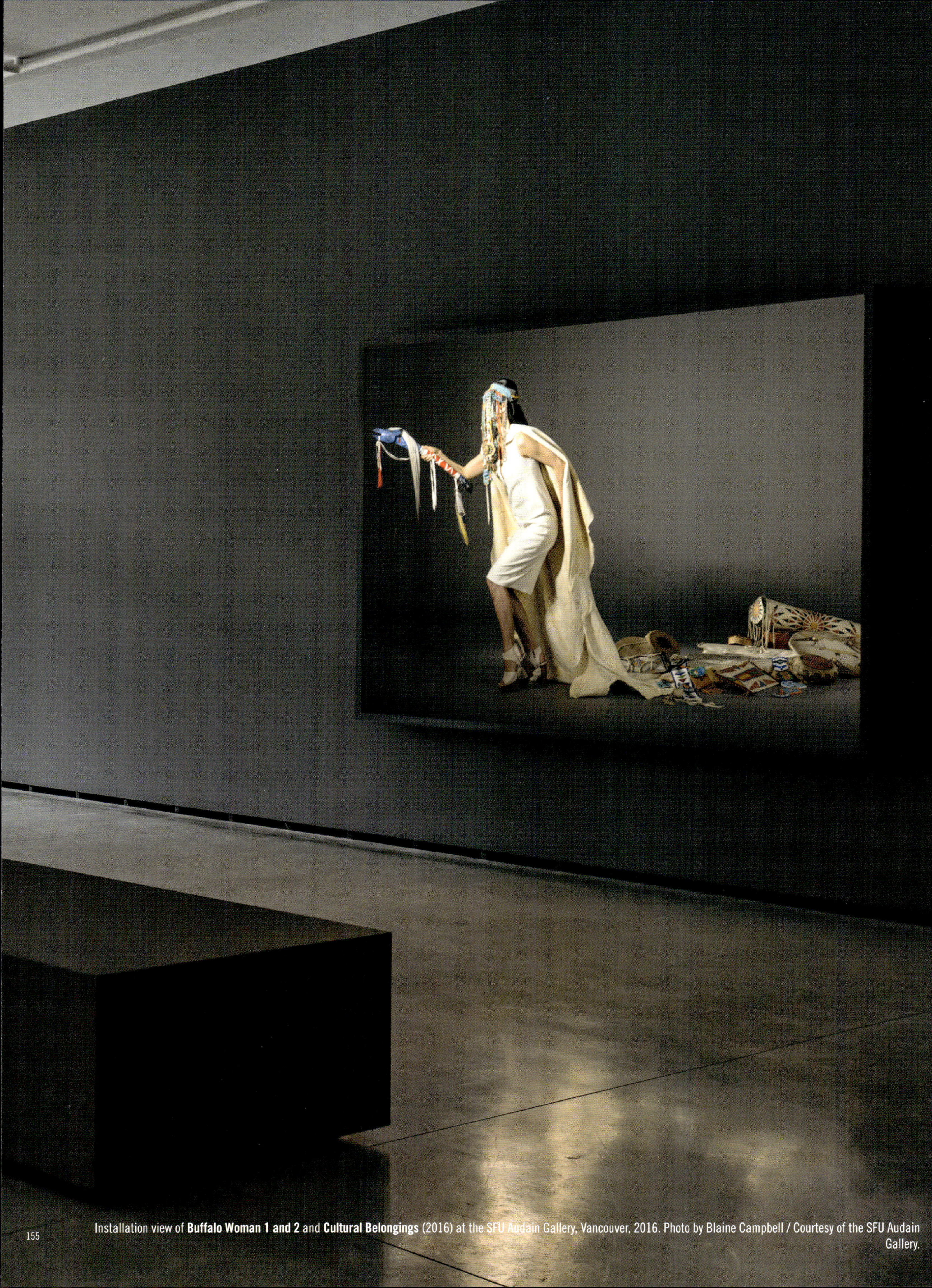

Installation view of **Buffalo Woman 1 and 2** and **Cultural Belongings** (2016) at the SFU Audain Gallery, Vancouver, 2016. Photo by Blaine Campbell / Courtesy of the SFU Audain Gallery.

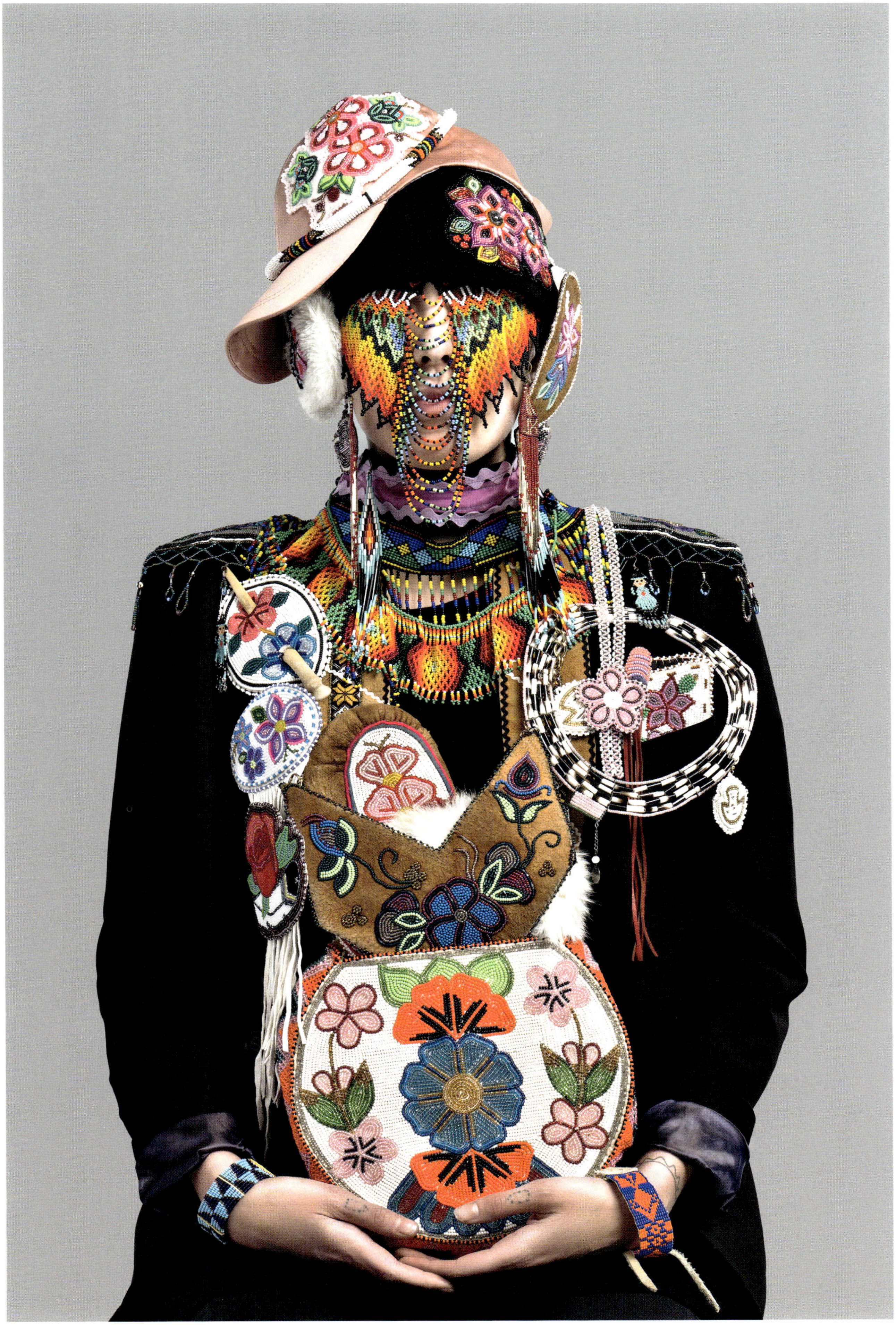

Headdress – Jeneen, 2018

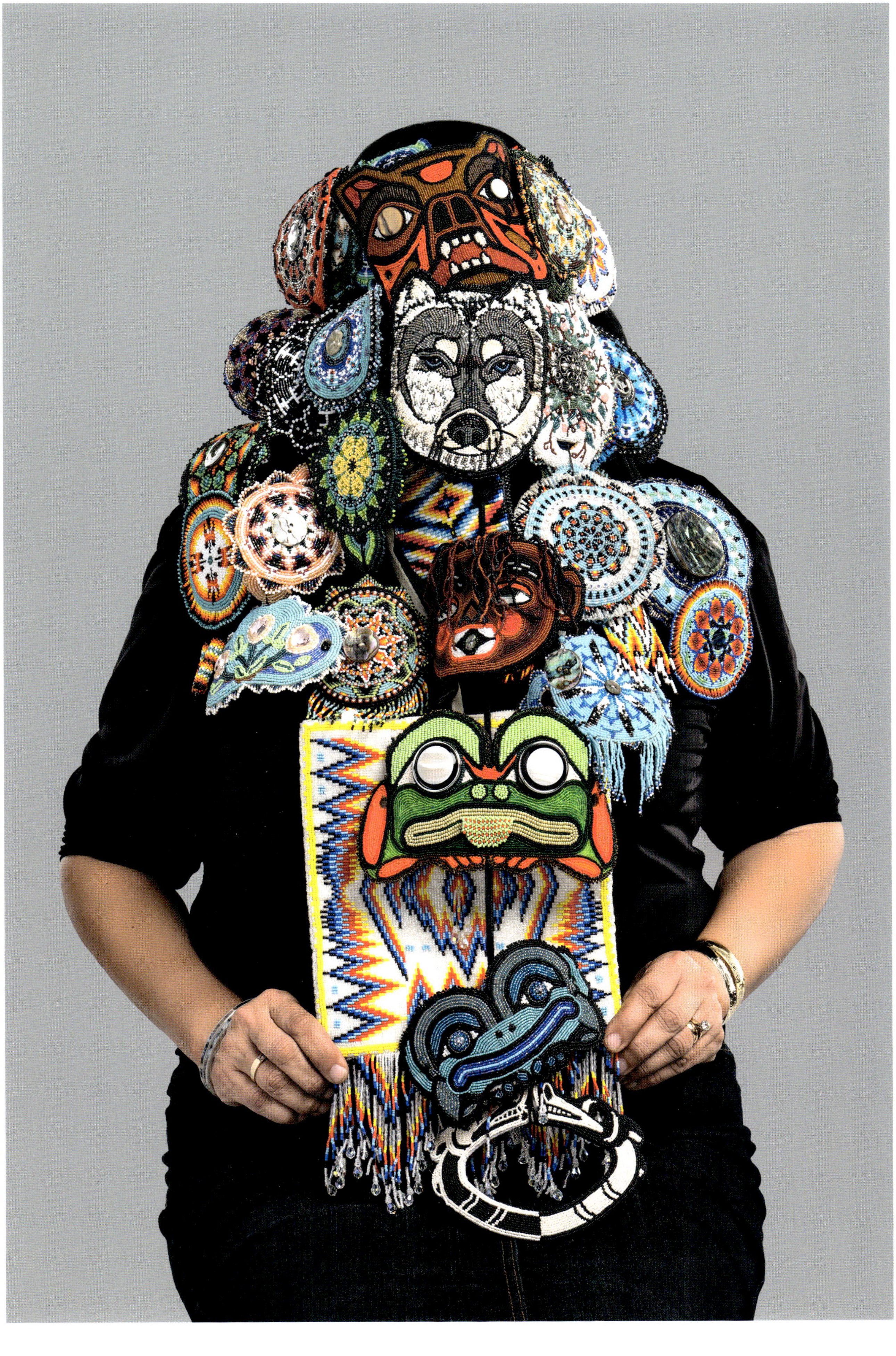

Headdress – Connie, 2019

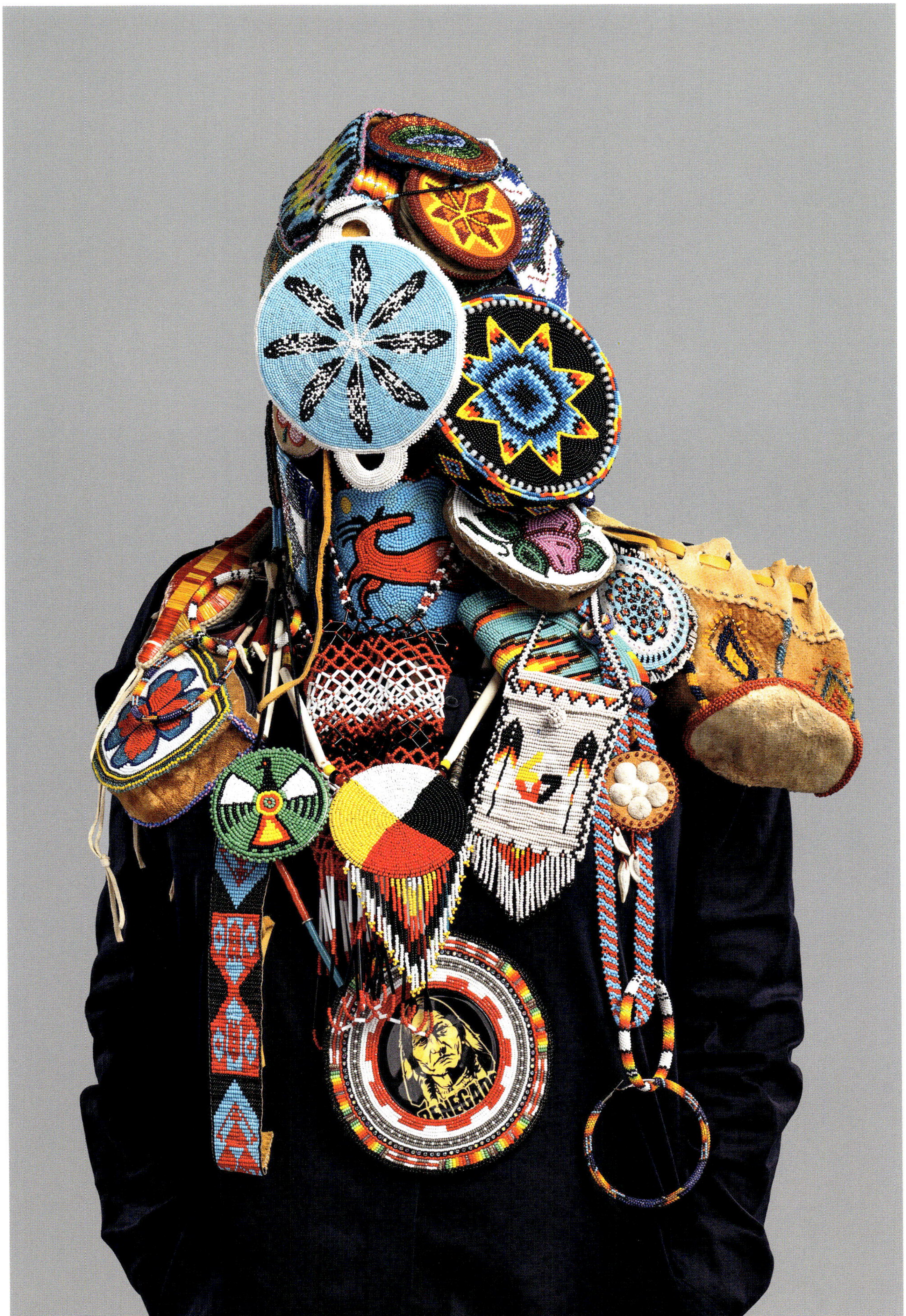

Headdress – Dana, 2019

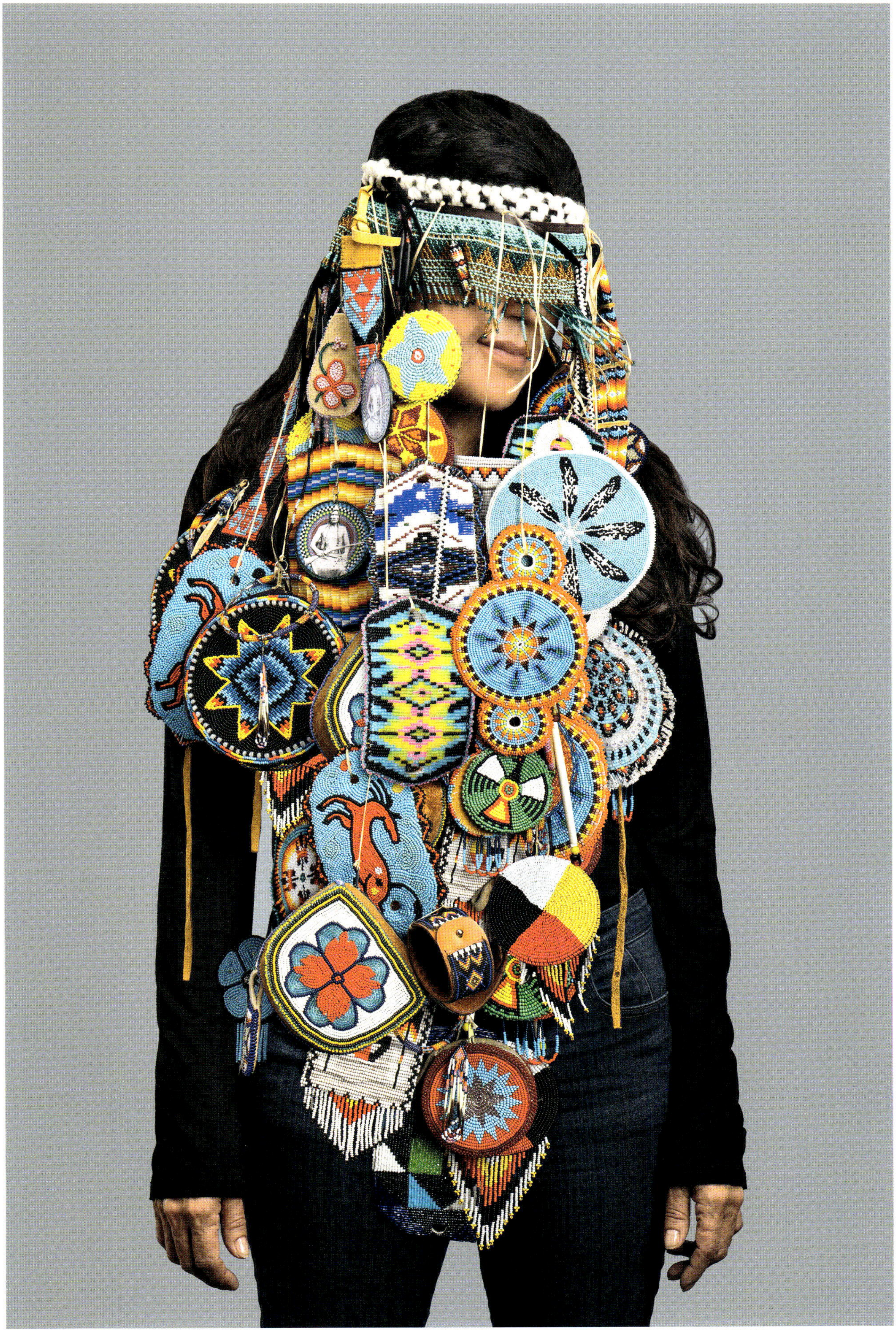

Headdress – Dee, 2019

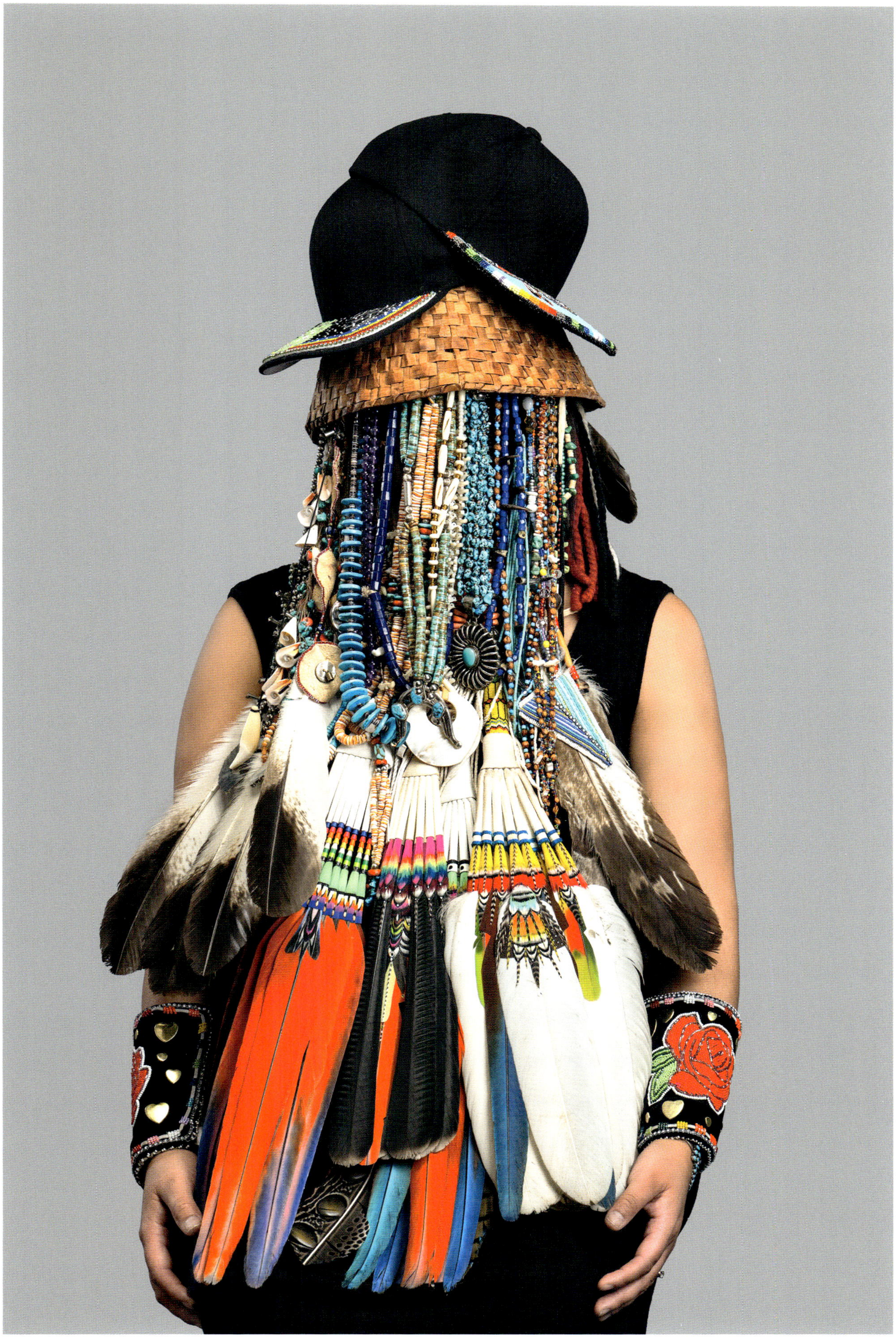

Headdress – Shadae, 2019

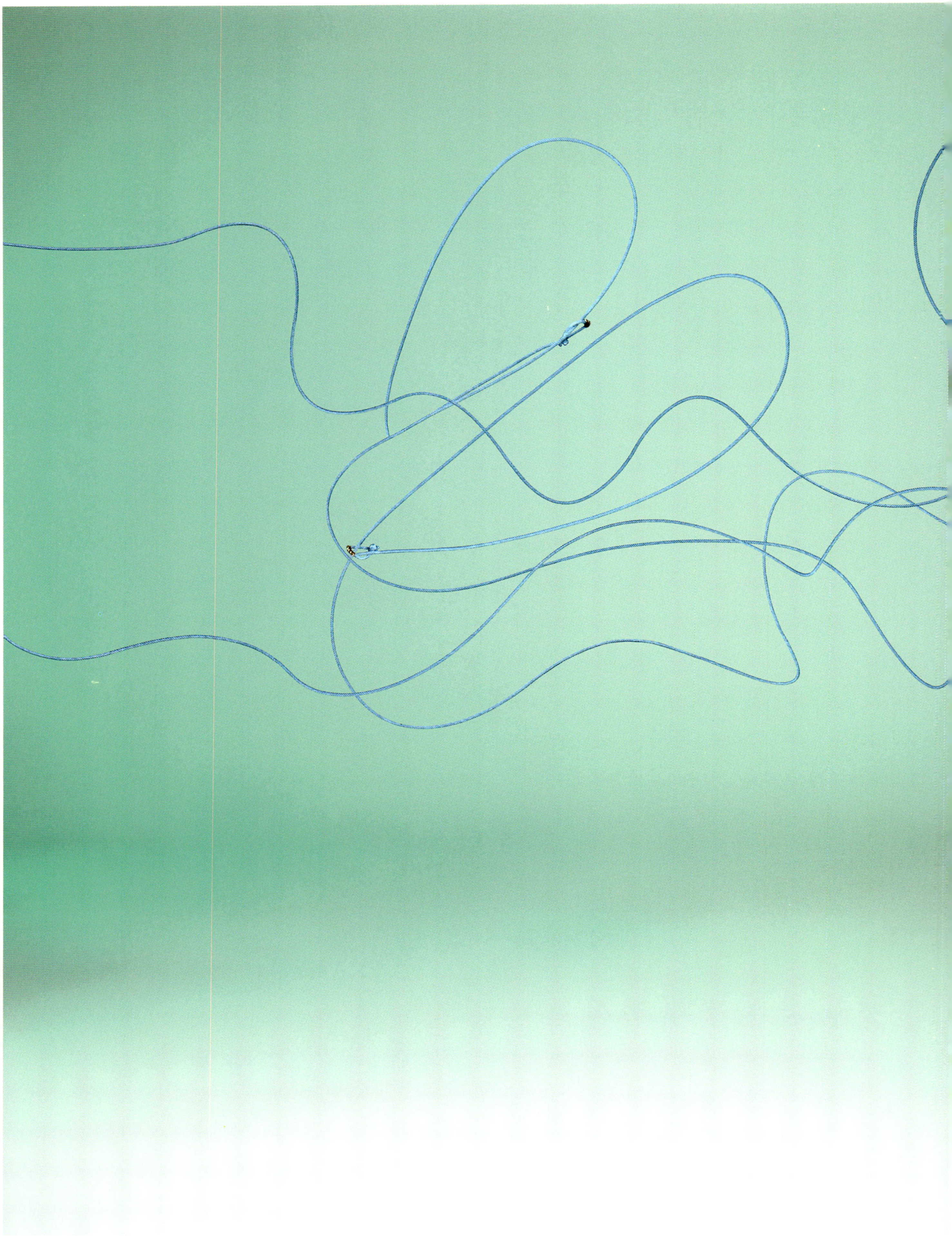

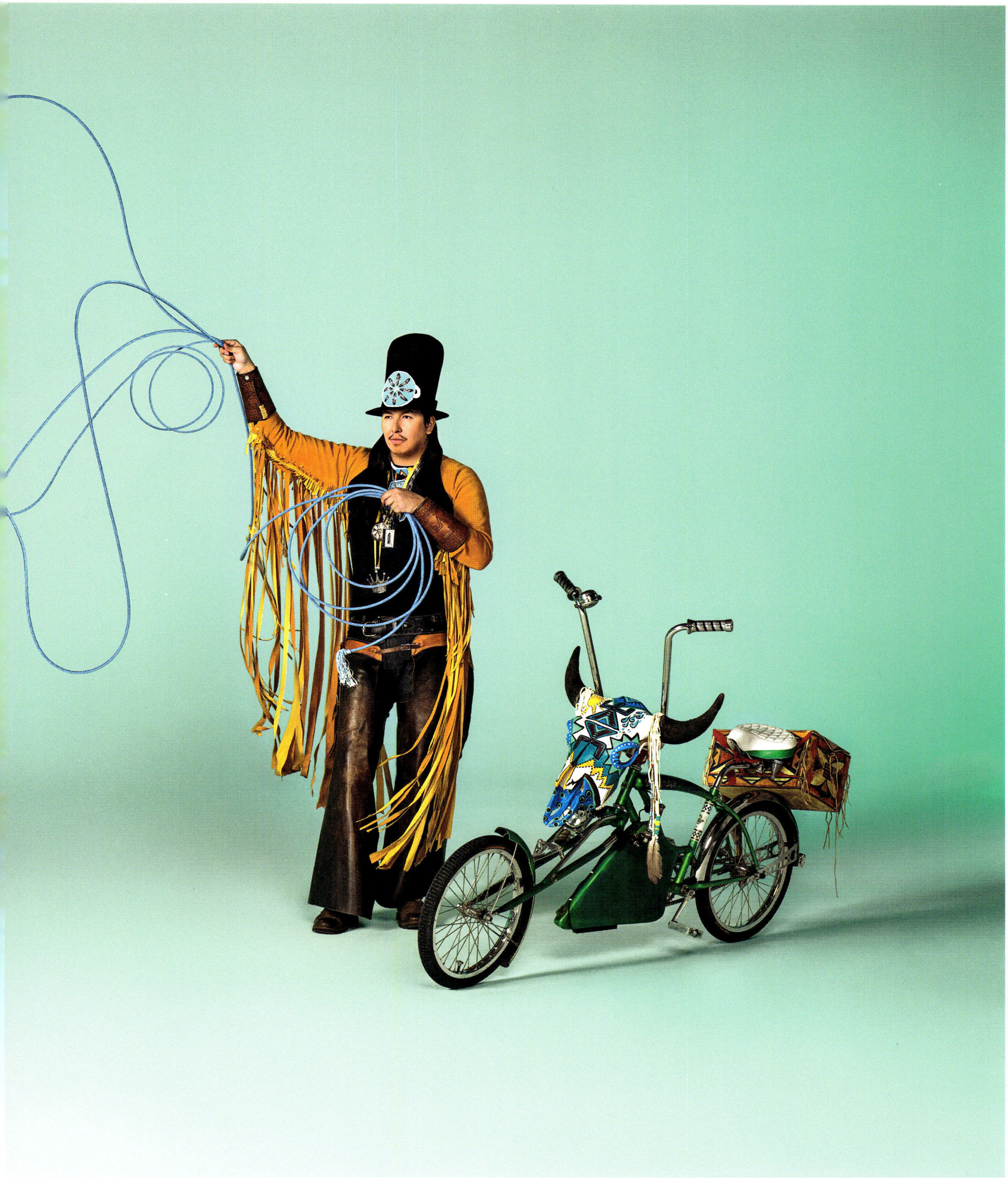

Lasso, 2018

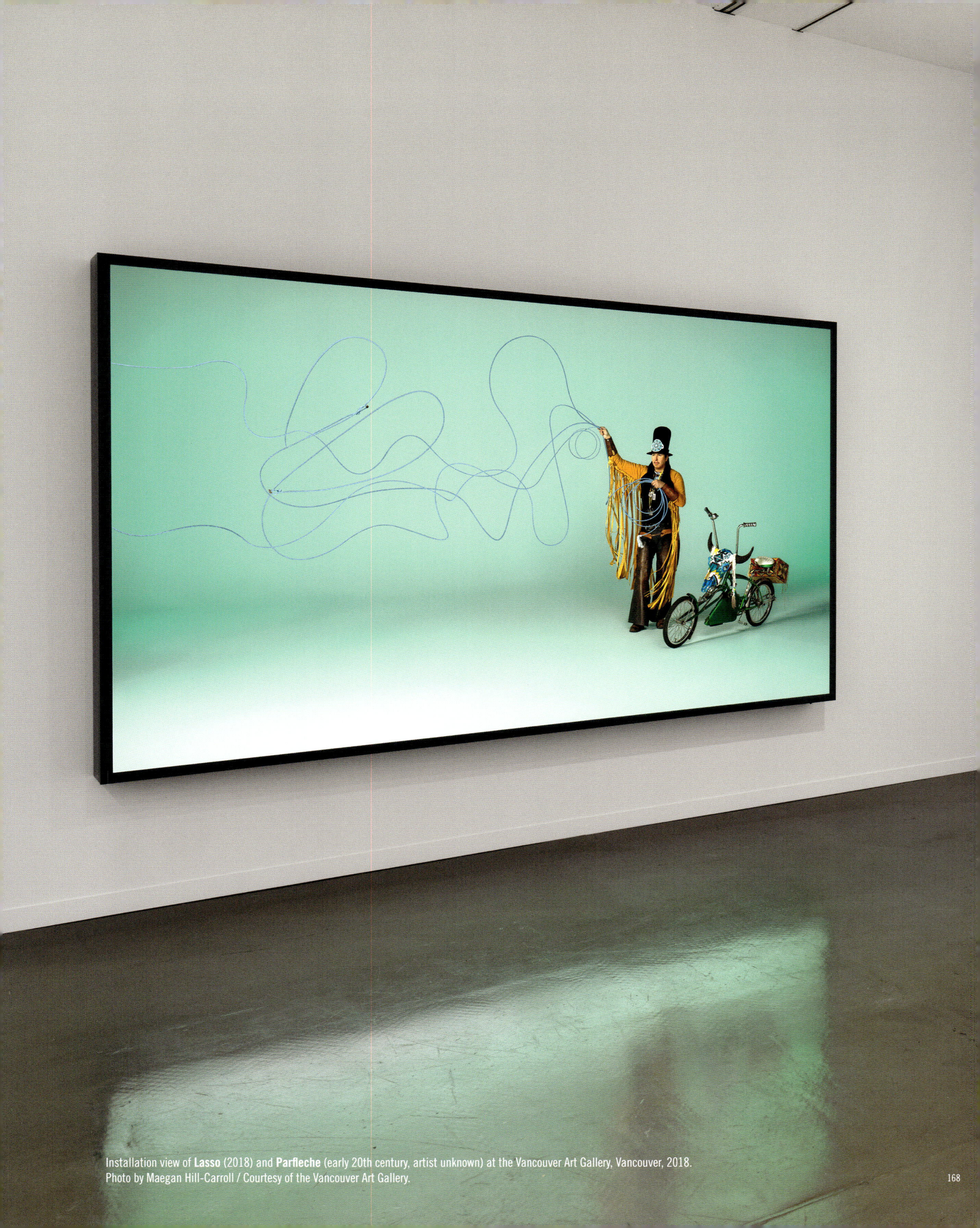

Installation view of **Lasso** (2018) and **Parfleche** (early 20th century, artist unknown) at the Vancouver Art Gallery, Vancouver, 2018.
Photo by Maegan Hill-Carroll / Courtesy of the Vancouver Art Gallery.

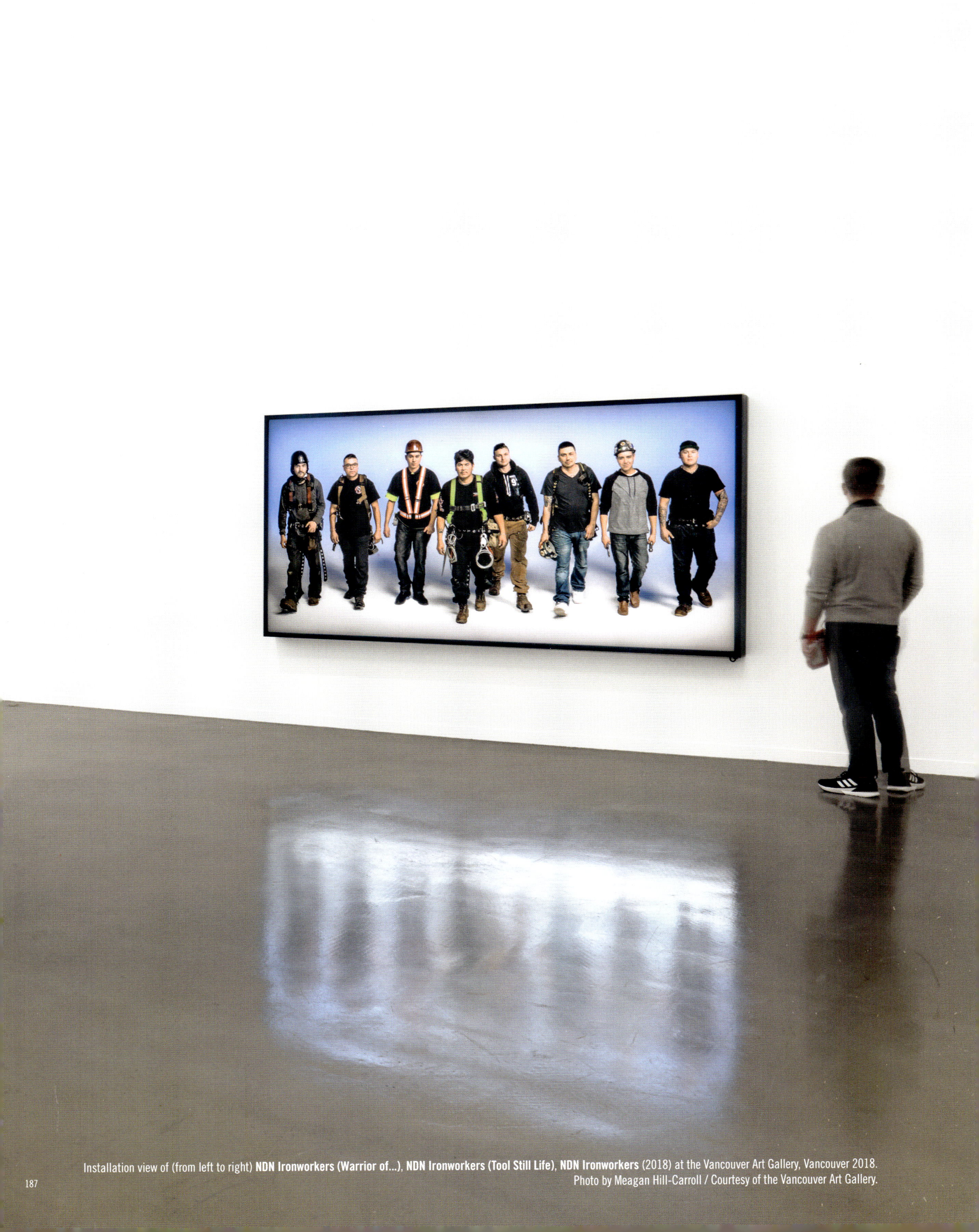

Installation view of (from left to right) **NDN Ironworkers (Warrior of...)**, **NDN Ironworkers (Tool Still Life)**, **NDN Ironworkers** (2018) at the Vancouver Art Gallery, Vancouver 2018.
Photo by Meagan Hill-Carroll / Courtesy of the Vancouver Art Gallery.

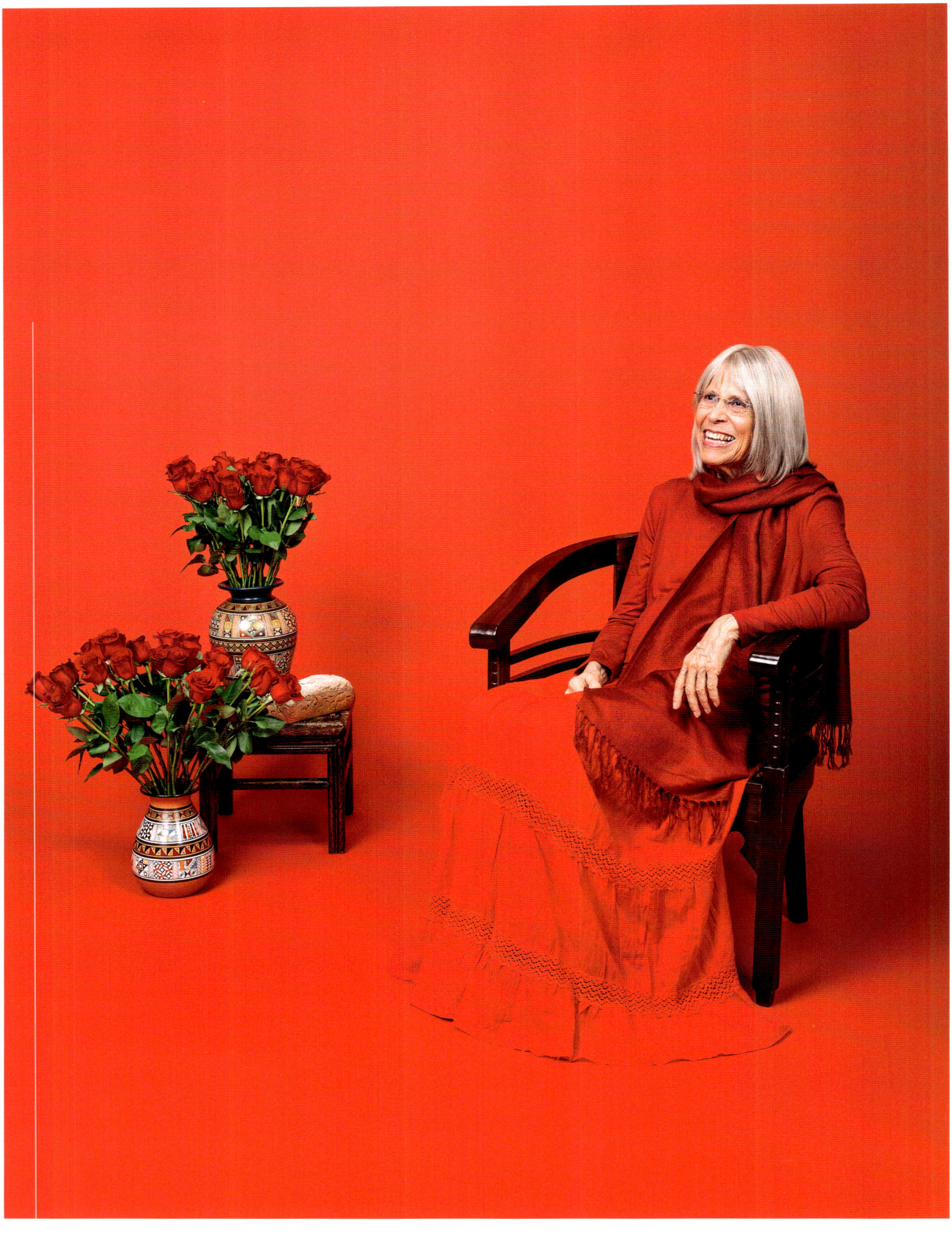

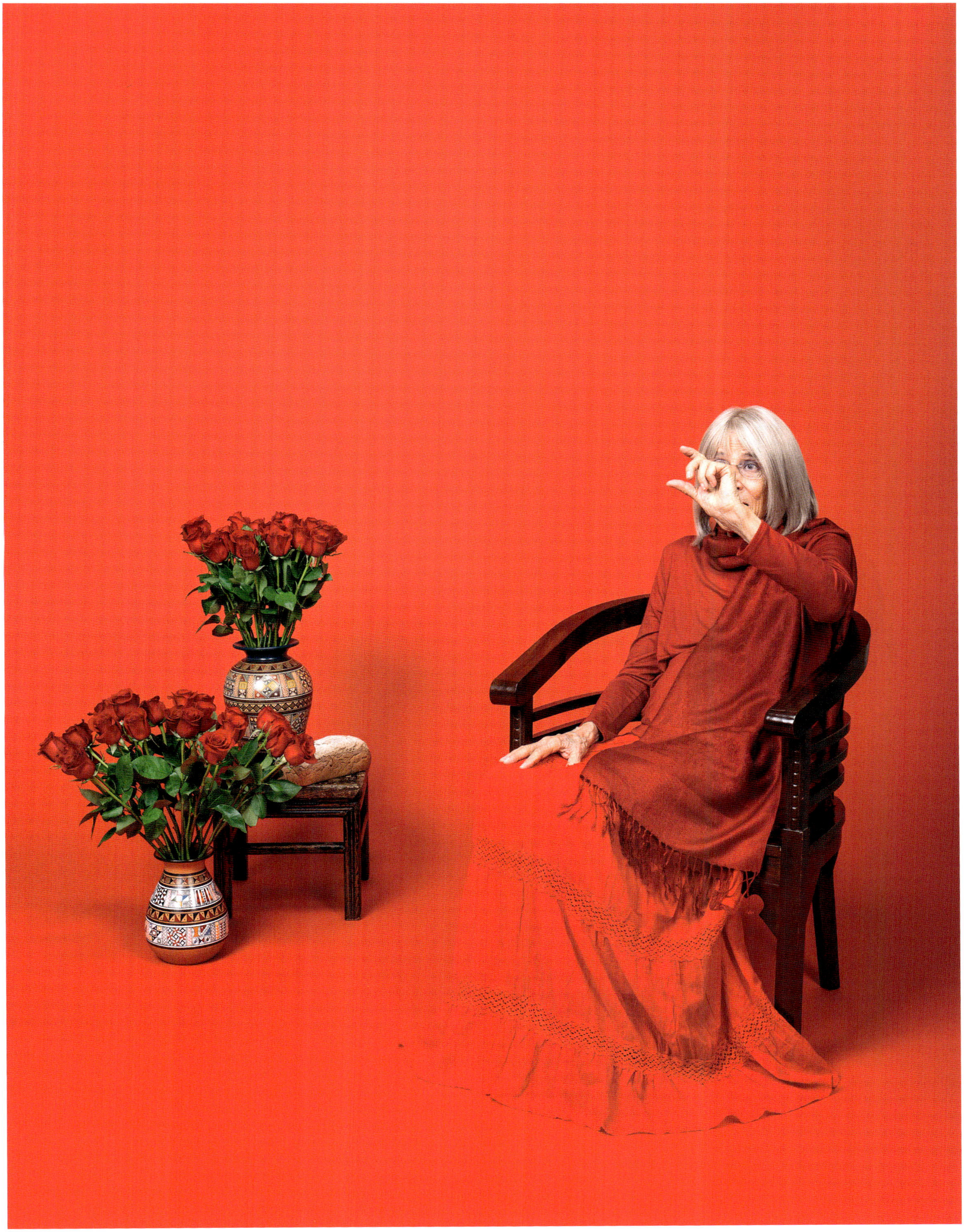

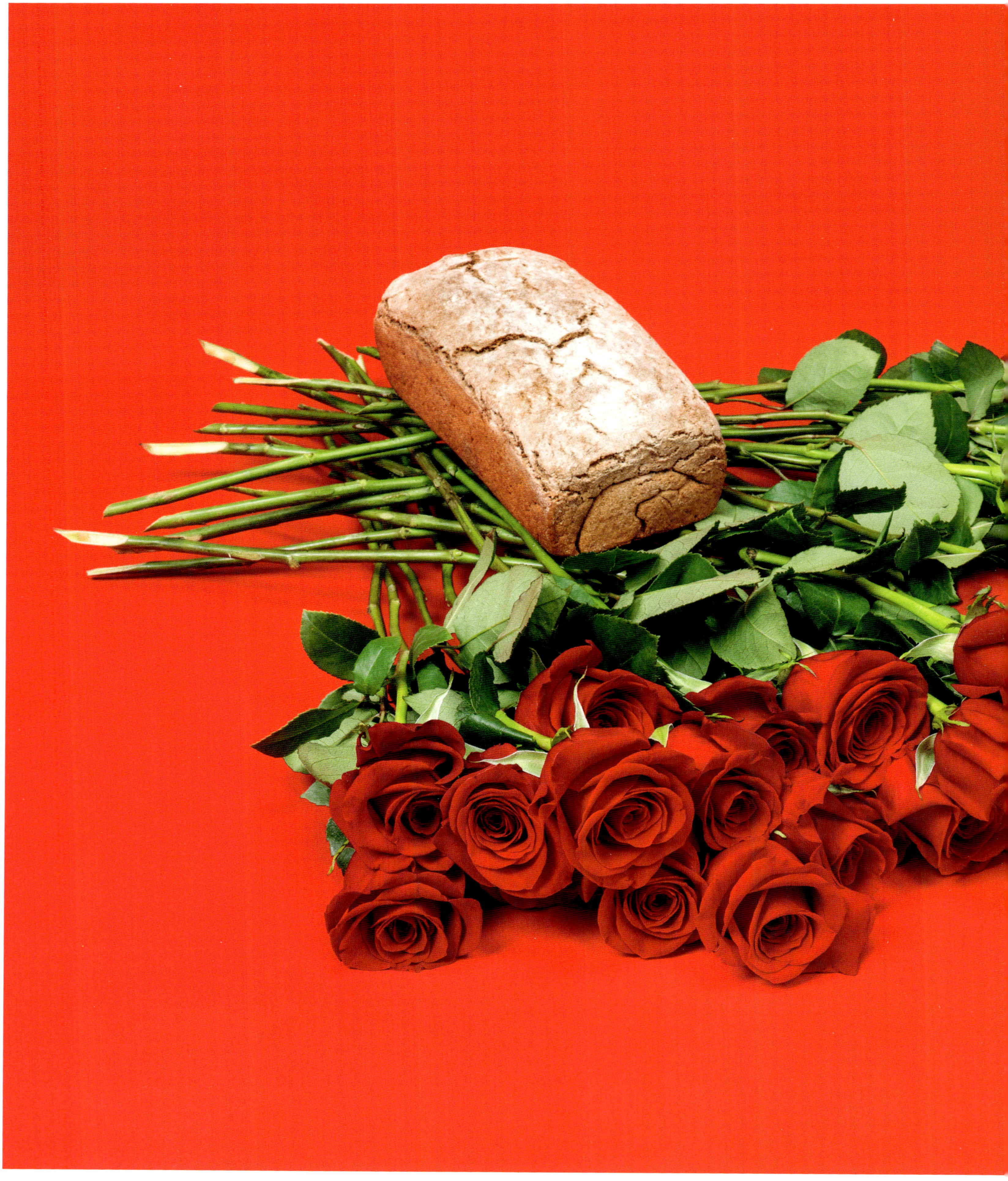

Bread and Roses, 2021

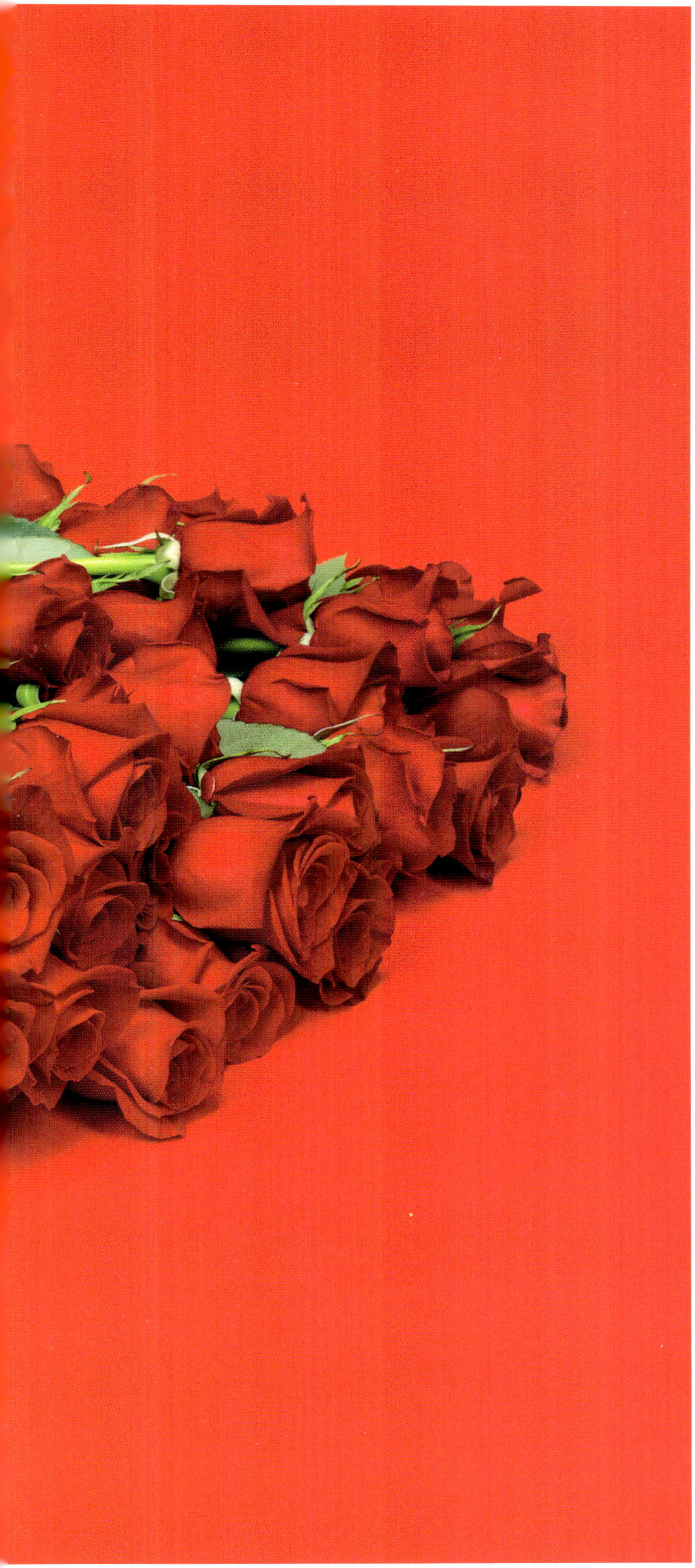

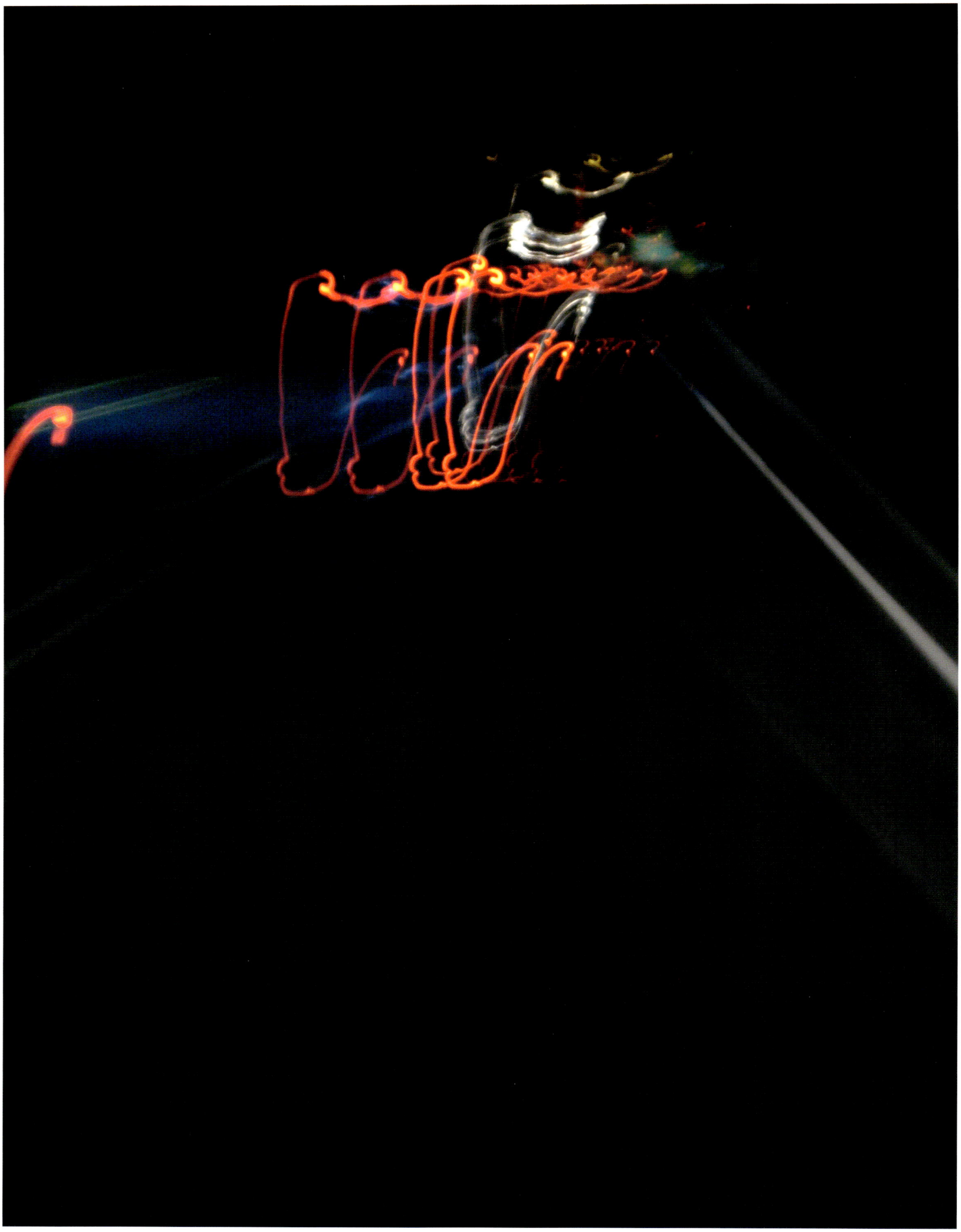

Tail Lights 1, 2005–2021

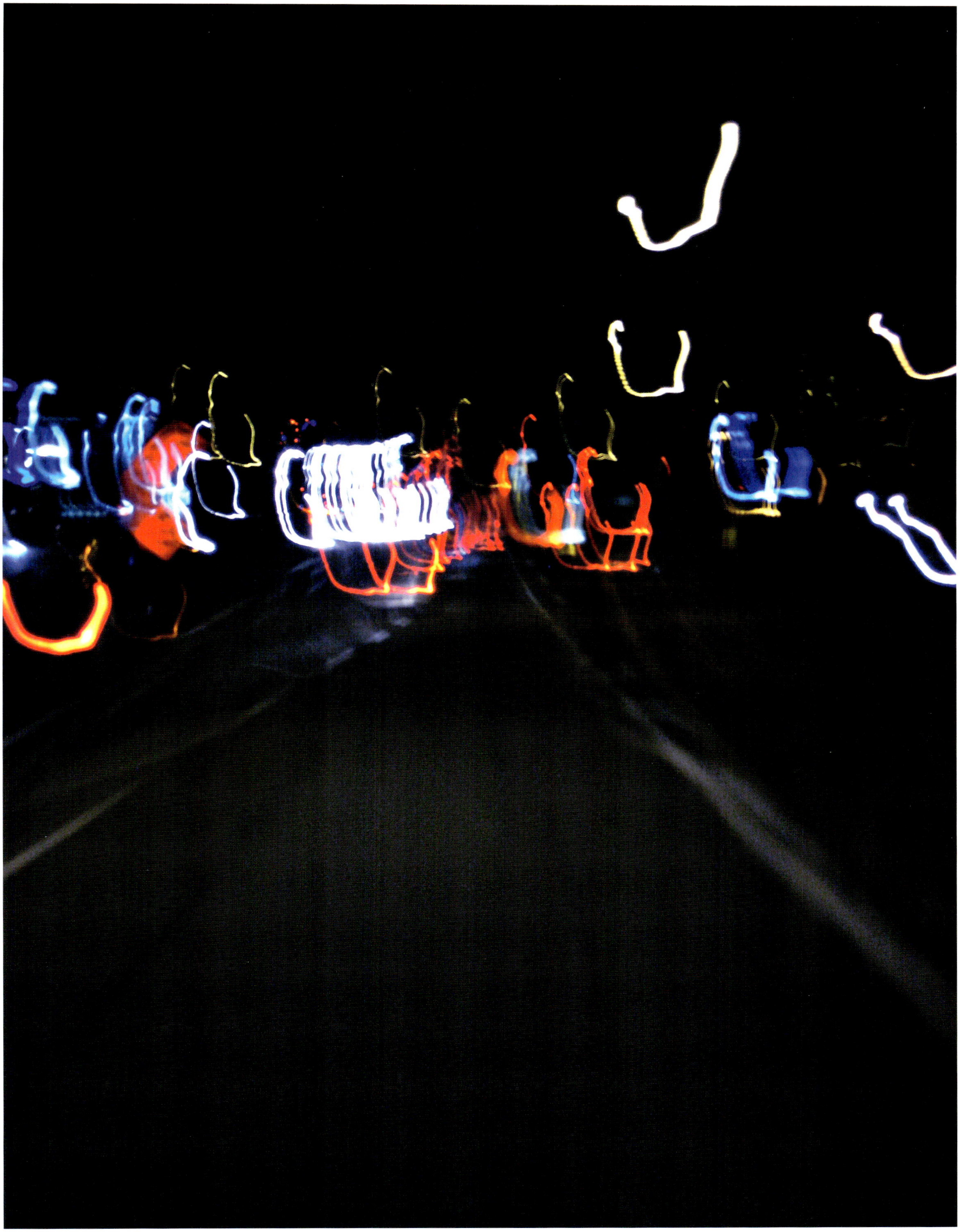

Tail Lights 2, 2005–2021

Sundancers' Gaze 1–4, 2021

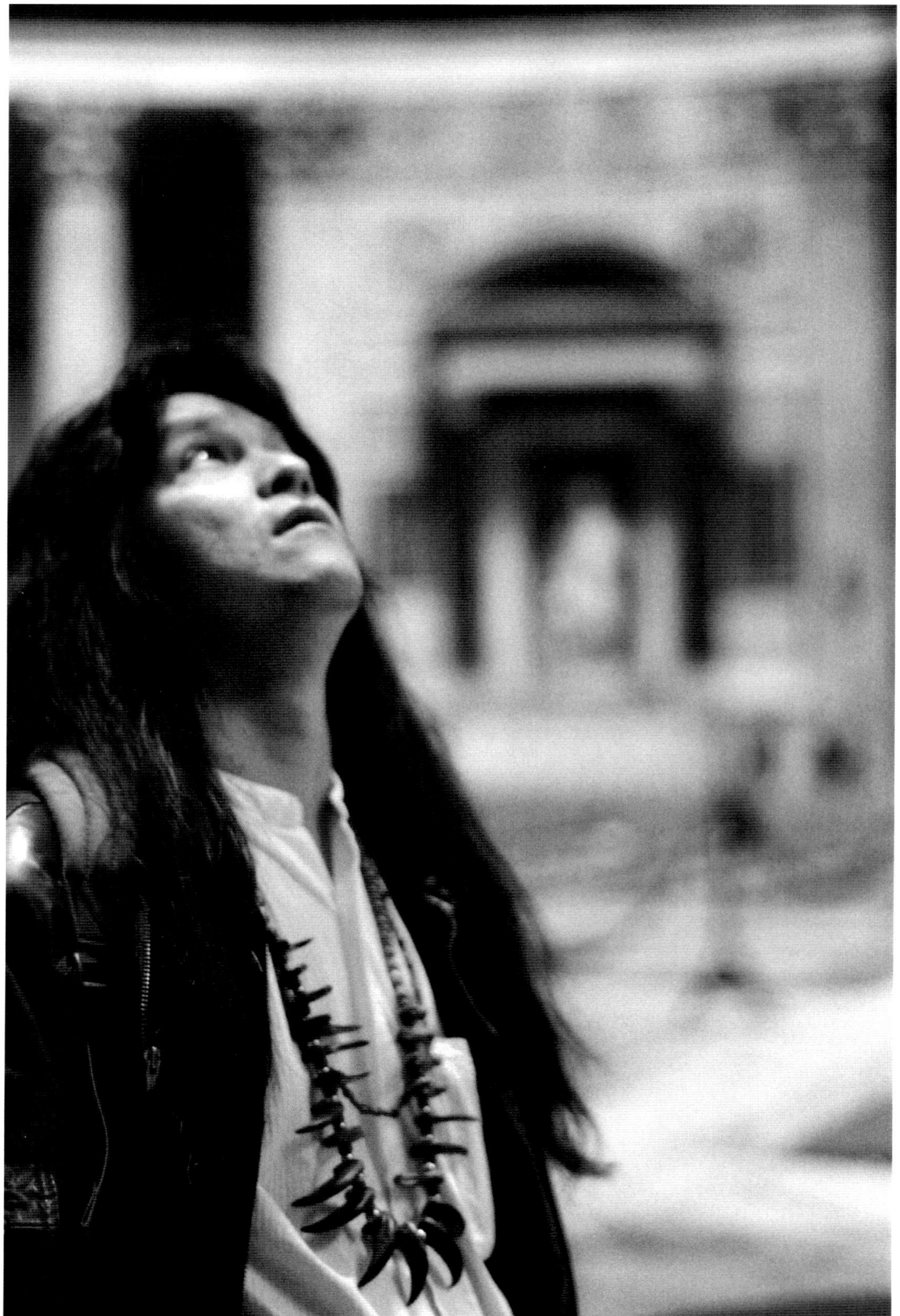

Sauvage au Musée 1, 1994–2021

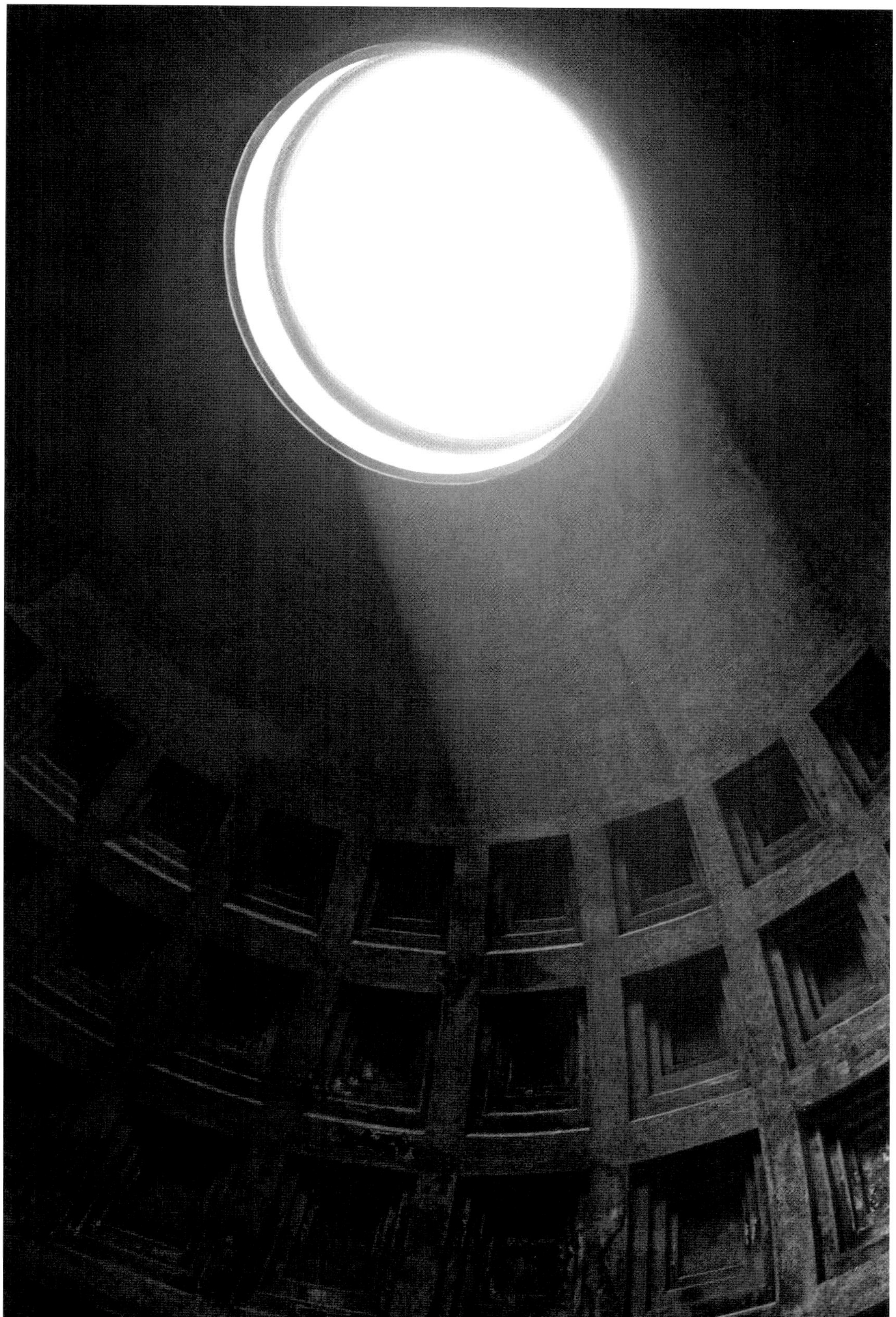

Sauvage au Musée 2, 1994–2021

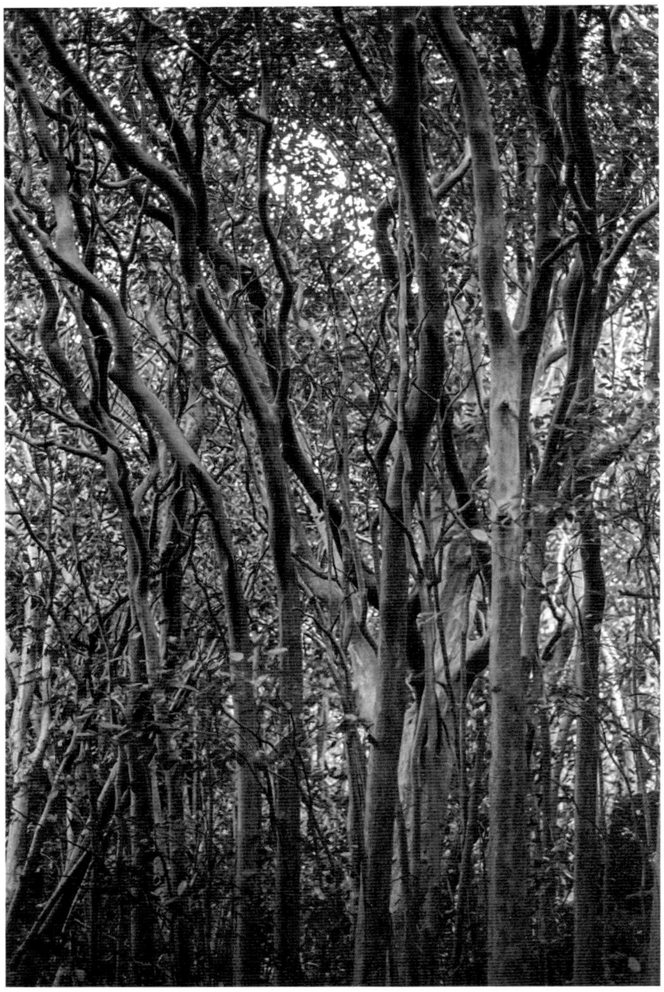

Kaui Trees, 2009–2021

LIST OF PLATES

ALL IMAGES COURTESY OF THE ARTIST, UNLESS OTHERWISE INDICATED

p. 6
Ayuta Najin Ktewin – Killed the Enemy Who Stood Standing – Her Moccasins (My Great Grandmother)
1993–2021
Inkjet print
40 × 48 inches / 101.6 × 122 cm

p. 9
Wood Mountain Moccasins 2 (For Grace Peigan Moccasin Maker), 2017–2021
Inkjet print
76 ¼ × 65 ¼ inches / 193.7 × 168.3 cm

p. 10
Wood Mountain Moccasins 1 (For Grace Peigan Moccasin Maker), 2017–2021
Inkjet print
130 ½ × 114 ¼ inches / 331.5 × 290.2 cm

p. 13
Cabri Lake 1, 1995–2021
C-print
28 × 41½ inches / 71.1 × 105.4 cm

p. 14
Cabri Lake 2, 1995–2021
C-print
28 × 41½ inches / 71.1 × 105.4 cm

p. 15
Cabri Lake 3, 1995–2021
C-print
41½ × 28 inches / 105.4 × 71.1 cm

p. 16
Self Portrait in Kaui, 2009–2021
Inkjet print
40 × 60 inches / 101.6 × 152.4 cm

pp. 18 and 33
Buffalo Bone China, 1997
Mixed-media installation with single-channel video, broken china, stanchions and rope
Dimensions vary
Collection of the MacKenzie Art Gallery, purchased with financial support of the Canada Council for the Arts Acquisition Assistance Program

pp. 20–21
Landscape Revisited, 2015
2 channel video installation
Dimensions vary
Collection John Cook

pp. 22–23
Landscape #1, 2004
2 channel video installation
Dimensions vary

pp. 24–25
Stones 1–3, 2000–2021
Inkjet prints
40 × 60 inches / 101.6 × 152.4 cm

pp. 26–28
Cabri Lake (BW Panorama), 2000-2021
Silver print
24¼ × 36 inches / 61.6 × 91.4 cm each

p. 35
The People Dance, 2001
Film
Running time 23:51 minutes

p. 39
Paris June Fourth, Fifth, and Sixth, Two Thousand and Six: She Loves Her, 2006
Silver print
Dimensions vary

p. 40
Paris June Fourth, Fifth, and Sixth, Two Thousand and Six: Nurse, 2006
Silver print
Dimensions vary

p. 41
Paris June Fourth, Fifth, and Sixth, Two Thousand and Six: Peasant Warrior, 2006
Silver print
Dimensions vary

p. 42
Paris June Fourth, Fifth, and Sixth, Two Thousand and Six: Cathedral Window 1, 2006
Silver print
Dimensions vary

p. 43
Paris June Fourth, Fifth, and Sixth, Two Thousand and Six: Candles at Notre Dame, 2006
Silver print
Dimensions vary

p. 44
Paris June Fourth, Fifth, and Sixth, Two Thousand and Six: This Took My Breath Away (Zapatista on the Seine River), 2006
Silver print
Dimensions vary

p. 45
Paris June Fourth, Fifth, and Sixth, Two Thousand and Six: Zapatista on the Bridge, 2006
Silver print
Dimensions vary

p. 46
Paris June Fourth, Fifth, and Sixth, Two Thousand and Six: Hostile, 2006
Silver print
Dimensions vary

p. 47
Paris June Fourth, Fifth, and Sixth, Two Thousand and Six: Canoe, 2006
Silver print
Dimensions vary

p. 48
Paris June Fourth, Fifth, and Sixth, Two Thousand and Six: Why, 2006
Silver print
Dimensions vary

p. 49
Paris June Fourth, Fifth, and Sixth, Two Thousand and Six: Kiss Me, 2006
Silver print
Dimensions vary

p. 50
Paris June Fourth, Fifth, and Sixth, Two Thousand and Six: Excess, 2006
Silver print
Dimensions vary

p. 51
Paris June Fourth, Fifth, and Sixth, Two Thousand and Six: Beaded Bras, 2006
Silver print
Dimensions vary

p. 52
Paris June Fourth, Fifth, and Sixth, Two Thousand and Six: More Cowboys and Indians, 2006
Silver print
Dimensions vary

p. 53
Paris June Fourth, Fifth, and Sixth, Two Thousand and Six: Beads and Feathers Head, 2006
Silver print
Dimensions vary

p. 54
Paris June Fourth, Fifth, and Sixth, Two Thousand and Six: Coloured White Collar, 2006
Silver print
Dimensions vary

p. 55
Paris June Fourth, Fifth, and Sixth, Two Thousand and Six: Nine Dollar Jacket, 2006
Silver print
Dimensions vary

p. 56
Paris June Fourth, Fifth, and Sixth, Two Thousand and Six: A Deity, 2006
Silver print
Dimensions vary

p. 57
Paris June Fourth, Fifth, and Sixth, Two Thousand and Six: Cowboys and Indians Magazine, 2006
Silver print
Dimensions vary

p. 58
Paris June Fourth, Fifth, and Sixth, Two Thousand and Six: Books, 2006
Silver print
Dimensions vary

p. 59
Paris June Fourth, Fifth, and Sixth, Two Thousand and Six: Book Seller Kills a NDN, 2006
Silver print
Dimensions vary

p. 60
Paris June Fourth, Fifth, and Sixth, Two Thousand and Six: A Horse and His Man or Woman, 2006
Silver print
Dimensions vary

p. 61
Paris June Fourth, Fifth, and Sixth, Two Thousand and Six: Paris Rooftop, 2006
Silver print
Dimensions vary

p. 62
Paris June Fourth, Fifth, and Sixth, Two Thousand and Six: Backwards Man, 2006
Silver print
Dimensions vary

p. 63
Paris June Fourth, Fifth, and Sixth, Two Thousand and Six: A Man and His Horse, 2006
Silver print
Dimensions vary

p. 64
Paris June Fourth, Fifth, and Sixth, Two Thousand and Six: A Man and His Horses, 2006
Silver print
Dimensions vary

p. 65
Paris June Fourth, Fifth, and Sixth, Two Thousand and Six: Jet in Sky 1, 2006
Silver print
Dimensions vary

p. 66
Paris June Fourth, Fifth, and Sixth, Two Thousand and Six: Two Dancing Clouds, 2006
Silver print
Dimensions vary

p. 67
Paris June Fourth, Fifth, and Sixth, Two Thousand and Six: Bird Clouds, 2006
Silver print
Dimensions vary

p. 68
Paris June Fourth, Fifth, and Sixth, Two Thousand and Six: The Sky, The Sky, 2006
Silver print
Dimensions vary

p. 69
Paris June Fourth, Fifth, and Sixth, Two Thousand and Six: Jet in Sky 2, 2006
Silver print
Dimensions vary

p. 70
Paris June Fourth, Fifth, and Sixth, Two Thousand and Six: Eastern Math, 2006
Silver print
Dimensions vary

p. 71
Paris June Fourth, Fifth, and Sixth, Two Thousand and Six: Protect Us, 2006
Silver print
Dimensions vary

p. 72
Paris June Fourth, Fifth, and Sixth, Two Thousand and Six: Paris Garden, 2006
Silver print
Dimensions vary

p. 74
Manhattan: Upper East Side 1, 2015–2021
C-print
47 × 40 inches / 119.4 × 101.6 cm

p. 75
Manhattan: Upper East Side 2, 2015–2021
C-print
47 × 40 inches / 119.4 × 101.6 cm

p. 76
Manhattan: American Elm 1, 2015–2021
C-print
47 × 40 inches / 119.4 × 101.6 cm

p. 77
Manhattan: American Elm 2, 2015–2021
C-print
47 × 40 inches / 119.4 × 101.6 cm

p. 78
Manhattan: Chelsea Hotel, 2015–2021
C-print
47 × 40 inches / 119.4 × 101.6 cm

p. 79
Manhattan: Empire State Building, 2015–2021
C-print
47 × 40 inches / 119.4 × 101.6 cm

p. 80
Manhattan: Black Fringe 1, 2015–2021
C-print
47 × 40 inches / 119.4 × 101.6 cm

p. 81
Manhattan: Black Fringe 2, 2015–2021
C-print
47 × 40 inches / 119.4 × 101.6 cm

pp. 82 and 30`
Manhattan: Fringe 1, 2015–2021
C-print
47 × 40 inches / 119.4 × 101.6 cm

pp. 83 and 30
Manhattan: Fringe 2, 2015–2021
C-print
47 × 40 inches / 119.4 × 101.6 cm

p. 84
Jingle Dress 1, 1998–2011
Black-and-white C-print
33 ¼ × 46 inches / 84.5 × 116.8 cm

p. 85
Jingle Dress 2, 1998–2011
Black-and-white C-print
33 ¼ × 46 inches / 84.5 × 116.8 cm

p. 86
The People Dance (The Camera), 1998–2011
Black-and-white C-print
26 ½ × 38 inches / 67.3 × 96.5 cm

p. 87
The People Dance (The Couch), 1998–2011
Black-and-white C-print
26 ½ × 38 inches / 67.3 × 96.5 cm

p. 88
The People Dance (The Stone), 1998–2011
Black-and-white C-print
26 ½ × 38 inches / 67.3 × 96.5 cm

p. 89
The People Dance (The Bundle), 1998–2011
Black-and-white C-print
26 ½ × 38 inches / 67.3 × 96.5 cm

p. 91
Tatanka Wanbli Chekpa Wicincala (Robe), 2006
C-print
30 × 40 inches / 76.2 × 101.6 cm

p. 92
Tatanka Wanbli Chekpa Wicincala (Eyes Open), 2006
C-print
30 × 40 inches / 76.2 × 101.6 cm

p. 93
Tatanka Wanbli Chekpa Wicincala (Eyes Closed)
2006
C-print
30 × 40 inches / 76.2 × 101.6 cm

p. 94
Tatanka Wanbli Chekpa Wicincala (Transformation)
2006
C-print
30 × 40 inches / 76.2 × 101.6 cm

p. 95
Tatanka Wanbli Chekpa Wicincala (Feather), 2006
C-print
30 × 40 inches / 76.2 × 101.6 cm

pp. 97–103
Onto the Red Road, 2006
Inkjet prints
72 × 60 inches / 182.9 × 152.4 cm each
Collection of the Eiteljorg Museum of American Indians and Western Art, Indianapolis, IN

pp. 105 and 110
The Mustang Suite: Family Portrait (Indians on a Blanket), 2008
C-print
48 × 60 inches / 121.9 × 152.4 cm

pp. 106 and 110–111
The Mustang Suite: Baby Girlz Gotta Mustang, 2008
C-print
48 × 60 inches / 121.9 × 152.4 cm

pp. 107 and 111
The Mustang Suite: Baby Boyz Gotta Indian Pony
2008
C-print
48 × 60 inches / 121.9 × 152.4 cm

pp. 108 and 110
Momma Has a Pony... (girl named History and sets her free), 2008
C-print
48 × 60 inches / 121.9 × 152.4 cm

pp. 109 and 111
The Mustang Suite: Daddy's Gotta New Ride, 2008
C-print
48 × 60 inches / 121.9 × 152.4 cm

pp. 112 and 114
Paint Up 1, 2009
Lightjet print
72 × 72 inches / 182.9 × 182.9 cm

pp. 113 and 115
Paint Up 2, 2009
Lightjet print
72 × 72 inches / 182.9 × 182.9 cm

pp. 116–119
Untitled 1–3, 1992–2018
Silver prints, triptych
60 × 40 inches / 152.4 × 101.6 cm each

pp. 120 and 22
AIM 1, 2010
Black-and-white C-print
60 × 42 inches / 152.4 × 106.7 cm

AIM 2, 2010
Black-and-white C-print
60 × 42 inches / 152.4 × 106.7 cm

pp. 121 and 123
AIM 3, 2010
Black-and-white C-print
60 × 42 inches / 152.4 × 106.7 cm

AIM 4, 2010
Black-and-white C-print
60 × 42 inches / 152.4 × 106.7 cm

pp. 124–125
Cigar Store NDN, 1994–2021
Silver print
24 ¼ × 36 inches / 61.6 × 91.4 cm

pp. 127–128
Indian Candy: Tatanka Buffalo, 2013
Metallic inkjet print
45 × 60 inches / 114.3 × 152.4 cm

p. 130
Indian Candy: Writing on Stone Blue Hands, 2013
Metallic inkjet print
34 ½ × 60 ½ inches / 87.6 × 153.7 cm

pp. 129 and 131
Indian Candy: Writing on Stone Headdress, 2013
Metallic inkjet print
24 × 42 inches / 61 × 106.7 cm

pp. 129 and 132
Indian Candy: Writing on Stone Blue Horse Man
2013
Metallic inkjet print
33 ¾ × 60 inches / 85.7 × 152.4 cm

p. 133
Indian Candy: Writing on Stone Aqua Blue Wall
2013
Metallic inkjet print
34 ½ × 60 ½ inches / 87.6 × 153.7 cm

p. 134
The Protector (Grid), 2020
Lightjet print
72 × 40 inches / 182.9 × 101.6 cm

p. 135
The Protector, 2017
LED firebox with transmounted lightjet Duratrans
96 × 48 inches / 243.8 × 121.9 cm

p. 137
Defiance 1 (rezthetics for Skeena), 2021
Metallic lightjet
64 × 48 inches / 162.6 × 121.9 cm
Edition of 2

p. 139
Defiance 2, 2021
Metallic lightjet
64 × 48 inches / 162.6 × 121.9 cm
Edition of 2

p. 141
Study for a Protest 1, 2018
Inkjet print
90 × 72 inches / 228.6 × 182.9 cm

p. 142
Muckamuch Strike Then and Now, 2018
Vinyl on wall
Dimensions vary

p. 143
Study for a Protest 2, 2018
Inkjet print
90 × 72 inches / 228.6 × 182.9 cm

pp. 144–147, 149 and 154
Buffalo Woman 1 and 2, 2016
Ink on silk windbox. Buffalo skull cast in polyurethane resin by Kevin Mackenzie.
108 × 42 inches / 274.3 × 106.7 cm each

pp. 148 and 151
Headdress, 2016
LED firebox with transmounted lightjet Duratrans
48 × 32 inches / 121.9 × 81.3 cm
Unique prototype
Collection of Rick Erickson and Donna Partridge

pp. 152–153 and 155
Cultural Belongings, 2016
LED firebox with transmounted lightjet Duratrans
72 × 96 inches / 182.9 × 243.8 cm

p. 157
Headdress – Jeneen, 2018
LED firebox with transmounted lightjet Duratrans
60 × 40 inches / 152.4 × 101.6 cm

p. 159
Headdress – Connie, 2019
LED firebox with transmounted lightjet Duratrans
60 × 40 inches / 152.4 × 101.6 cm

p. 161
Headdress – Dana, 2019
LED firebox with transmounted lightjet Duratrans
60 × 40 inches / 152.4 × 101.6 cm

p. 163
Headdress – Dee, 2019
LED firebox with transmounted lightjet Duratrans
60 × 40 inches / 152.4 × 101.6 cm

p. 165
Headdress – Shadae, 2019
LED firebox with transmounted lightjet Duratrans
60 × 40 inches / 152.4 × 101.6 cm

pp. 166–168 and cover
Lasso, 2018
LED firebox with transmounted lightjet Duratrans
72 × 120 inches / 182.9 × 304.8 cm

p. 171
Lasso Velour, 2021
LED firebox with transmounted lightjet print
48 × 30 inches / 121.9 × 76.2 cm

p. 172
Lasso Standing Velour, 2021
LED firebox with transmounted lightjet print
48 × 30 inches / 121.9 × 76.2 cm

p. 175
Lasso Easy Rider, 2021
LED firebox with transmounted lightjet print
48 × 30 inches / 121.9 × 76.2 cm

p. 176
Lasso Tomahawk, 2021
LED firebox with transmounted lightjet print
48 × 30 inches / 121.9 × 76.2 cm

p. 179
Hand Tooled (4 Ellen), 2021
Lightjet print
60 × 48 inches / 152.4 × 121.9 cm

pp. 181 and 186
NDN Ironworkers (Tool Still Life), 2018
Lightjet print
30 × 50 inches / 76.2 × 127 cm

pp. 182–183 and 187
NDN Ironworkers, 2018
LED firebox with transmounted lightjet Duratrans
72 × 120 inches / 182.9 × 304.8 cm

pp. 184 and 186
NDN Ironworkers (Warrior of...), 2018
LED firebox with transmounted lightjet Duratrans
84 × 48 inches / 213.4 × 121.9 cm

p. 185
NDN Ironworkers – Peter, 2021
LED firebox with transmounted lightjet Duratrans
50 × 37½ inches / 127 × 95.3 cm

p. 188
The Socialist 1, 2021
Inkjet print
72 × 54 inches / 182.9 × 137.2 cm

p. 189
The Socialist 4, 2021
Inkjet print
72 × 54 inches / 182.9 × 137.2 cm

pp. 190–191
Bread and Roses, 2021
Vinyl mural
Dimensions vary

p. 192
Tail Lights 1, 2021
Inkjet print
96 × 72 inches / 243.8 × 182.9 cm

p. 193
Tail Lights 2, 2021
Inkjet print
96 × 72 inches / 243.8 × 182.9 cm

pp. 194–195
Sundancers' Gaze 1–4, 2021
Inkjet prints
6 × 6 inches / 15.2 × 15.2 cm each

p. 196
Sauvage au Musée 1, 1994–2021
Silver print
36 × 24 ¼ inches / 91.4 × 61.6 cm

p. 197
Sauvage au Musée 2, 1994–2021
Silver print
36 × 24 ¼ inches / 91.4 × 61.6 cm

p. 198
Kaui Trees, 2009-2021
Silver print
36 × 24 ¼ inches / 91.4 × 61.6 cm

SELECTED BIOGRAPHY/BIBLIOGRAPHY

BORN 1959 IN YORKTON, SK • LIVES AND WORKS IN VANCOUVER, CANADA

EDUCATION

Traditional Lakota Teachings, Sitting Bull Sundance Circle, Standing Rock, South Dakota, with Isaac Dog Eagle, Joe Flying By and Dr. Bea Medicine

2009

Master of Arts, Liberal Studies, Simon Fraser University, Burnaby, Canada

1983

Certificate in Arts Administration, Spirit Song Native Indian Theatre Company, Vancouver, Canada

SELECTED SOLO EXHIBITIONS

2021

Dana Claxton, Scotiabank Photography Award, Ryerson Image Centre, Toronto, ON

2018

Fringing the Cube, Vancouver Art Gallery, Vancouver, Canada

A Forest of Canoes, The Bentway with Scotiabank CONTACT Photography Festival, Toronto, ON

2017

The Sioux Project, MacKenzie Art Gallery, Regina, SK

2016

Made to be Ready, Audain Gallery, Simon Fraser University, Vancouver, Canada

2015

Dana Claxton: Revisited, Tribe & AKA, Saskatoon, SK

2014

INDIAN CANDY, 28 Billboards Across Canada

INDIAN CANDY, Art Gallery of Greater Victoria, Victoria, Canada

Featured Artist, Your KONTINENT Media Arts Festival, Richmond, Canada

2013

ON SET – THE MUSTANG SUITE, Media Gallery, Concordia University, Montreal, QC

INDIAN CANDY, Winsor Gallery, Vancouver, Canada

2012

The People Dance, Wanuskewin Heritage Park Gallery, Saskatoon, SK

TXT4WPG, Urban Shaman Gallery, Winnipeg, MB

2011

Sitting Bull and the Moose Jaw Sioux, Gallery@501, Sherwood Park, AB

2010

New Works by Dana Claxton, Winsor Gallery, Vancouver, Canada

2009

To Mark on Surface, University of Lethbridge Gallery, Lethbridge, AB

The Barbarian, On Main, Vancouver, Canada

2008

Dana Claxton Video Art 1994-2007, Keyano Art Gallery, Fort McMurray, AB

The Mustang Suite, Alternator Gallery, Kelowna, Canada

2007

Starting From Home, Grunt Gallery, Vancouver, Canada (online retrospective)

Sitting Bull and the Moose Jaw Sioux, Thames Art Gallery, Chatham, ON

Sitting Bull and the Moose Jaw Sioux, Esplanade Art Gallery, Medicine Hat, AB

2006

Sitting Bull and the Moose Jaw Sioux, Prince Albert Art Gallery, Prince Albert, SK

Sitting Bull and the Moose Jaw Sioux, Swift Current Art Gallery, Swift Current, SK

2005

Art of the Canadian Landscape, Surrey Art Gallery, Surrey, Canada

2004

Sitting Bull and the Moose Jaw Sioux, Moose Jaw Art Gallery, Moose Jaw, SK

2003

Untitled, Rialto Gallery, Venice, Italy

The Heart of Everything That Is, Change Gallery, Rome, Italy

2002

Buffalo Bone China, Estevan Art Centre, Estevan, SK

Waterspeak, Oboro, Montreal, QC

2000

Waterspeak, Artspeak, Vancouver, Canada

The Heart of Everything That Is, Kamloops Art Gallery, Kamloops, Canada

1997

Buffalo Bone China, Tribe & AKA, Saskatoon, SK

SELECTED GROUP EXHIBITIONS

2020

Governor General's Awards in Visual and Media Arts 2020, Art Gallery of Alberta, Edmonton AB

Takuwe, The Brinton Museum, Big Horn, WY

Takuwe, Holter Museum of Art, Helena, MT

2019

Abadokone / Continous Fire, National Gallery of Canada, Ottawa, ON

The Shoreline Dilemma, Toronto Biennale, Toronto, ON

Hearts of Our People: Native Women Artists, Minneapolis Institute of Art, Minneapolis, MN

Carry Forward, Walter Phillips Gallery, Banff, AB

Art for a New Understanding: Native Voices, 1950 to Now, Nasher Museum of Art, Duke University, Durham, NC

Takuwe, Dahl Arts Centre, Rapid City, SD

2018

POP, Audain Art Museum, Whistler, Canada

Resilience, cross-country billboard art project, Canada

Carry Forward, Dunlop Gallery, Regina, SK

Through the Memory Atlas: 40 Years of Collecting, Kamloops Art Gallery, Kamloops, Canada

Beginning with the Seventies, Morris and Helen Belkin Art Gallery, Vancouver, Canada

Nanabozho's Sisters, Dalhousie Art Gallery, Halifax, NS

Art for a New Understanding: Native Voices, 1950s to Now, Crystal Bridges Museum of American Art, Bentonville, AR

2017

Walking Across, Talking Through, Art Gallery of Mississauga, Mississauga, ON

Since Then, Kamloops Art Gallery, Kamloops, Canada

Her Sugar Is?, Eastern Edge Gallery, St John's, NL

From the Vault: Recent Acquisitions to the Permanent Collection, Dalhousie Art Gallery, Halifax, NS

Resilience, cross-country billboard art project, Mentoring Artists for Women's Art, Canada

Carry Forward, Kitchener-Waterloo Art Gallery, Waterloo, ON

Raise a Flag: Works from the Indigenous Art Collection, Onsite Gallery, OCAD University, Toronto, ON

INSURGENCE/RESURGENCE, Winnipeg Art Gallery, Winnipeg, MB

STARE, Vancouver Art Gallery, Vancouver, Canada

What Does One Do With Such a Clairvoyant Image?, Gallery 44, Toronto, ON

2016

Inaugural Exhibition, Audain Art Museum, Whistler, Canada

Modest Eyes, Nuit Blanche, Montreal, QC

2015–2016

Traces That Resemble Us, Monte Clark Gallery, Vancouver, Canada

2015

Sky Doodle, Remai Modern, Saskatoon, SK

The Plains Indians Sky and Land, Metropolitan Museum of Art, New York, NY

You Are On Indian Land, IAIA Museum of Contemporary Native American Arts, Santa Fe, NM

The Rebel Yells: Dress and Political Re-dress in Contemporary Indigenous Art, FOFA Gallery, Concordia University, Montreal, QC

Wayward, Winsor Gallery, Vancouver, Canada

Women of Canadian Video, Open City Cinema/Video Pool, Ace Art, Winnipeg, MB

2014

In the Flesh, Ottawa Art Gallery, Ottawa, ON

GHOST DANCE: ACTIVISM. RESISTANCE. ART., Ryerson Image Centre, Toronto ON

Beat Nation, Musée d'art contemporain de Montréal, Montreal, QC

Counter Intelligence, Justina M Barnicke Gallery, University of Toronto, Toronto, ON

Politics of Representation, Slokum Galleries, Eastern Tennessee University, Johnson City, TN

Reflecting Light: 40 Years of Canadian Cinema, Winnipeg Film Group, Winnipeg, MB

2013

ABO VIDEO, University of Lethbridge Art Gallery, Lethbridge, AB

The Uplifting, The Offering, The Crawl, video installation, Nuit Blanche, Toronto, ON

Beat Nation, The Power Plant, Toronto, ON

Steeling the Gaze, Mendel Art Gallery, Saskatoon, SK

Western, Kamloops Art Gallery, Kamloops, Canada

Wild New Territories, Simon Fraser University Teck Gallery, Vancouver, Canada

SPLICE: Intersection of Art&Medicine, Pratt Institute, New York, NY

Contemporary Art & Indigenous Identities, Institut national d'histoire de l'art, Paris, France

2012

Fashionality, McMichael Canadian Art Collection, Kleinburg, ON

Wild New Territories, Camley Natural Park/Foundling Museum, London, UK

SPLICE: Intersection of Art&Medicine, University of Toronto Art Centre, Toronto, ON

Steeling the Gaze, Kelowna Art Gallery, Kelowna, Canada

2011
Beat Nation, Vancouver Art Gallery, Vancouver, Canada
The Audain Collection, Vancouver Art Gallery, Vancouver, Canada
Faces, Morris and Helen Belkin Art Gallery, UBC, Vancouver, Canada
Stop (the Gap): International Indigenous Art, Samstag Museum, Adelaide, Australia
Steeling the Gaze, Thunder Bay Art Gallery, Thunder Bay, ON
Steeling the Gaze, McMichael Canadian Art Collection, Kleinburg, ON
Steeling the Gaze, Dalhousie Art Gallery, Halifax, NS
Fierce: Women's Hot-Blooded Video and Film, Robert McLaughlin Gallery, Oshawa, ON
2010
Four Directions, Toronto Brickworks-No 9, Toronto, ON
Fierce: Women's Hot-Blooded Video and Film, McMaster Museum of Art, Hamilton, ON
Cue: Artists' Videos, Vancouver Art Gallery, Vancouver, Canada
Diabolique, Oakville Galleries, Oakville, ON
Diabolique, Galerie de l'UQAM, Université du Quebec, Montreal, QC
Resistance is Fertile, A Space, Toronto, ON
Acting Up, Acting Out, Galerie Sans Nom, Moncton, NB
Sistahood Celebration, Out on Screen, Vancouver, Canada
The Distance of Beauty Songs of Survival in a Precarious Age, Museum of Contemporary Art, 17th Biennale of Sydney, Sydney, Australia
2009
Cosmologies, Centre A, Vancouver, Canada
Steeling the Gaze, National Gallery of Canada, Ottawa, ON
Map(ing): Working Proof, Night Gallery, Tempe, AZ
Diabolique, Dunlop Art Gallery, Regina, SK
Native Visuality, C.N. Gorman Museum, University of Davis California, Davis, CA
Buffalo Bone China, Mackenzie Art Gallery, Regina, SK
2008
www.non-compliance.ca, Urban Shaman, Winnipeg, MB
Face the Nation, Art Gallery of Alberta, Edmonton, AB
Red Eye, Sir Wildred Grenfell College Art Gallery, Corner Brook, NL
18 Illuminations: Contemporary Art and Light, Winnipeg Art Gallery, Winnipeg, MB
2007
Eiteljorg Fellowship, Eiteljorg Museum, Indianapolis, IN
Vancouver InSight, King's Lynn Arts Centre, King's Lynn, Norfolk, UK
Les Rencontres Internationales, Babylon, Berlin, Germany
Starting From Home, Grunt Gallery, Vancouver, Canada
18 Illuminations: Contemporary Art and Light, St. Mary's University Gallery, Halifax, NS
18 Illuminations: Contemporary Art and Light, MacLaren Art Centre, Barrie, ON
Blink New Commissioned Works, Winnipeg Art Gallery, Winnipeg, MB
Testing Waters, PAVED Arts, Saskatoon, SK
Chinatown Night Market Screening, Cineworks, Vancouver, Canada
Limits of Tolerance, Morris & Helen Belkin Gallery, UBC, Vancouver, Canada
Crack the Sky, Biennale de Montréal, Montreal, QC
2006
Red Eye, Carleton University Art Gallery, Ottawa, ON
Canadian Video, CaixaForum, Fundacio la Caixa, Barcelona, Spain
75 Years of Collecting: First Nations Myths and Realities, Vancouver Art Gallery, Vancouver, Canada
Back/Flash, Dalhousie Art Gallery, Dalhousie University, Halifax, NS
Why I am So Unhappy, OR Gallery, Vancouver, Canada
18 Illuminations: Contemporary Art and Light, Robert McLaughlin Gallery, Oshawa, ON
18 Illuminations: Contemporary Art and Light, Art Gallery of Peterborough, Peterborough, ON
A History Show, Nuit Blanche, Toronto, ON
Emotional Geographies, University Art Gallery, St. Francis Xavier University, Antigonish, NS
Continuum, Musée Malraux, Biennale d'art contemporain du Havre, Le Havre, France
2005
18 Illuminations: Contemporary Art and Light, Tom Thomson Gallery, Owen Sound, ON
Neighbourhood, Centre A, Vancouver, Canada
Back/Flash, Winnipeg Art Gallery, Winnipeg, MB
Back/Flash, Walter Phillips Gallery, Banff, AB
Marking Time, Mendel Art Gallery, Saskatoon SK
Reclamations, McIntosh Gallery, University of Western Ontario, London, ON
Watch This: New Video From Indian Country, PAVED Art + New Media, Saskatoon, SK
Edges, MediaNet, Victoria, Canada
Fabulous Festival of Fringe Film, Durham Art Gallery, Durham, ON
Loss and Other Discoveries, Available Light c/o Arts Court, Ottawa, ON
Aboriginal Awareness Week, EM MEDIA, Calgary, AB
2004
A History Lesson, Museum of Canadian Contemporary Art, Toronto, ON
Gatherings: Aboriginal Art -WAG Collection, Guangdong Museum of Art, Guangzhou, China
Short Films and Videos from Aboriginal Artists, EM MEDIA, Calgary, AB

Electromediascope, Nelson-Atkins Museum of Art, Kansas City, MO
Photophobia, Art Gallery of Hamilton, Hamilton, ON
Reclaiming Squaw, Crazy Horse Theatre, Calgary, AB
Traplines, Urban Shaman Gallery, Winnipeg MB

2003

Language of Intercession, Dazibao, Montreal, QC
Back/Flash, Walter Phillips Gallery, Banff, AB
Gatherings: Aboriginal Art - WAG Collection, Museum of Natural History, Taipei, Taiwan.
Lessons in History, Mackenzie Art Gallery, Regina, SK
Language of Intercession, Hamilton Art Gallery, Hamilton ON
Vancouver Video, Folly Gallery, Lancaster, UK
Magnetic North, Huashan Arts District, Taipei, Taiwan
Magnetic North, The Power Plant, Toronto, ON
Video Art Plastique, Centre d'art contemporain de Basse-Normandie, Hérouville-Saint-Clair, France
Bluescreen Presents: Redscreen, Cube Microplex, Bristol, UK

2002

Vancouver Video, Galleria di Nuova Icona, Venice, Italy
Gatherings: Aboriginal Art from the Collection, Winnipeg Art Gallery, Winnipeg, MB

2001

Magnetic North, Plug In, Winnipeg, MB
Magnetic North, Art Gallery of Hamilton, Hamilton, ON
Abattoirs by Artists, Mendel Art Gallery, Saskatoon, SK
Magnetic North, Harvard Film Archives, Cambridge, MA
Exhibition, Canadian Trade Office, Taipei, Taiwan
Beyond Tonto II, TRIBE, Saskatoon, SK
States of Alterities: A Screen Capture of Vancouver Video, Pleasure Dome, Toronto, ON

2000

Magnetic North, Walker Arts Centre, Minneapolis, MN
Magnetic North, Video Pool, Winnipeg, MB
From the Collection – The Red Paper, Vancouver Art Gallery, Vancouver, Canada
New Acquisitions Buffalo Bone China, Mackenzie Art Gallery, Regina, SK
Centrifugal Vision – Video Circle, Hong Kong University of Science & Technology, Hong Kong, China
Selections from The Iskwew Festival, EM MEDIA, Calgary, AB
Super New, EM MEDIA, Calgary, AB
UK/Canadian Video Exchange 2000, Canada House, London, UK
Electronic Landscapes/Canadian Video Art, MonteVideo, Amsterdam, The Netherlands
Scope, Western Front, Vancouver, Canada

1999

Taste of Landscapes, Centre of Novi Sad, Novi Sad, Serbia
Past Life: Future Tense, Museo Nacional, Buenos Aires, Argentina
Private Properties, UCL Art Museum, University College, London, UK
Millennial Funk, Honolulu Academy of Art, University of Hawaii, Honolulu, HI
Video Binge III, Native Indian and Inuit Photographers Association, Hamilton, ON

1998

Material Zones, Walter Phillips Gallery, Banff, AB
Red Interiors, Open Space, Victoria, Canada
Beauty and the Beast, Walter Phillips Gallery, Banff, AB
Chaos & Disaster, Ed Video Media Arts Centre, Guelph, ON
Red Interiors, Surrey Art Gallery, Surrey, Canada
Red Interiors, EM MEDIA, Calgary, AB
Red Interiors, Nanaimo Art Gallery, Nanaimo, Canada
Beyond Tonto, Tribe, Saskatoon, SK

1997

New Works, Aboriginal Film & Video Art Alliance of Ontario, Native Canadian Friendship Centre, Edmonton, AB

1996

Topographies, Vancouver Art Gallery, Vancouver, Canada
Urban Fictions, Presentation House, North Vancouver, Canada
Turtle Island Storytellers Film and Video Screening, Saskatchewan Filmpool Co-op, Regina, SK
Contemporary Video Screening, Ed Video Media Arts Centre, Guelph ON

1994

Walking with the Ancients, Museum of Modern Art, New York, NY
Racing Thru Space, Artspeak Gallery, Vancouver, Canada

SELECTED BIBLIOGRAPHY

Abramson, Stacey. "In the Blink of an Eye." *C Magazine* 94, Summer 2007.
Alexandra, Kristi and Brittany Tiplady. "Dana Claxton: Fringing the Cube Takes a Cutting Gaze on Colonialism." *Loose Lips*, October 25, 2018.
Alteen, Glenn. "Liturgy for a New Secular World." Grunt Gallery, November 2000.
Anderson, Jack. "Exhibit Rewrites History." *Leader Post*, June 1, 2000.
Anderson, Jack. "Diabolique." *Canadian Art*, Winter 2009.
Andrews, Marke. "Filmmakers' plan to build native media gains support." *The Vancouver Sun*, June 24, 2005.
Arnold, Grant. *Audain Collection* (exhibition catalogue). Vancouver: Vancouver Art Gallery, 2011.
Arnold, Grant. "The Art of Dana Claxton: a Prologue." In *Dana Claxton: Fringing the Cube* (exhibition catalogue). Vancouver: Vancouver Art Gallery, 2018.
Baerwaldt, Wayne. *Remuer Ciel et Terre: La Biennale de Montréal 2007* (exhibition catalogue). Montreal: Centre International d'Art Contemporain, La Biennale de Montréal, 2007.

Bainas, Lexi. "Festival films cover culture to environment." *Cowichan Valley Citizen*, April 9, 2014.

Baltruschat, Doris. "Television and Canada's Aboriginal Communities." *Canadian Journal of Communication* (January 29, 2004).

Battiste, Marie, and Lynne Bell, Isobel M. Findlay, Len Findlay and James (Sákéj) Youngblood Henderson. "Thinking Place: Animating the Indigenous Humanities in Education." *The Australian Journal of Indigenous Education* 34 (2005).

Beatch, Lucas. "Reclamation, Beauty, and the Palindrome in Dana Claxton: Fringing the Cube." *Undergraduate Journal of Art History and Visual Culture* (Spring 2019).

Beesley, Ruby. "Photography & the pervasive influence." *Aesthetics* 34 (April/May 2010).

Beesley, Ruby. "Photography & the Pervasive Influence." *Aesthetica: The Art & Culture Magazine*, 2014.

Bell, G J. "Dana Claxton." *Canadian Art*. Spring 2014.

Bell, Lynne. "Taking a Walk in the City." *Urban Fictions*. Vancouver: Presentation House Gallery, 1997.

Bell, Lynne. "The Post/Colonial Photographic Archive and the Work of Memory." In *Image and Inscription: an Anthology of Contemporary Canadian Photography*. Toronto: YYZ Books, 2005.

Bell, Lynne. "Dana Claxton: Disturbing History." *Canadian Art*, Winter 2010.

Bell, Lynne. "From a Whisper to a Scream: Dana Claxton teaches art and a revised version of North American history." *Canadian Art*, Winter 2010.

Bell, Patricia. "Izzy's gift to the understanding of first nations people: this engagement with the concerns of indigenous people can take journalists far beyond the borders of Saskatchewan." *Media. Canadian Association of Journalists* 10, no. 2 (Fall 2002).

Berlo, Janet Catherine, and Ruth B. Phillips. "Encircles Everything: A Transformative History of Native Women's Arts." *Hearts of Our People: Native Women Artists*. Seattle: Minneapolis Institute of Art, in association with the University of Washington Press, 2019.

Berson, Amber. "Dana Claxton, The Mustang Suite and Hybrid Humour." *St. Andrews Journal of Art History and Museum Studies*. 14 (2010).

Besaw, Mindy N. "Dana Claxton." In *Art for a New Understanding: Native Voices, 1950s to Now*, edited by Mindy N. Besae, Candice Hopkins, Manuela Well-Off-Man. Fayetteville, NC: The University of Arkansas Press, 2018.

Birnie, Peter. "Kane is more than able; Aboriginal actor and dancer has come a long way from a troubled youth, now helps her people to heal." *The Vancouver Sun*, June 21, 2008.

Bissley, Jackie. "Dana Claxton." *Indian Cinema Entertainment*, Winter 2001.

Bodey, Michael. "Breaking out of cinema's dark cube." *The Australian*, February 9, 2011.

Boll, Natalie and LaTiesha Fazakas. *Maker of Monsters: The Extraordinary Life of Beau Dick*, Athene Films, 2017.

Bouvier, Denis. "Dana Claxton: Fringing the Cube." *The Source*, November 30, 2018.

Brackett, Donald. "Forest of Memory: the Provocative Art of Dana Claxton." *Vie des Arts*, April 2019.

Brophy, Sarah and Janice Hladki. *Embodied Politics in Visual Autobiography. Cultural Spaces.* Toronto: University of Toronto Press, 2014.

Burnham, Clint. "Dana Claxton: Made to be Ready." *Espace*, Spring-Summer 2016.

Burnham, Clint. "First nations art unites much and reality." *The Vancouver Sun*, September 16, 2006.

Cachia, Amanda. "Map of Blood." *Diabolique*. Regina: Dunlop Art Gallery, 2010.

Cochrane, Steven Leyden. "Remarkably unremarkable." *Winnipeg Free Press*, November 8, 2012.

Cotter, Holland. "America's Earliest Artists." *The New York Times*, March 13, 2015.

Cramp, Beverly. "Dana Claxton: Fringing the Cube. An exhibition at the Vancouver Art Gallery decries the oppressive legacy of colonialism and reclaims Indigenous culture." *Galleries West*, November 5, 2018.

Croft, Brenda L. "Sell-abrasion of our Nations." Samstag Museum, University of South Australia, 2010.

Croft, Brenda L. "Sell-abrasion of our Nations." *Artlink Contemporary Art of Australia & the Asia Pacific* 31 (2011).

Crowston, Catherine. *Beauty and the Beast. Dana Claxton, Isaac Julien and Alison Murray*. Banff: Walter Phillips Gallery, 1997.

Dahle, Sigrid. "Negative Space: Abattoirs by Artists and the Representation of Trauma." In *Obsession, Compulsion, Collection: On Objects, Display Culture, and Interpretation*. Banff: Banff Centre Press, 2004.

Davis, Jolene. "Time changes all things, including how we see ourselves." *Windspeaker*, January 1, 2000.

Deadman, Pat. "Dana Claxton: Sitting Bull and the Moose Jaw Sioux." Moose Jaw Museum and Art Gallery, 2007.

Dick, Terence. "What Does One Do With Such a Clairvoyant Image? At Gallery 44 & Trinity Square Video." *akimbo*, May 17, 2017.

Donnelly, Lauren. "Dana Claxton Flips the Colonial Script." *Beatroute*, November 2, 2018.

Dowell, Kristin. "Exploring the Sacred in Aboriginal Performance Art." *Hemispheric Institute, E-misferica* 2, no. 1 (Spring 2005).

Dowell, Kristin L. *Honoring Stories: Aboriginal Media, Art, and Activism in Vancouver*, New York University, September 2006.

Dowell, Kristin L. "Performance and 'Trickster Aesthetics' in the Work of Mohawk Filmmaker Shelley Niro." In *Native American Performance and Representation*. University of Arizona Press, 2011.

Dowell, Kristin L. *Sovereign Screens: Aboriginal Media on the Canadian West Coast*. University of Nebraska Press, 2013.
Dowell, Kristin. "Pushing Boundaries, Defying Categories." In *Native Art of the Northwest Coast: A History of Changing Ideas.* Vancouver: UBC Press, 2013.
Dowell, Kirstin L. "'The Future Looks Rad from Where I Stand': A Review of Claiming Space: Voices of Urban Aboriginal Youth at the University of British Columbia Museum of Anthropology." *Anthropologica* 57, no. 1 (2015).
Dunvely, T'Cha. "A Celebration of Aboriginal Culture; Montréal First People's Festival Showcases Film, Music, Theatre and Art." *The Montreal Gazette*, June 18, 2014.
Durand, Guy Sioui. "Steeling the Gaze: Portraits by Aboriginal Artists, Canadian Museum of Contemporary Photography at the National Gallery of Canada, Ottawa, October 31, 1008 – March 22, 2009." *Ciel Variable* 82, 2009.
Durand, Guy Sioui. "Look-Facebook-Auto'ado Texto-Photo ! Totem Hypermoderne." In *Rebelles. Photographie Actuelle et Considérations Insoumises Sur L'adolescence*. Quebec, QC: J'ai VU Editions, 2012.
Durand, Guy Sioui. "Edward Curtis, Un project démesuré, Musée McCord, Montréal, du 24 mai au 18 novembre 2012." *Ciel Variable* 93, 2013.
Elliot, David. *The Beauty of Distance: Songs of Survival in a Precarious Age*. Biennale of Sydney, 2010.
Fatona, Andrea. "From Sea to Sea: British Columbia." *Take One: Film & Television in Canada*, no. 5 (1994).
Fitzpatrick, Blake. "Four Directions." *Ciel Variable* 88, 2011.
Fuglerud, Ølivind. "Art and Ambiguity: An Extended Review of Border Zones at the Museum of Anthropology, British Columbia." *Museum Anthropology* 35, no. 2 (Fall 2012).
Fung, Richard. "If Walls Have Ears." *Reports Brochure*. Toronto: V Tape, 1998.
Gagnon, Monika Kin. "topographies." Vancouver Art Gallery, 1996.
Gagnon, Monika Kin. "Worldviews in Collision: Dana Claxton's Video Installations." In *Other Conundrums, Race & Canadian Art*. Vancouver: Arsenal Pulp Press with Vancouver Artspeak Gallery and Kamloops Art Gallery, 2000.
Gagnon, Monika Kin. *13 Conversations About Art and Cultural Race Politics*. Montreal: Artextes Editions, 2002.
Gagnon, Monika Kin and Olivia Michiko Gagnon. "Gifts of Fringe." In *Dana Claxton: Fringing the Cube*(exhibition catalogue). Vancouver: Figure 1 Publishing Inc., Vancouver Art Gallery, 2018.
Gale, Peggy. "Dana Claxton: In Search of Sitting Bull." Moose Jaw Museum & Art Gallery, 2007.
Garneau David. "Western Canada in Brief: Fall 1996 and Winter 1997." *C Magazine* 52, 1997.
Garneau, David. "Dana Claxton: Sitting Bull and the Moose Jaw Sioux." *Vie des Arts* 197, 2004.
Garneau, David. "Dana Claxton's Patient Storm." Urban Shaman, Winnipeg, 2005.
Garneau, David. "Little Distance Between Us." *Fuse Magazine*, Fall 2010.
Garneau, David. "Dana Claxton's Patient Storm." In *Dana Claxton: Fringing the Cube* (exhibition catalogue). Vancouver: Figure 1 Publishing Inc., Vancouver Art Gallery, 2018.
Gessell, Paul. "Native Creative and Contemplative; Aboriginal Artists Cast Their Lens on 'White' Culture." *National Post*, November 17, 2008.
Gessell, Paul."The Aboriginal Eye." *The Ottawa Citizen*, November 13, 2008.
Gessell, Paul. "The Beat goes on at Montreal Gallery; Beat Nation." *The Ottawa Citizen*, December 28, 2013.
Gillespie, James L. "Language of Intercession." *Canadian Art* 22, Summer 2005.
Goddard, Peter. "An Appetite for Destruction; Must-see Montreal Show Elves into Our Unending Fascination with War Imagery." *The Toronto Star*, February 6, 2010.
Goddard, Peter. "Fierce Fiery Female Filmmakers." *The Toronto Star*, January 28, 2010.
Green, Christopher. "The Plains Indians: Artists of Earth and Sky." *The Brooklyn Rail*, April 2015.
Griffin, Kevin. "Blockbuster Exhibitions, Public Installations Dominated the Vancouver Scene; Big and Bold Exhibitions Came to Traditional and Non-traditional Venues, Spurred in Part by a Need to Find New Revenue Sources." *The Vancouver Sun*, December 31, 2009.
Griffin, Kevin. "Beyond the Mask and Totem Pole; Vancouver is the Hub of a $100-Million-a-Year Market in the Contemporary Northwest Coast Native Art." *The Vancouver Sun*, October 9, 2010.
Griffin, Kevin. "Vancouver Curator to Take Part in Sydney Biennale; Tania Willard is One of Six Curators to Participate in Canada Council Initiative to Expand Skills and Raise Profile of First Nations Artists." *The Vancouver Sun*, May 3, 2010.
Griffin, Kevin. "Dana Claxton Explores Her 'Acceptable Edge'; First Nations Artist Repurposes Imagery from Her Heritage in a Modern Context." *The Vancouver Sun*, October 9, 2010.
Griffin, Kevin. "Seeing the Forest and the Trees; VAG Holds First Public Showing of Works from the Private Michael Audain Collection." *The Vancouver Sun*, October 29, 2011.
Griffin, Kevin. "Aboriginal Artists Stay on the Beat; Traditional Forms Find Contemporary Expression in Hip-Hop-Inflected Exhibition." *The Vancouver Sun*, February 25, 2012.
Griffin, Kevin. "ART SEEN: Only British Bone China Allowed for Buffalo Bone China." *The Vancouver Sun*, November 26, 2018.
Griffin, Kevin. "Dana Claxton Uses Beauty to Tell Difficult Truths About Colonialism." *The Vancouver Sun* and *The Province*, November 30, 2018.

Guglietti, Maria Victoria. *Imagining Drumbytes and Logging in Powwows: A History of Community Imagination in Canadian-based Aboriginal New Media Art.* Thesis for the degree of Doctor of Philosophy, Carleton University, May 2010.

Hewlett, Jason. "Wild Western; Kamloops Art Gallery Takes Stock of How the West was Settled." *Kamloops Daily News*, January 11, 2013.

Hladki, Janice. "Decolonizing Colonial Violence: The Subversive Practices of Aboriginal Film and Video." *Canadian Woman Studies* 25, no. 1-2 (2006).

Hladki, Janice. " Arrives Asking, Demanding Something of Us." In *Fierce Women's Hot-Blooded Film/Video*. Hamilton: McMaster University Museum of Art, 2010.

Hladki, Janice. "'Remembering Otherwise': Counter-Commemoration and Re-Territorialization in Indigenous Film and Video Art." *Revisita de Estudios Globales y Arte Contemporáneo* 2, no. 1 (2014).

Hoekstra, Matthew. "Your Kontinent Film Festival is on at Minoru Park." *Richmond Review*, July 19, 2013.

Holt, Jim. "Canadian First Nations Films Dominate at Sundance Fest." *The Province*, January 10, 2002.

Hood, Mary. "Map(ing): Multiple Artists Printing (Indigenous and Native Geographies)." *American Indian Art Magazine* 38, no. 4 (2013).

Hubbard, Tasha. "'The Buffaloes Are Gone' or 'Return: Buffalo'? The Relationship of the Buffalo to Indigenous Creative Expression." *Canadian Journal of Native Studies* 29, no. 1-2 (2009).

Issac, Jaimie and Leah Decter. "(Official Denial) Trade Value in Progress: Unsettling Narratives." *West Coast Lines* 46, no. 2 (Summer 2012).

Jones, Braeden. "Winnipeg Indigenous Women's Art to Be Displayed on Roadside Billboards Across Canada." *Metro*, August 2, 2017.

Jones, Marianne and Jeff Bear. "Hunkpapa Woman: Dana Claxton." In *The Indigenous Voice*. Vancouver: Urban Rez: Moving Images Distribution, 2006.

Kelsey, Penelope Myrtle. "Condolence Tropes and Haudenosaunee Visuality." In *American Indian Studies: Visualities*, Michigan State University Press, 2011.

Korniakova, Elena. *Canadian and Russian Animation on Northern Aboriginal Folklore*. MFA thesis. Concordia University, 2014.

Krivdova, Zofia. *Steeling the Gaze: Collaborative Curatorial Practices and Aboriginal Art.* Thesis in the department of Art History, MFA. Concordia University, 2014.

Kunard, Andrea, and Steve Loft. *Steeling the Gaze: Portraits by Aboriginal Artists*. Ottawa: Canadian Museum of Contemporary Photography, National Gallery of Canada, 2011.

Kunard, Andrea and Carol Payne. *The Cultural Work of Photography in Canada*. Montreal: McGill-Queen's University Press, 2011.

Labercane, Curranne. "Self-Identify." *Montecristo*, October 31, 2018.

La Flamme, Michelle. "Unsettling the West." In *Women Filmmakers: Refocusing*, Vancouver: UBC Press, 2003.

Laflamme, Michelle. "Dana Claxton: Reframing the Sacred and Indigenizing the White Cube." In *Diversity and Dialogue: the Eiteliorg Fellowship for Native American Fine Art*. Indianapolis: Eiteljorg Museum of American Indians and Western Art; Seattle, University of Washington Press, 2008.

Lanteri, Michelle. "Book Review." *First American Art Magazine*, Spring 2019.

LaPensée, Elizabeth and Jason Edward Lewis. "Timetraveller™: First Nations Nonverbal Communication in Second Life." In *Nonverbal Communication in Virtual Worlds: Understanding and Designing Expressive Characters*. Pittsburgh: ETC Press, 2014.

Laskaris, Sam. "Artist Proud of Multimedia Exhibit at Olympics 2010." *Saskatchewan Sage*, October 2009.

Laurence, Robin. "Exploring the Plight of Women in Urban Settings" "Visual Art." *Vancouver Sun,* January 27, 1996.

Laurence, Robin. " Visual Art." *Georgia Straight*. June 17, 2000.

Laurence, Robin. "River Run." *Canadian Art*, Fall 2000.

Laurence, Robin. " Wandering Spirit." *Georgia Straight*, March 24, 2005.

Laurence, Robin. "Visual Art." *Georgia Straight*, March 2006.

Laurence, Robin. "Claxton Mash-up." *Georgia Straight*, November 2010.

Laurence, Robin. "Dana Claxton Celebrates Major Vancouver Art Gallery Survey Fringing the Cube." *Georgia Straight*, October 24, 2018.

Lawrence, Toby. "Locating Sioux Aesthetics Through The Sioux Project – Tatanka Oyte: Conversations with Dana Claxton by Toby Katrine Lawrence." *Blackflash*, May 2018.

Lederman, Marsha. "Dana Claxton's Art Boldly Reclaims Narratives Around Indigenous Culture." *The Globe and Mail*, November 14, 2018.

Lee, James Jason. "Urban Fictions (Vancouver School, Exhibition)." *Parachute*, July/Sept 1996.

Lee, Vico. "Aboriginal Works of Art From Canada." *Taipei Times*, September 10, 2003.

Lewis, Randolph. *Indigenous Films: Navajo Talking Picture: Cinema on Native Ground*. University of Nebraska Press, 2012.

Lin, Brian. "Ablakela Invokes Calm and Innovation." *Windspeaker*, February 2002.

Lindner, Markus H. "'WE ALL HAVE TO PAY BILLS': Zeitgenössische Sioux-Künstler und der Markt." *Paideuma* 57, 2011.

Mahoney, Jeff. "Art is Not Always Pretty Pictures." *The Hamilton Spectator*, January 17, 2010.

Mansoor, Jaleh. "Rebar, or Subterranean Weaving: the Over-Written Foundational Matrix of 21st C. Vancouver." In *Dana Claxton: Fringing the Cube* (exhibition catalogue). Vancouver: Figure 1 Publishing Inc., Vancouver Art Gallery, 2018.

Marubbio, Elise. "Introduction to Native American/ Indigenous Film." *Post Script* 29, no. 3 (2010).

Mastai, Judith. "The Elevation of BC Art." *C Magazine* 52, 1997.

Mathur. Ashok. "Arts, Activism and the Academy: Resistance is Fertile." *Fuse Magazine*, Fall 2010.

Mathur, Ashok, Jonathan Dewar, and Mike DeGagné. *Cultivating Canada: Reconciliation Through the Lens of Cultural Diversity*. Ottawa: Aboriginal Healing Foundation, 2011.

Mathur, Ashok and Rita Wong. "Employing Equity in Post-Secondary Art Institutes." In *Retooling The Humanitites: The Culture of Research in Canadian Universities*. University of Alberta Press, 2011.

Mattes, Catherine. *Gatherings: Aboriginal Art from the Collection of the Winnipeg Art Gallery*. Winnipeg: Winnipeg Art Gallery, 2002.

McCreary, Cynthia. "Dana Claxton: Fringing the Cube." *Big City Art*, October 26, 2018.

McKegney, Sam. *Masculindians: Conversations about Indigenous Manhood*. University of Manitoba, 2014.

McKenna, Cara. "Fringing the Cube is Political with an Indigenous Sensibility." *The Windspeaker*, October 29, 2018.

McMahon, Finn. "Resilience." *MAWA Newsletter*, Summer 2017.

Methot, Suzanne. "Artists Explore Contemporary Idioms and Media." *Ontario Birchbark* 3, no. 8 (2004).

Milroy, Sarah. "Primeval Meets Postmodern in BC Art." *The Globe and Mail*, September 1996.

Morrill, Rebecca, et al. "Dana Claxton." In *Great Women Artists.* London: Phaidon, 2019.

Mulatz, Ryan. "Celebrate National Aboriginal Day in Regina." *Leader Post*, June 18, 2009.

Nixon, Lindsay. "Art in 2017: A View from Turtle Island." *Canada Art* online, December 28, 2017.

Oh, Susan. "Soaring Beyond the Totem Poles [Jack & Doris Shadbolt Foundation for the Visual Arts prize]." *Maclean's*, May 7, 2001.

O'Reilly, Finbarr. "A New Wave of Aboriginal Filmmakers is Determined to Leave Portrayals of Natives as Victims Where They Feel They Belong—in the Past." *The National Post*, June 18, 1999.

O'Riordan, Maurice. "Symmetry, Substance & Style." *Art Monthly Australia*, May 2011.

Perron, Annie. *La Photographie Comme Territoire Identitaire; L'Autoreprésentation photographique et les Technologies Web Comme Médium de Déploiement Identitaire et de Rencontre dans le Contexte Communautaire des Jeunes des Premières Nations*. Master of Arts Thesis, l'Université du Québec à Chicoutimi, 2010.

Pete, Coleman. "Dana Claxton's Fringing the Cube Challenges Viewers' Understand of Indigenous Art." *The Ubyssey*, January 8, 2019.

Pourtavaf, Leila. "Biennale de Montréal 2007. Can Art Exhibitions Have Upsets, Just Like a Sports Competition? Leila Pourtavaf Reports from Montreal" *C Magazine* 95, Fall 2007.

Redwood, Tom. "Indigenous Media Art: Complex Visions." *Real Time*, May 2011.

Rice, Ryan. "Into the Wild." *Face the Nation*. Art Gallery of Alberta, 2008.

Rico, Diana. "Cultures Crash." LA Freewaves Festival, 1998.

Ritter, Kathleen and Tania Willard. *Beat Nation: Art, Hip Hop and Aboriginal Culture* (exhibition catalogue). Vancouver: Vancouver Art Gallery, 2012.

Robertson, Sheila. "Show About Perceptions of Aboriginals and Others." *Star – Phoenix*, January 18, 1997.

Rosenberg, Ann. "Absence Creates Strong Presence." *The Vancouver Sun*, October 26, 1991.

Rondeau-Hoekstra, Cheryl. *Sharing the Cultural Experience: a Comprehensive Guide to First Nations Film and Video*. Artexte, 1996.

Roy, Marina. "Corporeal Returns: Feminism and Phenomenology in Vancouver Video and Performance, 1968-1983." *Canadian Art*, Summer 2001.

Ruiz, Cristina. "The European Enlightenment is Over." *Art Newspaper* 19, no. 214 (2010).

Rushing III, W. Jackson. "Manifest Sovereignty: 'Diversity and Dialogue' at the Eiteljorg Museum." *American Indian Art Magazine* 33, no. 3 (2008).

Sandals, Leah. "Dismantling the Shards of Past Identities." *The National Post*, July 7, 2008.

Scott, Michael. "BC Artists Emerge in Topographies." *The Vancouver Sun*, September 1996.

Sepsi, Enikö, Judith Nagy, Miklós Vassányi and János Kenyeres. *Indigenous Perspectives in North America: A Collection of Studies*. Cambridge Scholars Publishing, 2014.

Shaw, Nancy. "Tree of Consumption." *Video In 25th*, 2000.

Shepert, Elana. "This Provocative Indigenous Art Exhibition Will Take Your Breath Away." *Vancouver is Awesome*, October 25, 2018.

Smith, Charles C. *Pluralism in the Arts in Canada: A Change is Gonna Come*. Canadian Centre for Policy Alternatives, 2012.

Soldier, Layli Long. "Tribute to Dana Claxton and the Art of Generosity." In *Dana Claxton: Fringing the Cube* (exhibition catalogue). Vancouver: Figure 1 Publishing Inc., Vancouver Art Gallery, 2018.

Soldier, Layli Long. "38." In *Dana Claxton: Fringing the Cube* (exhibition catalogue). Vancouver: Figure 1 Publishing Inc., Vancouver Art Gallery, 2018.

Steele, Lisa. "Appropriate Behaviors." In *Toronto International Video Art Biennial*, 1999.

Stimson, Adrian A. "Two Spirited For You: The Absence of "Two Spirit" People in Western Culture and Media." *West Coast Line* 40, no. 1 (2006).

St-Jean Aubre, Anne Marie. "L'art contemporain Améridien s'expose." *Inter* 104, 2009.

St-Laurent, Jason. "History in Parts: The Work of Dana Claxton." In *Art Star 2: Video Art Biennial* (exhibition catalogue), Ottawa: SAW Gallery, 2005.

Stoffman, Judy. "Heirs to the Group of Seven." *The Toronto Star*, December 10, 2001.

Sugrue, Meagan. "Humour in Contemporary Indigenous Photography: Re-focusing the Colonial Gaze." *The Arbutus Review* 3, no. 2 (2012).

Tanzer, Ivan. "Ghost Dance: Activism. Resistance. Art., Ryerson Image Center, Toronto, 18 September to 15 December 2013." *Ciel Variable* 97, 2014.

Taunton, Carla. "PUSHING BOUNDARIES: 'Non Compliance' Short Experimental Program at imagineNATIVE Film + Media Arts Festival." *Fuse Magazine* 33, Winter 2010.

Taunton, Carla. "Indigenous (Re)memory and Resistance: Video Works by Dana Claxton." *Post Script* 29, no. 3, (Summer 2010).

Taunton, Carla Jane. "Performing Resistance/Negotiation Sovereignty: Indigenous Women's Performance Art in Canada." Art history graduate thesis, Queen's University, 2011.

Taunton, Carla. "(Re)memory and Resistance: Video Works by Dana Claxton." In *Native Americans on Film: Conversations, Teaching, and Theory*. Lexington: University of Kentucky, 2013.

Timmins, Leila, cheyanne turions, and Jayne Wikinson. *What Does One Do with Such a Clairvoyant Image?*, Gallery 44, Toronto, 2017.

Todd, Jeremy. "The Ongoing Powers of Dana Claxton." In *Fierce: Women's Hot-Blooded Film/Video*, Hamilton: McMaster Museum of Art, 2010.

Townsend-Gault, Charlotte. "topographies." *Canadian Art*, March 1997.

Townsend-Gault, Charlotte. "Dana Claxton." In *St. James Guide to Native North American Artists*. St James Press, 1997.

Townsend-Gault, Charlotte. "Let X = Audience." In *Reservation X*. Gatineau: Canadian Museum of Civilization, Goose Lane, 1998.

Townsend-Gault, Charlotte. *Native Art of the Northwest Coast: a History of Changing Ideas*. Vancouver: UBC Press, 2013.

Turnbull, Glenna. "Showcase of Indigenous Art." *Kelowna Capital News*, June 11, 2008.

Turner, Michael. "Ester Shalev-Gerz." *Canadian Art*, Fall 2012.

Walker, Morley. "Poetry in Motion Pictures WAG Exhibit Strives to Open Winnipeggers' Eyes to Avant-Garde Filmmaking." *Winnipeg Free Press*, January 15, 2007.

Walsh, Andrea Naomi. *Contemporary Aboriginal Art Texts: Intersections of Visual Culture*. Toronto: York University, September 2000.

Walsh, Andrea. "Complex Sightings Aboriginal Art and Intercultural Spectatorship." In *On Aboriginal Representation in the Gallery*, Gatineau: Canadian Museum of Civilization, 2002.

Weder, Adele. "The Art of Medicine." *CMAJ* 184, no. 15 (October 2012).

Wemigwans, Jennifer. "Indigenous Worldview: Cultural Expression on the World Wide Web." *Canadian Woman Studies* 26, no. 3/4 (Winter/Spring 2008).

White, Sara. "Tracey Moffatt: Narratives; Stop (the) Gap: International Indigenous Art in Motion." *Artlink* 31, no. 2, (2011).

Whyte, Murray. "The True North: Strong, Conflicted, Free." *The Toronto Star*, April 27, 2017.

Whyte, Murray. "Subverting the Cliches: A Mixed Show of Aboriginal Artists both Challenges and is Subsumed by the Dominant Culture." *The Toronto Star*, July 19, 2011.

Whyte, Murray. "Medium Delivers a New Message Contact Fest Probes Marshall McLuhan's Overlooked Notions of Photography." *The Toronto Star*, May 1, 2010.

Wild, Paula. "Star Spirit Festival has Potential." *The Courtenay Comox Valley Record*, March 19, 2006.

Willard, Tania. "Beginning From Home." Grunt Gallery, Vancouver, Canada, 2007.

Wine, Rachel. "Northern Exposure." *The Globe and Mail*, May 5, 2017.

Yohe, Hill Ahlberg, and Teri Greeves (ed.). *Hearts of Our People: Native Women Artists*. Seattle: Minneapolis Institute of Art, in association with the University of Washington Press, 2019.

Youds, Mike. "Walking in Two Worlds; Inaugural Aboriginal Film Fest Set for Weekend." *Kamloops Daily News*, February 14, 2008.

Yusuf, Farah. *Raise a Flag: Works from the Indigenous Art Collection*, Onsite Gallery, OCAD University, Toronto, 2017.

Zimmerman, Patricia. "Ardent Spaces, Formidable Environments." In *Fierce: Women's Hot-Blooded Film/Video*. Hamilton: Robert McLaughlin Gallery, McMaster University Museum of Art, 2010.

PUBLISHED WRITING

"A Poem for Beau." In *Remembering Beau Dick (1955-2017)*. Vancouver: Fazakas Gallery, March 30, 2017.

"Ode to Gramsci #1, 2, 3, 8 – RED on RED." *GRAMSCIANA: Rivista Internazionale di Studi su Antonio Gramsci* 2 (2016).

"Together Doings: Presence in the Work of Guadalupe Martinez." In *Supermoon*. Vancouver: Brick Press, Morris and Helen Belkin Art Gallery, 2014.

“Dana Claxton and Tania Willard, Imperfect Compliance: A Trajectory of Transformation.” In *Arcpost: A Project of the Pacific Association of Artist Run Centres*, 2013.
“NWC on the Up-load: Surfing for Northwest Coast Art.” In *Native Art of the Northwest Coast : A History of Changing Ideas*. Vancouver: UBC Press, 2013.
“Lawrence Paul Yuxweluptun: Master Mixer, Man of Many Colors.” In *RED*, 21-41. Indianapolis: Eiteljorg Museum of American Indians and Western Art, 2013.
“NDN AXE/IONS — A Collaborative Essay with Tania Willard.” In *Indianacts*. Vancouver: Grunt Gallery, 2011.
“My Best Shot: ‘Aim #1’.” *Blackflash* 29, 2012.
“Making Medicine.” In *The Medicine Project*. Vancouver: Grunt Gallery, 2011.
“Going to the Centre: Performance Works and Other Thoughts.” *Canadian Theatre Review* 146 (2011).
“A Decade In Retrospect: 10 Years of Dramatic Programming at ImagineNATIVE.” In *ImagineNATIVE: Aboriginally Produced Film & Video*. Toronto: V Tape, 2009.
“Re: Wind.” In *Transference, Tradition, Technology: Native New Media Exploring Visual & Digital Culture*. Banff: Walter Phillips Gallery, 2005.

PERFORMANCES

2017
Don’t Betta Work Bitch!, performance intervention at book launch for *Marshall Plan Modernism* by Jaleh Mansoor, REDMAY Seattle, Seattle, WA
2016
Follow the Red Sinew, UBC, Vancouver, Canada
2015
Dirt Worshipper, Faculty Exhibition, Audain Centre for the Arts, UBC, Vancouver, Canada
Fringed, in *The Plains Indians: Artists of Earth and Sky*, Metropolitan Museum of Art, New York, NY
2013
Recoil, Imagine Day, UBC, Vancouver, Canada
The Beat/The Tear/The Crumple, UBC, Vancouver, Canada
2011
The Elsewhere, LIVE Bienale, Western Front, Vancouver, Canada
2010
WACKO – A Disco Ceremony for Michael Jackson, Open Space, Victoria, Canada
1999
Ablakela with Primeaux and Mike, *Live At the End of the Century*, Grunt Gallery, Vancouver, Canada
1997
Buffalo Bone China, A Tribe Project with AKA, Saskatoon, SK
1994
SA—(work in progress), Western Front, Vancouver, Canada
1993
Tree of Consumption, Grunt Gallery, Vancouver, Canada
1991
10 Little Poems, in *Neo-Nativist*, Pitt Gallery, Vancouver, Canada

SELECTED CURATORIAL PROEJCTS

2019
50 works selected from the Vancouver Art Gallery’s permanent collection and exhibited with the exhibition *Dana Claxton: Fringing the Cube*, Vancouver Art Gallery, Vancouver, Canada
2017
Indigenous Perspectives, Victoria Film Festival, Victoria, Canada
2013
Curatorial team, *Witnesses: Art and Canada’s Indian Residential Schools*, Morris and Helen Belkin Gallery, UBC, Vancouver, Canada
2011
Indian Acts on Line, co-curated with Tania Willard, Grunt Gallery, Vancouver, Canada (online exhibition)
2009
Danger in Paradise, Or Gallery, Vancouver, Canada
2008
The Medicine Project, Grunt Gallery, Vancouver, Canada (online exhibition)
2006
Back/Flash, Aboriginal New Media, Winnipeg, MB; Walter Phillips Gallery, Banff, AB; Winnipeg Art Gallery, Winnipeg, MB; and Dalhousie University, Halifax, NS
2004
Inside Focus, Work from the Pacific Region, IMAA Conference, Montreal, QC
2003
RumiNATIONS, Doxa Festival, Vancouver, Canada
2002
Duking It Out on the Northwest Coast, ImagiNATIVE Festival, Toronto, ON
2001
RE:Place, Vtape and Art System, Toronto, ON
1998–1999
Red Interiors – A Look into First Nations Video (travelling group exhibition)
1994
Leah Modigliani, To Suffer is to Shine, Pitt Gallery, Vancouver, Canada
1993
Sharyn Yuen, Like A Plague of Locusts, Pitt Gallery, Vancouver, Canada
Faye Heavyshield, The Heart Is, Pitt Gallery, Vancouver, Canada, and Saw Gallery, Ottawa, ON
1992
First Ladies, Pitt Gallery, Vancouver, Canada

Kate Smith's Bed Show, Pitt Gallery, Vancouver, Canada
ABO – Aboriginal Videos that Unmask Colonialism, Video In, Vancouver, Canada
1991
Neo Nativist, Pitt Gallery, Vancouver, Canada

AWARDS AND DISTINCTIONS

2020
Governor General's Award in Visual and Media Arts
Scotiabank Photography Award
2019
Hnatyshyn Foundation Mid-Career Award
YWCA Woman of Distinction Award, Arts, Culture & Design
2016
Mayor's Award for Art, City of Vancouver
2014
Best Cinematography for *He Who Dreams*, Montreal First Peoples Festival
2013
Best Experimental Feature for *He Who Dreams*, ImagiNATIVE Film and Media Arts Festival
2012
Artistic Innovation Award, WIFT (Woman in Film and Television)
2007
Eiteljorg Fellowship for Native American Fine Art, Ford and Lily Foundations, Eiteljorg Museum for American Indians and Western Art
2006
Outstanding Contribution, Aboriginal Screen Culture, Indigenous Media Arts Group
2005
VIVA Award, Jack and Doris Shadbolt Foundation
2002
Best Multi Media for *Ablakela – CDROM of Performance Work*, ImagiNATIVE Film and Media Arts Festival
1997
Best Experimental Short Drama for *The Red Paper*, Dreamspeakers First Nations Film and Video Festival

COLLECTIONS

Art Gallery of Alberta, Edmonton, AB
Audain Art Museum, Whistler, Canada
Morris and Helen Belkin Art Gallery, UBC, Vancouver, Canada
CaixaForum, Fundacio la Caixa, Barcelona, Spain
Canada Council Art Bank, Ottawa, ON
CDN Trade Office, Taipei, Taiwan
Dalhousie University Art Gallery, Halifax, NS
Eiteljorg Museum, Indianapolis, IN
Foreign Affairs and International Trade Canada, Ottawa, ON
Kamloops Art Gallery, Kamloops, Canada
MacKenzie Art Gallery, Regina, SK
McMichael Canadian Art Collection, Kleinburg, ON
Moose Jaw Museum and Art Gallery, Moose Jaw, SK
National Gallery of Canada, Ottawa, ON
Native and Inuit Art Collection, Ottawa ON
Private and corporate collections
Remai Modern, Saskatoon, SK
Saskatchewan Arts Board, Regina, SK
University of Arizona State Gallery, Tucson, AZ
Vancouver Art Gallery, Vancouver, Canada
Winnipeg Art Gallery, Winnipeg, MB

The artist has requested that BC (for British Columbia) not be used in her CV—in solidarity with Indigenous communities (and their allies) who would like to renew discussions of Indigenous land and title, and determine who has the right to name and claim the land known as BC.

ACKNOWLEDGEMENTS

DANA CLAXTON

Many thanks to Ed Burtynsky, who initiated this award, for his in/sight and desire to honour Canadian artists. Thank you to Scotiabank for valuing artists and creating this opportunity, and Barr Gilmore and his team for the details with the image and text—it's been a pleasure to work with you. An enormous thanks to Leila Timmins, who was steadfast in nominating me, for her devotion to art and culture in Canada. I am thankful to Amy Kazmerchyk, who left her research desk to travel to my birthplace of the Great Plains to embody her eloquent words and analysis, and to Candice Hopkins for her significant relations with indigenous art and artists and for editing Amy's essay. Thanks also to Valérie Matteau and Gaëlle Morel of Ryerson Image Centre for the lovely zooming to organize the show that accompanies this award and book, and all the staff at the gallery.

Wopila to the talented, funny, beautiful and deeply intelligent Pauline Petit who inspires me and keeps me organized. I have worked with exceptional photographers and thank Geoff Neufeld, Robert Keziere, Carole Segal and Henry Robideau. I am grateful to Launie Fairbairn, Roy Ng and their crew at ABC Colour Lab who so graciously prepare my work with such dedication and care. I am thankful to Jennifer Winsor, who has assisted with getting my work out into the world, and Robin Laurence for bringing it to life on the page. I would like to thank my colleagues in the Department of Art History, Visual Art and Theory at UBC for supporting me as an artist, professor and Head of the Department, especially Trey Le, Andrea Tuele and Scott Watson.

I thank Reid Shier and the Polygon Gallery for my Paris book, as well as Glenn Alteen, Paul Wong, Sara Diamond, grunt gallery, VIVO, Video In, /n/ and all of the artist run centres across Canada who have been foundational to my praxis and learning. To scholar/curators Daina Augaitis, Catherine Crowston, Lynne Bell, Kristin Dowell, David Elliot, Janice Hladki, Heather Smith, Carla Taunton, Andrea Walsh and Monika Kin Gagnon—thanks so very much. And to all of the collectors, museums, galleries and art workers I have worked with—thanks so very much. I hold my hands up to Samaya Jardey, whom I have photographed for 30 years, and to everyone else who has let me take a picture of them. And to my dear friends—love! I am in awe of Ted Douglas of Eatonia, Saskatchewan, who brought me to Cabri Lake many times and showed me the Stone Man and medicine wheels. You are now in your 95th year and I dedicate my Cabri Lake work to you dear man.

I also thank my family where love is profound—Dad and Lynda, my late mother Ellen, Kim, Ron, Don, Megan, Mitchell, David and fam, Shadae and fam, and my god son Leo. And my dear mate Robert, whose wry humour is nourishing.

Skan, (sky) thank you for lifting me up with the enormity of all your teachings—you are a magnificent being. I am grateful to Sundance teachings, my late Auntie Dr. Bea Medicine, the late Joe Flying By and Isaac Dog Eagle—mitakuye oyasin. My art is a Plains practice, infused with a life that has given and shown me many tragedies, many joys, many gifts and many views of existence. I am grateful to be able to see. The camera brings that seeing/knowing/being forward to art, to the gallery and to this book. I thank the spirit of art.